SCHOLASTIC

100 SCIENCE LESSONS

NEW EDITION

TERMS AND CONDITIONS

IMPORTANT - PERMITTED USE AND WARNINGS - READ CAREFULLY BEFORE USING

SCOTTISH PRIMARY 6

YEAR 5

Minimum specification:
- PC with a CD-ROM drive and 512 Mb RAM (recommended)
- Windows 98SE or above/Mac OSX.1 or above
- Recommended minimum processor speed: 1 GHz

For all technical support queries, please phone Scholastic Customer Services on 0845 603 9091.

WS 2252726 5

O 507 ONE

David Glover, Ian Mitchell, Louise Petheram and Peter Riley

Authors
David Glover
Ian Mitchell
Louise Petheram
Peter Riley

Series Editor
Peter Riley

Editors
Tracy Kewley
Kate Pedlar

Project Editor
Fabia Lewis

Illustrators
Robin Lawrie
Tony O'Donnell, Sarah Wimperis
Theresa Tibbets c/o Beehive Illustrations

Series Designers
Catherine Perera and Joy Monkhouse

Designer
Catherine Perera

CD-ROM developed in association with
Vivid Interactive

ACKNOWLEDGEMENTS

With thanks to Clifford Hibbard and Tom Rugg for the use of some lessons in Chapter 1, Chapter 2 and Chapter 7 of this book, taken from *100 Science Lessons – Year 6*, by Clifford Hibbard Karen Mallinson-Yates and Tom Rugg, © 2001, Clifford Hibbard, Karen Mallinson-Yates and Tom Rugg (2001, Scholastic Ltd) revised by Clifford Hibbard and Tom Rugg, for this edition.

With thanks to Malcolm Anderson for the use of 'Sound survey' in Chapter 7 of this book taken from *100 Science Lessons - Year 3* by Malcolm Anderson © 2001, Malcolm Anderson (2001, Scholastic Ltd) revised by Malcolm Anderson, for this edition.

With thanks to Kendra McMahon for use of some lessons in Chapter 6 and Chapter 7 of this book, taken from *100 Science Lessons – Year 4*, by Kendra McMahon© 2001, Kendra McMahon (2001, Scholastic Ltd) revised by Kendra McMahon, for this edition.

All Flash activities developed by Vivid Interactive

Material from the National Curriculum © Crown copyright. Reproduced under the terms of the Click Use Licence.

Extracts from the QCA Scheme of Work © Qualifications and Curriculum Authority.

Extracts from the Primary School Curriculum for Ireland, www.ncca.ie, National Council for Curriculum and Assessment.

LEGO® is a brand name and the property of the LEGO Group © 2007 The LEGO Group.

Every effort has been made to trace copyright holders for the works reproduced in this book, and the publishers apologise for any inadvertent omissions.

Published by Scholastic Ltd
Villiers House
Clarendon Avenue
Leamington Spa
Warwickshire CV32 5PR

www.scholastic.co.uk

Designed using Adobe InDesign.

Printed by Bell and Bain Ltd, Glasgow

2 3 4 5 6 7 8 9   7 8 9 0 1 2 3 4 5 6

Text © 2007 David Glover, Ian Mitchell, Louise Petheram and Peter Riley

© 2007 Scholastic Ltd

British Library Cataloguing-in-Publication Data
A catalogue record for this book is available from the British Library.

ISBN 978-0439-94507-3

The rights of David Glover, Ian Mitchell, Louise Petheram and Peter Riley to be identified as the authors of this work have been asserted by them in accordance with the Copyright, Designs and Patents Act 1988.

This new edition of *100 Science Lessons* follows the QCA Science Scheme of Work and also meets many of the demands of the curricula for England, Wales, Scotland, Northern Ireland and Eire. The book is divided into seven units - one unit to match each unit of the QCA scheme for Year 5, and one enrichment unit.

The planning grid at the start of each unit shows the objectives and outcomes of each lesson, and gives a quick overview of the lesson content (starter, main activity, group activities and plenary). The QCA objectives for Year 5 provide the basis for the lesson objectives used throughout the book.

After the planning grid is a short section on Scientific Enquiry. It is based on a QCA activity and provides a context for children to develop certain enquiry skills and for you to assess them. The section ends by showing where the activity can be embedded within one of the lessons.

Each unit is divided into a number of key lessons, which closely support the QCA scheme and all units end with an assessment lesson which is based on those key lessons. In addition to the key lessons, a unit may also contain one or more enrichment lessons to provide greater depth or a broader perspective. They may follow on from a key lesson or form a whole section, near the end of the unit, before the assessment lesson. The lesson objectives are based on the statements of the national curricula for England, Wales, Scotland, Northern Ireland and Eire, which are provided, in grid format, on the CD-ROM.

Lesson plans

There are detailed and short lesson plans for the key and enrichment lessons. About 60 per cent of the lesson plans in this book are detailed lesson plans. The short lesson plans are closely related to them and cover similar topics and concepts. They contain the essential features of the detailed lesson plans, allowing you to plan for progression and assessment. The detailed lesson plans have the following structure:

OBJECTIVES

The objectives are stated in a way that helps to focus on each lesson plan. At least one objective is related to content knowledge and there may be one or more relating to Scientific Enquiry. When you have read through the lesson you may wish to add your own objectives. You can find out how these objectives relate to those of the various national curricula by looking at the relevant grids on the CD-ROM. You can also edit the planning grids to fit with your own objectives (for more information see 'How to use the CD-ROM' on page 6).

RESOURCES AND PREPARATION

The Resources section provides a list of everything you will need to deliver the lesson, including any photocopiables presented in this book. The Preparation section describes anything that needs to be done in advance of the lesson, such as collecting environmental data.

As part of the preparation of all practical work, you should consult your school's policies on practical work and select activities for which you are confident to take responsibility. The ASE publication *Be Safe!* gives very useful guidance on health and safety issues in primary science.

BACKGROUND

This section may briefly refer to the science concepts which underpin the teaching of individual lessons. It may also highlight specific concepts which children tend to find difficult and gives some ideas on how to address these during the lesson. Suggestions may be given for classroom displays as well as useful tips for obtaining resources. Safety points and sensitive issues may also be addressed in this sections, where appropriate.

VOCABULARY

There is a vocabulary list of science words associated with the lesson which children should use in discussing and presenting their work. Time should be spent defining each word at an appropriate point in the lesson.

STARTER

This introductory section contains ideas to build up interest at the beginning of the lesson and set the scene.

MAIN TEACHING ACTIVITY

This section presents a direct, whole-class (or occasionally group) teaching session that will help you deliver the content knowledge outlined in the lesson objectives before group activities begin. It may include guidance on discussion, or on performing one or more demonstrations or class investigations to help the children understand the work ahead.

The relative proportions of the lesson given to the starter, main teaching activity and group activities vary. If you are reminding the children of their previous work and getting them onto their own investigations, the group work may dominate the lesson time; if you are introducing a new topic or concept, you might wish to spend all or most of the lesson engaged in whole-class teaching.

GROUP ACTIVITIES

The group activities are very flexible. Some may be best suited to individual work, while others may be suitable for work in pairs or larger groupings. There are usually two group activities provided for each lesson. You may wish to use one after the other; use both together (to reduce demand on resources and your attention); or, where one is a practical activity, use the other for children who successfully complete their practical work early. You may even wish to use activities as follow-up homework tasks.

Some of the group activities are supported by a photocopiable sheet. These sheets can be found in the book as well as on the CD-ROM. For some activities, there are also accompanying differentiated ideas, interactive activities and diagrams – all available on the CD-ROM (for more information, see 'How to use the CD-ROM' on page 6).

The group activities may include some writing. These activities are also aimed at strengthening the children's science literacy and supporting their English literacy skills. They may involve writing labels and captions, developing scientific vocabulary, writing about or recording investigations, presenting data, explaining what they have observed, or using appropriate secondary sources. The children's mathematical skills are also developed through number and data handling work in the context of science investigations.

ICT LINKS

Many lessons have this section in which suggestions for incorporating ICT are given. ICT links might include: using the internet and CD-ROMs for research; preparing graphs and tables using a computer; using the graphing tool, interactive activities and worksheets from the CD-ROM.

DIFFERENTIATION

Where appropriate, there are suggestions for differentiated work to support less able learners or extend more able learners in your class. Some of the photocopiable sheets are also differentiated into less able support, core ability, and more able extension to support you in this work. The book contains the worksheets for the core ability while the differentiated worksheets are found on the accompanying CD-ROM.

ASSESSMENT

This section includes advice on how to assess the children's learning against the lesson objectives. This may include suggestions for questioning or observation opportunities, to help you build up a picture of the children's developing ideas and guide your future planning. A separate summative assessment lesson is provided at the end of each unit of work. One may also be provided for a group of enrichment lessons if they form a section towards the end of a unit.

PLENARY

Suggestions are given for drawing together the various strands of the lesson in this section. The lesson objectives and outcomes may be reviewed and key learning points may be highlighted. The scene may also be set for another lesson.

HOMEWORK

On occasions, tasks may be suggested for the children to do at home. These may involve using photocopiables or the setting of a research project, perhaps involving the use the books on display (as suggested in the background section) to broaden the knowledge of the topic being studied.

OUTCOMES

These are statements related to the objectives; they describe what the children should have achieved by the end of the lesson.

LINKS

These are included where appropriate. They may refer to subjects closely related to science, such as technology or maths, or to content and skills from subjects such as art, history or geography.

ASSESSMENT LESSONS

The last lesson in every unit focuses on summative assessment. This assessment samples the content of the unit, focusing on its key theme(s); its results should be used in conjunction with other assessments you have made during the teaching of the unit. The lesson usually comprises of two assessment activities, which may take the form of photocopiable sheets to complete or practical activities with suggested assessment questions for you to use while you are observing the children. These activities may include a mark scheme, but this will not be related directly to curriculum attainment targets and level descriptors. These tasks are intended to provide you with a guide to assessing the children's performance.

PHOTOCOPIABLE SHEETS

These are an integral part of many of the lessons. They may provide resources such as quizzes, instructions for practical work, worksheets to complete whilst undertaking a task, information, guidance for written assignments and so on.

Photocopiable sheets printed in the book are suitable for most children. The CD-ROM includes differentiated versions of many photocopiables to support less confident learners and stretch more confident learners.

How to use the CD-ROM

SYSTEM REQUIREMENTS

Minimum specifications:
- PC or Mac with CD-ROM drive and at least 512 MB RAM (recommended)
- Microsoft Windows 98SE or above/Mac OSX.1 or above
- Recommended minimum processor speed: 1GHz

GETTING STARTED

The accompanying CD-ROM includes a range of lesson and planning resources. The first screen requires the user to select the relevant country (England, Scotland, Wales, Northern Ireland, Eire). There are then several menus enabling the user to search the material according to various criteria, including lesson name, QCA unit, National Curriculum topic and resource type.

Searching by lesson name enables the user to see all resources associated with that particular lesson. The coloured tabs on the left-hand side of this screen indicate the differentiated worksheets; the tabs at the top of the page lead to different *types* of resource (diagram, interactive or photocopiable).

PHOTOCOPIABLES

The photocopiables that are printed in the book are also provided on the CD-ROM, as PDF files. In addition, differentiated versions of the photocopiables are provided where relevant:
- green indicates a support worksheet for less confident children;
- red indicates the core photocopiable, as printed in the book;
- blue indicates an extension worksheet for more confident children.

There are no differentiated photocopiables for assessment activities.

The PDF files can be annotated on screen using the panel tool provided (see below). The tools allow the user to add notes, highlight items and draw lines and boxes.

PDF files of photocopiables can be printed from the CD-ROM and there is also an option to print the full screen, including any drawings and annotations that have been added using the tools. (NB where PDF files are landscape, printer settings may need to be adjusted.)

INTERACTIVE ACTIVITIES

The CD-ROM includes twelve activities for children to complete using an interactive whiteboard or individual computers. Each activity is based on one of the photocopiables taken from across the units. Activities include: dragging and dropping the body parts into the correct place, to show the digestive system; clicking on creatures to answer questions about pond life; sequencing a baby's development, in the womb.

GRAPHING TOOL

The graphing tool supports lessons where the children are asked to gather and record data. The tool enables children to enter data into a table, which can then be used to create a block graph, pie chart or line graph.

When inserting data into the table, the left-hand column should be used for labels for charts; the right-hand column is for numeric data only (see example below). The pop-up keypad can be used to enter numbers into the table.

DIAGRAMS

Where appropriate, diagrams printed in the book have been included as separate files on the CD-ROM. These include examples of tables and diagrams for children to refer to when undertaking experiments or building objects, such as earth models, in 'Earth, Sun and Moon'. These can be displayed on an interactive whiteboard.

GENERAL RESOURCES

In addition to lesson resources, the CD-ROM also includes the planning grids for each unit, as printed in the book, and the relevant curriculum grid for England, Scotland, Wales, Northern Ireland and Eire. The curriculum grids indicate how elements of each country's National Curriculum are addressed by lessons in the book. The planning grids are supplied as editable Word files; the curriculum grids are supplied as Word and PDF files. Selection of a planning grid leads to a link, which opens the document in a separate window; this then needs to be saved to the computer or network before editing.

CHAPTER 1 Keeping healthy

Lesson	Objectives	Main activity	Group activities	Plenary	Outcomes
Lesson 1 Food groups	• To know that some foods are needed for activity and others for growth. • To use a table to record and interpret data.	Discuss how foods are graded on the nutrients they contain. Use scales to compare the relative weights of nutrients in food samples.	Interpret a table of the nutritional values of different foods. Analyse the contents of packaged food according to given criteria.	Compare judgements on the nutritional content of foods.	• Can recognise and name some foods for activity (carbohydrates). • Can recognise and name some foods for growth (proteins). • Can group foods according to their relative nutritional content. • Can interpret data in a table.
Lesson 2 Healthy meals	• To be able to plan healthy meals.	Plan healthy meals from information about food groups.		Assess the healthiness of the planned meals. Consider extreme versions.	• Can plan a healthy meal. • Can display the components of a meal clearly and know their value to health. • Can distinguish between a healthy meal and an unhealthy meal.
Lesson 3 What's in a dish?	• To identify foods for activity and for growth in prepared dishes.	Identify foods for growth and activity in pictures of prepared meals.		Assess each group's work as a class.	• Can identify foods for energy and growth (in prepared dishes).
Lesson 4 Digestion	• To know that food is digested by a number of organs, together called the digestive system.	Identify parts of the digestive system and place them on a body outline.	Identify parts of the digestive system and place them within a body outline. Match captions to parts of a diagram of the digestive system. Use a stethoscope to listen to chewing, swallowing and stomach digestion.	Trace the path of a sandwich through the digestive system.	• Can recognise parts of the digestive system and have some understanding of what each part does.
Lesson 5 Breathing	• To know the basic structure of the respiratory system. • To know that exercise increases the breathing rate. • To make comparisons and identify simple patterns. • To make predictions.	Measure breathing rates at rest and after light exercise.	Investigate how activity affects breathing rate. Answer questions on the breathing mechanism.	Groups report on their results. Compare findings and look for overall conclusions.	• Can describe how the body draws in and expels air. • Can measure the breathing rate at rest and after exercise. • Can plan an investigation to answer a given question. • Can make predictions. • Can recognise patterns in the results, and suggest explanations.
Lesson 6 The heart	• To know about the structure and function of the heart and the circulatory system.	Use a balloon pump and diagrams to consider the form and function of the heart.	Use diagrams to look at the mechanism of the heart. Use a diagram to consider the circulation of the blood.	Describe the path of the blood around the body.	• Can describe the action of the heart. • Can describe the path of the blood through the circulatory system.
Lesson 7 The pulse	• To know that the pulse is produced by the heartbeat. • To plan and carry out an investigation: make a prediction, make observations and measurements, check them by repeating, compare results with the prediction and draw conclusions. • To use tables and bar graphs to communicate data (perhaps using ICT).	Measure pulse rates at rest and after varying amounts of exercise. Explain the results.		Collate results to identify and explain the overall pattern.	• Can find the pulse and measure its rate. • Can plan and carry out an investigation: make a prediction, carry out observations and measurements, check by repeating them, record results in an appropriate and systematic manner, compare results with prediction and draw conclusions. • Can use tables and bar graphs to communicate data (perhaps using ICT).

Lesson	Objectives	Main activity	Group activities	Plenary	Outcomes
Lesson 8 How fit am I?	• To plan and carry out an investigation. • To use tables and bar graphs to communicate data (perhaps using ICT).	Use pulse rates to investigate 'fitness'.		Discuss the effects of lifestyle on fitness.	• Can plan and carry out an investigation. • Can use tables and bar graphs to communicate data (perhaps using ICT).
Enrichment Lesson 9 Healthy living	• To construct a plan for a healthy lifestyle.	Examine aspects of a healthy lifestyle through discussion. Key points to be raised: diet, exercise, hygiene.	Construct their own lifestyle chart, including diet, exercise and sleep. Examine their lifestyle critically to consider improvements.	The class vote on who has the healthiest lifestyle. Discuss TV-watching habits.	• Can plan a regime for a healthy lifestyle. • Can explain the need for each item in such a regime.
Lesson 10 Harmful drugs	• To know that some drugs can help the body recover from illness. • To know that people can persuade others to take harmful drugs.	Discuss how medicines and drugs can make people who are ill feel better and aid recovery.	Categorise medicines and drugs according to the parts of the body they help. Use role-play to explore the effects of peer pressure.	Assess the children's posters. Repeat the role-play once with an imbalance of numbers.	• Recognise some medicines are helpful drugs and know how they assist recovery from illness. • Recognise how peer pressure can introduce young people to harmful drugs.
Lesson 11 The effects of tobacco	• To know how tobacco affects the body.	Use a 'smoking machine' to demonstrate how smoking affects the lungs.		Discuss why people start smoking and why they should stop.	• Can explain why smoking is harmful.
Lesson 12 The effects of alcohol	• To know how alcohol affects the body.	Use secondary sources to find out about the dangers of alcohol and the treatment of alcoholism.		Display posters. Some children report back on how alcoholic drinks are made.	• Can describe the effects of alcohol on the body. • Can explain why drinking alcohol can be harmful.
Lesson 13 The effects of drugs and solvents	• To know how solvents affect the body. • To know how illegal drugs affect the body.	Use secondary sources (or a visit from a health professional) to find out about the dangers of solvent abuse and illegal drugs.		Display posters. Repeat the role-play as in Lesson 11.	• Can explain how solvents affect the body. • Can explain the dangers of using illegal drugs.
Enrichment Lesson 14 Things to avoid	• To identify activities and substances that may be harmful to health. • To develop skills in collaborative research, discussion and presentation of ideas.	Discuss activities that are hazardous to health.	Use a range of sources to research different health risks and prepare a presentation. Deliver the talk. Make brief notes on each topic covered by the other groups.	Assess each presentation. Encourage the children to do the same thing.	• Understand that drugs, solvents, alcohol, loud music and overexposure to sunlight can damage their health.
Enrichment Lesson 15 Health promises	• To assess the healthy and unhealthy aspects of a lifestyle. • To suggest lifestyle changes to improve the health of an individual.	The children write about their lifestyle, then prepare and perform a doctor–patient role-play in which lifestyle changes are recommended.		The children choose three lifestyle changes to adopt as 'resolutions'.	• Can assess a lifestyle and suggest changes to improve the health of the individual. • Recognise that the decisions they make may affect the quality of their lifestyle.

Assessment	Objectives	Activity 1	Activity 2
Lesson 16	• To assess the children's knowledge of the foods needed for growth and activity. • To assess the children's knowledge of the position and action of the heart. • To assess the children's ability to make a prediction and plan a fair test.	Answer questions on nutrition, the heart and the pulse rate.	Plan an investigation into pulse rates. Predict findings.

SC1 SCIENTIFIC ENQUIRY

Does the pulse vary at rest?

LEARNING OBJECTIVES AND OUTCOMES
- Measure the pulse rate.
- Relate the pulse rate to heart beat.
- Repeat measurements.
- Construct a bar chart and interpret it.

ACTIVITY
The children measure their pulse when at rest and record the result in a table. They repeat the measurement several times and each time record their result in a table. They then convert the data in the table into a bar chart and say what the chart shows.

LESSON LINKS
This Sc1 activity forms an integral part of the introduction to Lesson 7.

Lesson 1 ▪ Food groups

Objective
- To know that some foods are needed for activity and others for growth.
- To use a table to record and interpret data.

Vocabulary
fats, oils, sugar, starch, translucent, protein, carbohydrate, nutrient

RESOURCES 💿
Main activity: Cheese (such as Edam) that cuts without crumbling; rice; weighing scales; an A3-sized copy of photocopiable page 27 (also 'Food groups' (red) available on the CD-ROM); a flipchart and marker pen.
Group activities: 1 Photocopiable page 27. **2** Empty packets of cereal, soup, crisps and biscuits, showing tables of nutritional values; pens or pencils.

PREPARATION
Display an enlarged copy of photocopiable page 27 where the children can easily see it. You may prefer to sit them around the flipchart initially.

BACKGROUND
The nutrients we need from food to grow and remain healthy are divided into five groups: carbohydrates, lipids (fats and oils), proteins, vitamins and minerals. Carbohydrates provide energy that is ready for use; fats provide energy that is stored; proteins provide materials for growth; vitamins and minerals keep the body healthy. The body also needs water and fibre.

No one food provides all the requirements for the body (except milk for an infant), so we have to eat a combination of different foods. If the combination provides all the requirements, the diet is healthy and balanced. If one or more nutrients are missing, or too much of some nutrients (such as fats) are eaten, the diet is not balanced and ill-health can result.

To help provide people with information to choose a healthy diet, all packaged foods are analysed and the amounts of different nutrients in a 100g sample displayed on the label. In this lesson, the information is simplified to a star rating so the children can easily see that there are different quantities of nutrients in different foods.

STARTER
Start by saying that the biggest changes to our bodies occur from the age of around 10 to 16, when we are changing into adults. Food affects the way we grow, so we are going to look at food in some detail. Ask the class: *What are your favourite foods? What foods would you eat all the time if you could?* Develop the idea that it may not be a good thing just to live on a few foods such as chips. Discuss why not. The children should realise that they

Differentiation
Group activity 1
Support children by giving them 'Food groups' (green), from the CD-ROM, which includes fewer foods and simplified questions. Extend children with 'Food groups' (blue), which includes more open-ended questioning.

need a variety of foods for good health. Build on this by explaining that foods can be divided into foods for growth and foods for energy. Foods for energy can be split into two groups: 'carbohydrate' and 'protein'.

MAIN ACTIVITY

Explain that the amounts of nutrients in foods can be worked out and that for this lesson, a star rating has been used. Show them the enlarged copy of photocopiable page 27. The star rating is based on the contents of 100g of the food. One star represents up to 10g of the substance present, two stars represent 11–20g, three stars 21–30g, four stars 31–40g, and five stars above 41g (write this on the board so it can be used in Group activity 2).

Ask some of the children to help you in the following weighing activities. Weigh 100g of cheese and cut it into two pieces, one slightly larger than the other. Say that although the food substances are mixed throughout the cheese, if you could separate the fat and protein they would form two pieces as shown. In this case, both parts are over 41g, so the cheese has a five-star rating for both fat and protein. Weigh out 100g of rice; remove a small pinch (about 1g) to represent fat and a larger pinch (about 6g) to represent protein. The remaining rice represents starch – so the rice has a one-star rating for fat and for protein, but a five-star rating for starch.

GROUP ACTIVITIES

1 Give each child a copy of photocopiable page 27 and let them work through it. The answers for the core sheet (red) are: 1. jam, spaghetti, rice; 2. butter, peanuts, cheese; 3. cheese, peanuts, chicken, lentils; 4. milk. **2** Refer the children to the star rating system you have written on the board. Ask them to use this to give star ratings to packaged foods by reading their ingredients lists, and then to record their findings in a table.

ASSESSMENT

Can the children generalise about the foods needed for growth and activity? Ask them, for example: *What nutrients do you think beef and cod contain?*

PLENARY

Draw the children's attention to the judgements that are made when allocating a food to a group. (Refer to Group activity 1.) What foods would they recommend to someone who needed more food for activity (such as an athlete). Check the children's star ratings for packaged foods with the class.

OUTCOMES

- Can recognise foods for activity (carbohydrates) and growth (proteins).
- Can group foods according to their relative nutritional content.
- Can interpret data in a table.

Lesson 2 ▸ Healthy meals

Objective
- To be able to plan healthy meals.

RESOURCES

A large selection of magazines containing pictures of food; paper plates to which pictures can be stuck; plain paper; coloured pencils; scissors; adhesive.

MAIN ACTIVITY

Food can be divided into five main groups: 1. meat and eggs, 2. dairy products, 3. cereals, 4. fruit and vegetables, 5. sweets and cakes. Many health authorities recommend that each day, we eat one 'serving' of each of groups 1 and 2, three 'servings' of group 3 and five 'servings' of group 4. Group 5 should only be an occasional treat. With this information, let groups

Differentiation
Let children who need support use pictures and paste them on to sheets of paper or paper plates. Extend children by asking them to cross-reference these food groups to those considered in the previous lesson.

plan and display one or more meals. They should draw and label their own pictures of foods, or cut out pictures and stick them onto paper plates.

ICT LINK
Children could make an illustrated menu by scanning in pictures of food.

ASSESSMENT
Examine the meals planned and displayed by the children. Do they follow the recommendations given?

PLENARY
Each group should display their work and have it assessed for healthiness by other groups. Consider possible meals for 'healthy' and 'unhealthy' weeks.

OUTCOME
● Can plan a healthy meal.

Lesson 3 ▪ What's in a dish?

Objective
● To identify foods for activity and for growth in prepared dishes.

RESOURCES
Pictures of well-known dishes such as vegetable curry, chilli con carne or spaghetti bolognese; access to cookery books; paper; pencils.

MAIN ACTIVITY
Ask the children to work in groups to look at pictures of dishes, write down the names of the main food items, identify foods for growth and foods for activity, and record these in a table. Provide cookery books for the children to find out how to make similar dishes, if it is not clear from the pictures.

ICT LINK 💿
Children could make a spreadsheet of ingredients in a recipe, identify them as foods for growth or activity and make a bar chart to show the results. They could use the graphing tool from the CD-ROM to create their graphs.

Differentiation
Some children could label pictures of dishes with the names and food groups of the main items. Other children can examine dishes more critically, looking for a limited content of meat, eggs or dairy products and a higher content of cereals, fruit or vegetables. *Does the dish seem to have lots of sugar or fat in it?* They can go on to consider the sources of the ingredients.

ASSESSMENT
Note how quickly and easily the children can identify foods for activity (sugars and starches) and for growth (proteins) in each prepared dish. Are they confident about which foods are in each group?

PLENARY
Assess together each group's identification of the foods in each dish and their nutritional composition.

OUTCOME
● Can identify foods for energy and for growth (in prepared dishes).

Lesson 4 ▪ Digestion

Objective
● To know that food is digested by a number of organs, together called the digestive system.

RESOURCES 💿
Main activity: A large piece of paper on which to draw the outline of a child; a thick cord or rope about 5-6m long; adhesive tape; carpeted area; cardboard for shapes; large labels on cards ('mouth', 'gullet', 'stomach', 'small intestine', 'large intestine', 'rectum', 'liver', 'pancreas'), Blu-Tack®; photocopiable page 28 (also 'Digestion - 1' (red), available on the CD-ROM).
Group activities: 1 Photocopiable pages 29 and 30 (also 'Digestion - 2' and

Vocabulary
gullet (or oesophagus), stomach, liver, pancreas, small intestine, large intestine (or colon), rectum, anus, enzyme, stethoscope

'Digestion – 3' available on the CD-ROM); colouring pencils; scissors; adhesive. **2** Pencils; small pieces of food (such as squares of bread); a stethoscope. Make sure that the pieces of food are prepared hygienically. If bread is used, check that none of the children are coeliacs. Be aware of other food allergies.

ICT link: 'Digestion – 1' and 'Digestion – 2' interactives from the CD-ROM.

PREPARATION
Make two sets of large cardboard shapes of the mouth, gullet, stomach, liver, pancreas and large intestine (including the rectum), using the illustration below as a guide. Do not make shapes for the small intestine: the coiled rope will give a better effect. Make large labels for the various parts. Make a cardboard sandwich shape for the Plenary.

BACKGROUND
The body can only take in nutrients that are dissolved in water, so that they can be carried round the body in the blood and supplied to the parts where they are needed. In many foods, the nutrients are insoluble in water and so must be broken down into soluble forms by the process of digestion. Digestion is a two-stage process. In the first stage, the food is physically broken down by the action of the teeth; in the second stage, it is chemically broken down by the action of enzymes. You may like to invite the children to examine their teeth in the introduction to this lesson, consolidating their work in Year 3/Primary 4.

On photocopiable page 28, the idea of dissolving the nutrients is greatly simplified. The following is for your information, but may be useful if the children are researching from secondary sources and come across more detailed descriptions. Digestive chemicals called enzymes are produced by various parts of the digestive system. Each enzyme breaks down a specific part of the food. For example, the salivary glands secrete an enzyme which breaks down starch to sugar. The stomach produces an enzyme which begins the digestion of protein, and the pancreas produces three enzymes – for the digestion of protein, fat and carbohydrate. The liver produces bile, which makes fat droplets in food very small so that the enzyme can work on them more effectively. When the nutrients are soluble, they are absorbed through the wall of the small intestine into the blood.

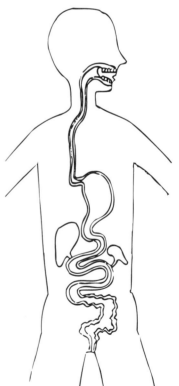

Food does not move on its own through the digestive system: it is pushed by muscles in the walls of the gullet, stomach and intestine. Fibre does not dissolve, but forms a solid mass on which the gut muscles can push. The digestive system of an adult is a tube about 7m long, through which a meal passes in about 18 hours.

The answers to the core sheet (red) are: 1. The sight and smell of the cooking burger; 2. In the salivary glands; 3. Incisors bit into it, premolars and molars chewed it up; 4. The gullet; 5. It was churned up; 6. They helped the food dissolve; 7. It went into the blood and around the body; 8. Undigested food.

STARTER
Explain that the class are going to find out where food goes when it enters our bodies. As the food passes through the body, it is digested. It is made into substances which

the body can use for energy, growth and keeping healthy.

MAIN ACTIVITY

Divide the class into two and set one half to work individually on copies of page 28. Take the other half of the class, place a large piece of paper on top of the carpet and ask a girl to lie on the paper while two friends draw around her outline. Arrange the cord on the outline to represent the digestive tract (see diagram) and stick each end to the paper with tape. Say that the cord represents a tube - 7m long in adults - in which the food is digested. Present each cardboard organ and ask the children where they should go. Steer their responses towards the correct ones and let a child stick each organ in place on the cord. Say that although we cannot see what is happening to food, inside our body, we can listen to what is happening with a stethoscope. Demonstrate listening to chewing (place the stethoscope next to the jaw), swallowing (place it on the throat) and churning (place it on the stomach). Say that the children will be able to try this for themselves later in the lesson.

Let the second half of the class construct a digestive system while the first half work on page 28. When constructing the second digestive system, select a boy to be drawn around.

GROUP ACTIVITIES

1 Give the children a copy each of pages 29 and 30 to complete.
2 Working in pairs, with adult help, taking turns to eat a little food and listen to their partner's jaw, throat and stomach with a stethoscope.

ICT LINK

Children can use the 'Digestion - 1' and 'Digestion - 2' interactives from the CD-ROM.

ASSESSMENT

During the group work, note those children who can position and label the organs accurately. Can they tell you the correct sequence of events in the passage of food through the digestive system? Can they name the different organs that make up the digestive system?

PLENARY

Put a cardboard sandwich on the mouth of a body outline and ask the class what will happen to it there. Move the sandwich through the different parts of the digestive system, asking what happens to it at each place.

OUTCOME

● Can recognise the parts of the digestive system and have some understanding of what each part does.

LINKS

Unit 5b, Lesson 11, 'Growing cabbages'.

Lesson 5 ▪ Breathing

Objective
● To know the basic structure of the respiratory system.
● To know that exercise increases the breathing rate.
● To make comparisons and identify simple patterns.
● To make predictions.

RESOURCES

Main activity: A 2-litre clear plastic bottle; the barrel of a ballpoint pen; a small balloon; a larger balloon; Plasticine®; adhesive tape; modelling clay, string; scissors; a stopclock; paper; pencils.
Group activities: 1 Stopclocks; paper; pencils. **2** Photocopiable page 31 (also 'Breathing' (red) on the CD-ROM); pencils.
ICT link: 'Breathing' interactive and graphing tool on the CD-ROM.

Vocabulary

nostril, nasal cavity, voice box (larynx), windpipe (trachea), lung, rib, diaphragm, inhale, exhale, oxygen, carbon dioxide.

PREPARATION

Cut the bottom off the plastic bottle. This represents the chest. Attach the small balloon to one end of the pen barrel with adhesive tape. This represents the windpipe and a lung. Secure the pen barrel in the neck of the bottle with modelling clay. Cut open the large balloon and stretch it over the bottom of the bottle. Fasten it in place with adhesive tape. This piece of balloon represents the diaphragm. Nip the balloon skin (diaphragm) between the finger and thumb, then push it in and pull it out gently so that the small balloon (lung) inflates and deflates.

BACKGROUND

The respiratory system consists of the windpipe, lungs, chest wall and diaphragm. This system draws air into the body, extracts some oxygen from it, releases carbon dioxide into it and then releases it to the outside - a process commonly known as breathing. At a chemical level, the process of respiration occurs in all living cells.

All life processes, including those that make our bodies grow and change, require energy. This enters the body in a chemical form, stored within food. In digestion it is broken down into a soluble chemical called glucose - a type of sugar. In order for the energy to be released from the glucose, oxygen has to be taken into the body and combined with glucose in a chemical reaction called respiration, which causes energy to be released. This reaction produces carbon dioxide, a poison that must be removed from the body.

In exercise, the muscles use more oxygen and more carbon dioxide is produced. This stimulates the brain to make the muscles in the chest and diaphragm work faster, so increasing the frequency and depth of breathing. In the circulatory system, the heart is stimulated to pump more quickly. These changes increase the amount of oxygen entering the blood and the amount of carbon dioxide leaving the body.

STARTER

Remind the children that food provides the body with energy. Explain that the body also needs oxygen from the air to release energy from food. When energy is released using oxygen, carbon dioxide is produced. The body contains a group of organs called the respiratory system which take in oxygen from the air and release carbon dioxide into it.

Use the bottle model of the chest to explain how we work. When the diaphragm is pushed in (the larger balloon is pushed up and in), the air in the chest (the bottle) is squashed and the air in our lungs (the small balloon) is pushed out. When the diaphragm is pulled down, there is more space for the air in the chest and air is pulled into the lungs.

Ask the children to hold their rib cage and breathe in and out, looking for signs of change in the rib cage. They should feel the ribs go upwards and outwards when breathing in, and downwards and inwards when breathing out. Ask them to put a hand on their body just below their ribs and breathe in and out. They should feel the body pushing outwards when breathing out, due to the diaphragm pushing down, and feel the body drawn inwards when the diaphragm relaxes and the muscles in the lower body push the body contents back up (see illustration on page 15).

MAIN ACTIVITY

Ask the children: *How could we measure how often we breathe?* The children should suggest that the number of breaths in a certain time could be measured. There may be some discussion about how long the time should be; help them to decide on a minute. Let the children sit quietly for a minute and count their breaths. You may wish them to work in pairs. Tell them to relax and breathe naturally, and not force their breathing to reach a high score or hold their breath to reach a low one. After they have counted

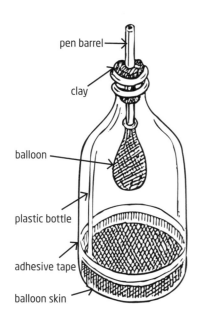

pen barrel

clay

balloon

plastic bottle

adhesive tape

balloon skin

Differentiation 💿

Group activity 1
Some children may need guiding through the planning stage and help with counting the number of breaths in a certain time. Other children will be able to plan their investigation and carry it out after it has been checked. They may also like to investigate how the breathing rate changes with time after stopping exercise. This will involve counting the breaths for a one-minute period several times.

Group activity 2
Support children by giving them 'Breathing' (green), from the CD-ROM, which includes fewer questions than the core sheet. Extend children by giving them 'Breathing' (blue), which includes a wider range of questions and asks them to write a story about air going in and out of the lungs.

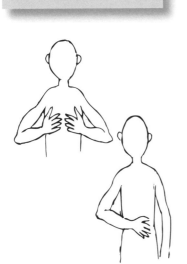

their breaths for a minute, put their results on the board. Note the variation, and state that such variation is natural.

Ask the children how they think their breathing rate would change if they walked about for two minutes. Write down their predictions on the board and write a simple plan for the investigation together. Let the children walk about for two minutes and then record their breaths for a minute as before. Collect their results and discuss what they have found. Remind the children about the structure and action of the respiratory system, and the way they planned the investigation.

GROUP ACTIVITIES

1 Ask the children to develop the class plan into an investigation of how activity affects breathing rate. They should investigate activities such as resting (lying down), walking and running. The time for breathing should be measured with a stopclock. Remind them of the need to keep the tests fair. They should predict the results before carrying out the tests they have planned. Several children in each group should take part, to reduce the effect of individual variations. They should look for patterns in their results.
2 Give the children a copy each of page 31 and let them work through it. The answers for the core sheet (red) are: 1. a rib; 2. upwards and outwards; 3. downwards and inwards; 4. diaphragm; 5. downwards; 6. upwards; 7. nostril, nasal cavity, voice box, windpipe, bronchus, lung.

ICT LINK 💿

Children could plan and carry out an investigation to find out if tall people have bigger lungs (larger chests) than short people, then record the results in a spread sheet and make a bar chart using the graphing tool on the CD-ROM.

'Breathing' interactive on the CD-ROM requires the children to label the different parts of the respiratory system. This could be completed in small groups or as a whole-class activity.

ASSESSMENT

Look for logical structure in the investigation plans, and for reasons for children's predictions. For example: 'The breathing rate will increase more for faster exercise, because more energy is needed for the movement.' Look for the use of 'per minute' in the results, not just numbers without units. Look for patterns being described in results obtained from different people. Look for a mention of 'variation' to explain why everyone does not have the same breathing rate. Ask each child to describe the movements made as they breathe; look for confident use of the correct vocabulary in a description.

PLENARY

Ask each group to report on the results of their investigation. Look for similarities and differences in the results from different groups. Ask the class what they can conclude from all the results they have seen.

OUTCOMES
- Can describe how the body draws in and expels air.
- Can measure the breathing rate at rest and after exercise.
- Can plan an investigation to answer a given question.
- Can recognise patterns in the results, and suggest explanations.

LINKS
PSHE: keeping healthy.

Lesson 6 ▫ The heart

RESOURCES

Main activity: Three 2-litre bottles of water (coloured red for dramatic effect if you wish); lumps of Plasticine®; wallpaper; a marker pen; a poster showing the position and structure of the heart; a balloon and balloon pump; an empty plastic bottle; a piece of paper.
Group activities: 1 Photocopiable page 32 (also 'The heart – 1' (red), available on the CD-ROM); pencils; scissors; adhesive; a CD-ROM showing heart action (if available). **2** Photocopiable page 33 (also 'The heart – 2' (red), available on the CD-ROM); pencils; a CD-ROM showing blood circulation (if available).
ICT link: 'The heart' interactive on CD-ROM.

BACKGROUND

The children will have studied the skeleton and muscles in Year 4/Primary 5, and may have studied exercise. They may have been introduced to the pulse and its dependence on the heart. Children often have difficulty with the structure of the heart because of the way it is represented in books: the convention is to show the heart as it would appear in a person facing you, so that the left side of the heart appears on your right. The children should be made aware of this straight away.

STARTER

Remind the children that nutrients are taken into the blood from the small intestine and that oxygen enters the body from the lungs, which have a rich blood supply. Nutrients and oxygen are transported around the body so that they can release energy for activity and for growth and change in the body. There are six litres of blood in the body (show the class the three bottles of water), and it does not move on its own. It is moved by a pump, the heart, through blood vessels. The pumping action of the heart can be felt as a regular pulse in some blood vessels (called arteries). Let the children find their pulses; then say that the pulse will be investigated in the next lesson.

MAIN ACTIVITY

Ask a child to lie on a piece of wallpaper while one or two friends draw around them. Put the outline drawing on the wall. Ask the first child to clench his or her fist, and ask another friend to mould a piece of Plasticine about the same size as the fist. Say: *Your heart is about the same size as your clenched fist.* Give the first child the Plasticine 'heart'; ask him or her to hold it in the correct place within the body outline, then mark the spot with a cross or draw around the heart. Ask other class members if they can place it more accurately. Finally, compare their efforts with a poster showing the position of the heart and ask them to assess their accuracy.

Show the class a balloon pump and demonstrate how it works. Point out that the air does not leave the balloon when the pump is pulled back, because a valve in the pump stops the air from escaping. Demonstrate how a valve stops the flow of air by holding a piece of paper close to the open neck of an empty plastic bottle: when you press in the sides of the bottle, the paper is blown outwards; when you let the bottle expand again, the paper settles over the open neck and stops air flowing in.

Say that in the heart there are two pumps, each with two valves. One pumps blood from all parts of the body to the lungs, and the other pumps it back from the lungs to the rest of the body. Copy diagram A onto the board. *Do you think your heart might look like this?* Draw diagram B on the board to show how the pumps are more 'bent round' in reality, then show the children a picture of a real heart with the two pumps joined together. Explain that the muscles in the walls of the heart squeeze the blood, and

A

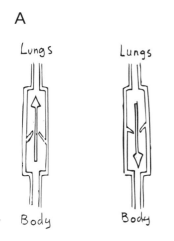

B

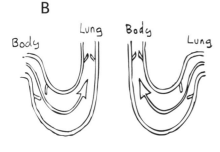

Differentiation 💿
Group activity 1
Some children may need more help in recognising the arrangement of the two pumps in the heart, and may need to be shown again how the two pumps are 'bent'. Other children may be able to use secondary sources to label the blood vessels connected to the heart.
Group activity 2
To support children, give them 'The heart – 2' (green) from the CD-ROM, a simplified version of the core sheet.

the valves open and close to make the blood move in one direction only.

If appropriate, say that blood leaving the heart is pushed very strongly into tubes called arteries that have thick, stretchy walls. Blood returning to the heart from the lungs or the rest of the body is pushed less strongly, and travels in thin-walled tubes called veins. Ask the children to look at the veins in their wrists or on the underside of their lower arm.

GROUP ACTIVITIES

1 If you have a CD-ROM that shows the heart beating, let the children watch it before they work individually to complete photocopiable page 32.
2 If you have a CD-ROM that shows how blood flows around the body, let the children watch it before they work individually to complete photocopiable page 33. The answers to the core sheet (red) are: 1. Arrows along A to the lungs; 2. Arrows along C to the heart; 3. Arrows along D to the body; 4. Arrows along B to the heart; 5. Could include brain, muscles, gut, kidneys, liver; 6. A artery, B vein, C vein, D artery.

ICT LINK 💿

Press a sound sensor to your chest and let the children listen to your heart beat. Use a portable heart rate monitor and wrist watch (the type used by joggers) to show how the heart beat can be recorded and displayed.

Some children can complete 'The heart' interactive, on the CD-ROM.

ASSESSMENT

At an appropriate time in the lesson, ask each child to explain how the heart moves blood around the body. In the Plenary session, ask the class to describe the path taken by the blood in the body.

PLENARY

Enlarge the diagram on page 33. Ask the children who completed 'The heart – 2' (green) to describe the path of the blood around the body. Then let other children identify the arteries and veins and read parts of their accounts.

OUTCOMES
- Can describe the action of the heart.
- Can describe the path of the blood through the circulatory system.

Lesson 7 ▫ The pulse

Objective
- To know that the pulse is produced by the heartbeat.
- To plan and carry out an investigation: make a prediction, make observations and measurements, check them by repeating, compare results with the prediction and draw conclusions.
- To use tables and bar graphs to communicate data (perhaps using ICT).

RESOURCES
Stopclocks; paper; pencils; a computer (optional).

MAIN ACTIVITY
Show the children how to take their pulse. They should count the beats for a minute. Ask them to predict how the pulse rate may vary with exercise, and then to plan an investigation. They should take the pulse when lying down, sitting, standing, after walking and after running, taking each reading several times and recording the results in a table. They should produce a bar graph of their results and compare their prediction with their data. From their data they should see that the pulse rate is least when lying down and greatest when exercising vigorously. Remind them about the blood carrying food and oxygen which the muscles use to release energy; ask them how this fact could be used to explain their results. (The heart beats faster to provide more food and oxygen for energy as the muscles become more active.) They should also note that there is variation in pulse rate between children.

Differentiation

Support children by asking them to take counts for 15 seconds and (with help) multiply by four, or double and double again, to find the number of beats per minute. They could take one measurement for each activity. Challenge children by asking them to explain the different pulse rates under different conditions (excitement, muscles used to hold body up, blood moving horizontally when lying down, and so on).

ICT LINK

Children could record the results of their investigations in a spread sheet and make a bar chart. They may wish to use the graphing tool, from the CD-ROM to create these.

ASSESSMENT

Note whether the children can find a pulse and measure the pulse rate. Examine their investigation plan for logical sequence and an appropriate level of detail. Look for tables of results. Examine the graphs for accuracy.

PLENARY

Evaluate the children's investigation plans. Collate the group data and try plotting a class graph for each physical activity. Ask the class to make a statement about heart activity based on these results. Treat the interpretation of the results with care and sensitivity.

OUTCOMES

- Can find the pulse and measure its rate.
- Can plan and carry out an investigation: make a prediction, carry out observations and measurements, record results in an appropriate and systematic manner, compare results with predictions and draw conclusions.
- Can use tables and bar graphs to communicate data (perhaps using ICT).

Lesson 8 How fit am I?

Objective

- To plan and carry out an investigation.
- To use tables and bar graphs to communicate data (perhaps using ICT).

RESOURCES

Stopclocks; paper; pencils; a computer and data-handling software (optional).

MAIN ACTIVITY

In a fit person with a healthy heart, the heart returns quickly to a 'resting' rate after activity. Challenge the children to use this fact to plan an investigation to check how fit they are. They may need some guidance (including an explanation of what 'fit' means in this context). The essential features of the investigation are taking the pulse when resting, immediately after a short period of exercise and at short (30-second or one-minute) intervals after the exercise has ceased until the 'resting' pulse rate returns.

ICT LINK

Children could display the results as a line graph, using the graphing tool on the CD-ROM.

ASSESSMENT

Look for clear recording in tables and accurately constructed graphs.

PLENARY

Review the results and say that the heart becomes healthier if a person takes regular exercise. Ask the children to speculate on how people's hearts might be affected if they take no exercise and spend all their free time watching television or playing on computers. They might like to review their own lifestyle. This discussion needs to be handled with care and sensitivity.

Differentiation

Support children by asking them to take the pulse three times only - before exercise, immediately after and one or two minutes later. Extend children by asking them to repeat the whole investigation and compare the results.

OUTCOMES

- Can plan and carry out an investigation.
- Can use tables and bar graphs to communicate data, perhaps using ICT.

ENRICHMENT
Lesson 9 ▪ Healthy living

Objective
● To construct a plan for a healthy lifestyle.

Vocabulary
healthy, unhealthy, hygiene, heart disease, exercise, diet, obesity, fibre

RESOURCES
Group activity: A3 paper; pens; pencils.
ICT link: Graphing tool and the diagram 'Lifestyle plan', from the CD-ROM

BACKGROUND
Aspects of diet, exercise and hygiene are targeted in this lesson. Good personal hygiene prevents the build-up of body odour – the sweat we produce provides an ideal breeding ground for microbes living on our skin, and these microbes can react with sweat to make us smell. 'Athlete's foot' is caused by a fungus that thrives on moist, sweaty skin between the toes; washing and drying thoroughly helps to prevent this. Microbes thrive on food deposits left between our teeth; they feed on sugars and produce acids that attack the enamel of the teeth and cause cavities to form. Regular brushing is important for keeping teeth healthy.

STARTER
Gather the children together. Ask them to imagine how their lives would have been different if they had lived 200 years ago. Explain that people in Britain now live almost twice as long (on average) as they once did.

MAIN ACTIVITY
Explain that this lesson is about looking at our lifestyles and trying to decide whether they are healthy. *What does 'healthy' mean?* Explain that for many people who live in relatively wealthy parts of the world, such as Britain, the quality of life has greatly improved; but that some diseases, including heart disease, have become more common as a result of an unhealthy lifestyle. *What things are important for staying healthy?* Responses should include diet, exercise, sleeping enough and good hygiene.

What should a healthy diet include? A healthy diet should include plenty of fresh fruit and vegetables, fish or lean meat (or beans), wholemeal foods containing fibre, foods rich in minerals (such as calcium) and vitamins, and so on. Foods to avoid should include foods that are high in fat, or that have added salt, sugar, colourings, preservatives and so on.

Now ask the children why exercise is important. Hopefully, answers will include: 'it makes your muscles and bones stronger'; 'it strengthens the heart and improves the circulation of the blood'; 'it reduces stress'; 'it helps to prevent obesity' (becoming overweight, which increases blood pressure and the strain on the heart).

GROUP ACTIVITY
Using A3 paper, the children should each draw a 'My Lifestyle' circle to represent their day, showing what time they wake, wash, eat breakfast and so on (see illustration on page 20 or diagram on the CD-ROM). Emphasise that they must show exactly what they eat – for example, not just 'sandwiches' but 'ham sandwiches (white bread) with butter, tomatoes and lettuce'. They must mention milk and sugar if these are added to cereals. They should also include whether (and for how long) they watch TV; what time they go to bed and so on. At the bottom of the page, they should draw two boxes entitled 'Good points' and 'Bad points'.

The children should then swap their charts and look critically at each other's day. When they have agreed on the main points, they should write these ideas and some of their own in the boxes, under the chart (still using the swapped copies).

Ask them to compare their lifestyles and discuss (in groups), how they could improve the quality of their diet, exercise and general lifestyles to become healthier. They should add their suggestions to their charts.

Differentiation
Some children will need help with setting out their day as an A3 chart. You may want to give a rough guide on the board. Alternatively, you could draw the circles in advance with key activities (such as 'Eat breakfast') added at the bottom, allowing the children to sort out the events.

ICT LINK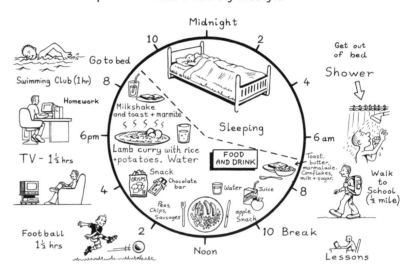

Children could work out the times they spend activities in a typical day and record them in a spread sheet, bar chart or pie chart .They could use the graphing tool to create their graphs.

ASSESSMENT

Go through the charts as a class, checking the aspects of lifestyle that have been recognised as healthy and unhealthy. Check that each child recognises exercise, a balanced diet and hygiene as key aspects of a healthy lifestyle.

PLENARY

Have a class vote on who has the healthiest lifestyle based on their daily plan. Take care not to encourage comments that refer to children's upbringing. Explain that many national groups in the USA and in Britain are campaigning for measures that will lead children to watch less TV. *Can you think why this might be a good idea?* Generate discussion by asking: *Do you believe that TV should be abolished? What would the advantages and disadvantages be?*

OUTCOMES

- Can plan a regime for a healthy lifestyle.
- Can explain the need for each item in such a regime.

LINKS

PSHE and citizenship: what makes a healthy lifestyle.

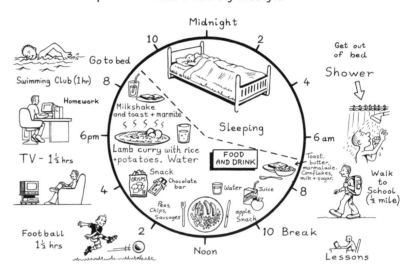

Lesson 10 ◼ Harmful drugs

Objective
- To know that some drugs can help the body recover from illness.
- To know that people can persuade others to take harmful drugs.

Vocabulary
medicine, drug, solvent, addict, nicotine, cigarette, alcohol

RESOURCES

A collection of advertisements (see Preparation); a plastic tumbler; water.

PREPARATION

Look through a selection of magazines and make a collection of advertisements relating to medicines and other chemicals that we apply to our bodies: foot powders, spot treatments, mouthwash and so on.

BACKGROUND

This lesson and the three that follow it deal with drugs. This issue can be a sensitive one, and care must be taken to take into account the health and domestic circumstances of the children. This lesson presents drugs in a medicinal context, and introduces the idea of harmful drugs.

Tobacco

Nicotine is the addictive drug in tobacco, but there other chemicals in cigarette smoke that are harmful to the body. The lining of the windpipe has microscopic hairs that move inhaled dust up and out of the respiratory system. Harmful chemicals in smoke stop the action of the hairs, so the dust accumulates in the lungs and has to be removed by continual coughing. The smoke can also cause bronchitis and cancers to develop. Smoking also increases the chances of heart disease and lost limbs in later life.

Alcohol

Alcohol drunk in moderation is believed to help keep the circulatory system of an adult healthy. The effect of alcohol on the nervous system of the body is related to body size. A large person can drink more alcohol than a small person before the nervous system is affected. The serious danger of alcohol for children is related to their small body size: they may become quickly intoxicated if they drink adult measures. At the very least, intoxication leads to impaired judgement and a 'hangover' with headaches and nausea. The major danger to young people from drinking alcohol in excess is becoming unconscious and choking on their own vomit. Addiction in adults increases the chances of developing heart disease, hepatitis and cirrhosis of the liver. Heavy drinking can also cause violent and irrational behaviour.

Solvents and illegal 'recreational' drugs

Children of this age may be more at risk of coming in to contact with dangerous solvents than illegal drugs. Some everyday substances such as glues and correcting fluids are made with chemical solvents that evaporate readily. If these are sniffed, they produce an effect similar to drunkenness.

Some children have died the first time they sniffed solvents; others, through prolonged use, have experienced damage to the face, lungs, liver and kidneys. The children's exposure to illegal drugs may vary widely, and you may wish to consult with health professionals working in your area to decide on an appropriate approach to the topic.

STARTER

Start by saying that while we try to keep ourselves healthy by eating a balanced diet and taking exercise, sometimes we may become ill and need to visit the doctor or the hospital to help make us better. A doctor may give us drugs to help us. Ask the children to describe treatments they have received. Talk about taking medicines at home to control a condition. Highlight that it is important to take your prescribed dosage, as taking too much of a medicine can be harmful. Ask what other drugs are used by people. If the children do not suggest them, explain that there are also some drugs that people take that can be harmful – including nicotine in tobacco and alcohol in alcoholic drinks. Say that this lesson will look at drugs that help us and how young people may come to take drugs that harm them.

MAIN ACTIVITY

Start by asking: *What do people take when they suffer from colds or 'flu? What do they hope these substances will do for them?* Say that for thousands of years, people have taken substances to make themselves feel better, and some of these can aid recovery.

GROUP ACTIVITIES

1 The children should examine some advertisements for medicines and chemicals that we apply to our bodies, and make a table to categorise them according to the parts of the body they help.

2 Arrange the children into groups of three for an 'Oh, go on' role-play: one child as persuader, one as resister and one as an observer. The persuader has to try to get the resister to take a drink of water (pretending that it is alcoholic). After three minutes, the groups can reflect on the activity and ask each other questions such as: 'When did you think I might take a drink?', 'If you had more time, could you have persuaded me to take a drink?', 'How would the observer have felt if they were a friend of the resister or the persuader?' The observer should be prepared to report back to the class.

ICT
As part of the Starter, children could make a spreadsheet of parts of the body that are helped by medicines (for example the mouth – mouthwash).

ASSESSMENT
Examine how the children categorise medicines and helpful drugs. Look for clear reasons why a persuader thinks a person should take a drink, and clear reasons for resisting. Look for expression of the observer's feelings.

PLENARY
Examine any posters that have been made and decide which are the most effective. Select three children who are good persuaders and two children who are good resisters, and let them re-enact Group activity 2 with the rest of the class acting as observers. Evaluate the effect of having more persuaders than resisters.

OUTCOMES
● Recognise some medicines and helpful drugs and know how they assist recovery from illness.
● Recognise how peer pressure can introduce young people to drugs.

Lesson 11 ▪ The effects of tobacco

Objective
● To know how tobacco affects the body.

RESOURCES
A 'smoking machine' (can be obtained from educational suppliers or borrowed from a secondary school or teachers' centre); a large open space (such as the school hall or playground); a selection of leaflets and posters about the dangers of smoking; paper; writing and drawing materials; a computer. Some local authorities have health initiatives aimed at young people and can provide useful additional resources.

MAIN ACTIVITY
Demonstrate the smoking machine in a large open space. Explain that the syringe represents the chest and the damp filter paper placed in the machine represents the lungs (and the lining of the windpipe). Follow the instructions provided. Place a cigarette in the holder and light it. Repeat the 'breathing' actions as described until the cigarette is 'smoked'. With each 'breath', the syringe will fill with smoke. Remove the filter paper and display the tar. Discuss the dangers of smoking. Relate this to the 'Oh, go on' activity in Lesson 10. Look together at any leaflets about smoking then ask the children to design their own anti-smoking poster or leaflet.

ASSESSMENT
Display the posters and leaflets the children have made.

Differentiation
Extend children by asking them to assess the impact of the various leaflets and posters, as well as making their own.

PLENARY
Lead a discussion on why people start and stop smoking.

OUTCOME
● Can explain why smoking is harmful.

Lesson 12 ▪ The effects of alcohol

Objective
● To know how alcohol affects the body.

RESOURCES
Leaflets on the dangers of alcohol; library books on alcohol and related social issues; paper; writing and drawing materials. Several local authorities have health initiatives aimed at young people and can provide useful additional resources.

MAIN ACTIVITY
Use secondary sources to find out how alcohol affects the body and why it can be a danger to young people. *What is an alcoholic? What help is available for alcoholics?* Let the children design a poster about the dangers of alcohol.

ASSESSMENT
Examine some children's posters. Check the children's research methods and findings on how alcoholic drinks are made. Look for accuracy and impact in the posters, and accurate details and sequences in the written findings.

PLENARY
Display the posters. Ask some children to report back on how alcoholic drinks are made.

Differentiation
Extend children by asking them to find out how alcoholic drinks are made.

OUTCOMES
● Can describe the effects of alcohol on the body.
● Can explain why drinking alcohol can be harmful.

Lesson 13 ▪ The effects of drugs and solvents

Objective
● To know how solvents affect the body.
● To know how illegal drugs affect the body.

RESOURCES
Leaflets, if available, on solvent and drug abuse; a visitor such as a health visitor or, if appropriate, a police officer specialising in drug education.

MAIN ACTIVITY
Arrange your classroom visitor in advance. Let the children examine secondary sources about solvent abuse. Then discuss: *Why do people sniff glue? How dangerous is sniffing solvents?* If appropriate, use secondary sources and your visitor to discuss the dangers of illegal drugs and how to avoid dangerous drugs. Ask the children to work in groups to make posters warning about the dangers of solvent (or drug) abuse.

ASSESSMENT
Examine the messages of the posters for accuracy and impact. Through discussion, determine the children's awareness of dangers.

PLENARY
Exhibit the children's posters. If appropriate, carry out a role-play 'Oh, go on' exercise as in Lesson 11, with the class as observers. Highlight major points from the role-play on the board.

Differentiation
The children should work in mixed-ability groups to make the posters.

OUTCOMES
● Can explain how solvents affect the body.
● Can explain the dangers of using illegal drugs.

ENRICHMENT
Lesson 14 ▪ Things to avoid

Objective
● To identify activities and substances that may be harmful to health.
● To develop skills in collaborative research, discussion and presentation of ideas.

Vocabulary
medicines, symptoms, liver, brain, addicted, ozone layer, ultra-violet rays, decibels, hertz (Hz), mucus, cilia, cancer, toxic

RESOURCES
Group activity: A4 paper; access to the school library; CD-ROMs such as *Encarta*® (Microsoft); young people's health advice booklets concerning drugs from your local health authority; photocopiable pages 34, 35 and 36 (also 'Things to avoid – 1, 2 and 3' (red), available on the CD-ROM).

PREPARATION
Make one copy per child of photocopiable pages 34, 35, 36.

BACKGROUND
Smoking claims thousands of lives in the UK each year. Alcohol is linked to many of the accidents treated by hospitals, to violence in the home, to liver disease and to many other problems. Solvents and 'recreational' drugs ruin the health of many young people and are linked to fatalities. Overexposure to sunlight can lead to cancer and the premature ageing of unprotected skin. Prolonged exposure to very loud music damages the hearing.

STARTER
Gather the class together. Remind them that in Lesson 9 they looked at their lifestyles to see how healthy they were. Explain that today they are going to look at some activities that can be harmful to our health.

MAIN ACTIVITY
Ask the children to name some activities that can damage our bodies. Focus on ones that are intrinsically harmful, rather than ones that carry a risk of accidental injury. Hopefully suggestions will include smoking, taking drugs and drinking too much alcohol; you may have to prompt the children to mention overexposure to the sun and listening to very loud music.

Tell the class that they will be working in groups, looking at one topic and then presenting it to the rest of the class. They will have 30 minutes to write their ideas on a sheet of A4 paper, and the presentation by each group should last about two minutes. Say that you will give each group a mark out of 10, based upon how effectively they present their ideas.

GROUP ACTIVITY
Write the topic titles below on sheets of A4 paper. Split the class into six groups and each one a topic to discuss and research. They should use photocopies of pages 34 and 35 as well as other sources. Advise them to share their ideas within the group. Suggest that they brainstorm ideas, with one person writing them down, then decide how they are going to present them. They can use reference materials to find information. Encourage them to try to be entertaining and imaginative when they present their ideas – perhaps they might like to present a role-play, or give their audience a quiz at the end of their talk. Tell them that they have 30 minutes to prepare.

Group 1: Avoid drugs!   Group 2: Avoid solvents!
Group 3: Avoid sunburn!   Group 4: Avoid alcohol!
Group 5: Avoid loud music!   Group 6: Don't smoke!

Differentiation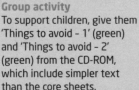
Group activity
To support children, give them 'Things to avoid – 1' (green) and 'Things to avoid – 2' (green) from the CD-ROM, which include simpler text than the core sheets.

Ask each group to come up to the front of the room in turn and present their talk. Give the 'audience' copies of page 36. After each talk, they should write down what they have learned in the appropriate space.

ASSESSMENT
Ask the children to design a poster for other children (perhaps for homework), telling them what they should do and what they should avoid to live a healthy life. This will provide a summary of what they have learned.

PLENARY

Give each group a mark out of 5 for the content of their talk, with higher marks for those who have used a number of information sources. Give them another mark out of 5 for the style of their talk: was it engaging, humorous, imaginative? Share your marks with the children, as it will help them to develop their presentation skills. The 'audience' could also give each group's talk a mark out of 10 to help them develop their critical appreciation skills.

OUTCOME

● Understand that drugs, solvents, alcohol, loud music and overexposure to sunlight can damage their health.

LINKS

PSHE and citizenship: effects and risks of drugs.

ENRICHMENT
Lesson 15 ▫ Health promises

Objective
● To assess the healthy and unhealthy aspects of a lifestyle.
● To suggest lifestyle changes to improve the health of an individual.

RESOURCES

Paper; writing materials; notes from previous lessons; space for the children to perform sketches; a white coat (optional).

MAIN ACTIVITY

Ask the children to put together a role-play in pairs: as a doctor and a patient. They should start by writing individually about their lifestyle: what they eat, how often they exercise, whether they listen to loud music and so on. They should try to balance the good and bad points. At the end of this, they should work in pairs: the doctor giving advice, the patient seeking advice. They should prepare and act out the consultation, then swap over. The 'doctor' should draw on the knowledge gained in previous lessons to provide a 'prescription' for a healthier life. Select pairs to act out their piece in front of the class (if you have a white coat, the 'doctors' can take turns to wear it). Check whether there is general agreement about the 'prescriptions' given by the doctors. If there is disagreement, explore the suggestions made and discuss any alternatives there might be. Some of the role-plays could be repeated in an assembly.

ASSESSMENT

Note if the children can identify healthy and unhealthy aspects of a lifestyle, and whether they can recommend appropriate changes to improve the quality of an individual's health.

PLENARY

With the class, check the key issues that have arisen. Ask the children to choose three resolutions they can make to improve their health. These should be realistic! They shouldn't aim to give up all sweets, for example, but they could aim to eat one apple every day in place of one sugary snack. You can put up the children's names on a 'health promises' chart on the wall and give them a gold star for each week they keep up their resolution.

Differentiation
Main activity
Support children by asking them to provide extreme examples of poor lifestyle so that they can start to consider possible improvements - for example, someone who chain-smokes, eats nothing but chips and sausages and drinks heavily.

OUTCOMES

● Can assess a lifestyle and suggest changes to improve the health of the individual.
● Recognise that decisions they make may affect the quality of their lifestyle.

Lesson 16 ◾ Assessment

Objective
● To assess the children's knowledge of the foods needed for growth and activity.
● To assess the children's knowledge of the position and action of the heart.
● To assess the children's ability to make a prediction and plan a fair test.

RESOURCES ◉
Photocopiable pages 37 and 38 (also 'Assessment - 1' (red) and 'Assessment - 2' (red), available on the CD-ROM); pencils; blue and red colouring pencils.

STARTER
You may wish to begin the Assessment activities straight away, or start by giving an oral vocabulary test. You could either give words and ask the children for definitions or give definitions and ask for suitable words. Refer to the vocabulary lists for the appropriate lessons.

ASSESSMENT ACTIVITY 1
Give the children a copy each of page 37 to complete individually. You may wish to mark the sheets yourself, or to swap them around the class and let the children mark each other's sheets.

ANSWERS
1. Chicken, fish (2 marks).
2. Two from spaghetti, rice, bread, potato (2 marks).
3. Label lines should be included (4 marks).
4. Slightly to the right side of the chest (true left) (2 marks) or in the centre of the chest (1 mark). The heart should be about 0.5 cm long on this scale.
5. In your wrist, side of the neck, at your temple, in your thumb (any of these for 1 mark).
6. The beating of the heart (1 mark).
7. The number of times the heart beats in a certain amount of time (1 mark), usually in beats per minute (1 mark).
8. It increases (1 mark).
9. The heart beats faster to send more blood to the muscles (1 mark). The blood contains food and oxygen that the muscles need. When muscles exercise they need more food and oxygen, so the heart beats faster (1 mark for some appropriate explanation). (Total marks: 17.)

LOOKING FOR LEVELS
All the children should be able to answer questions 3 and 8. Most children will answer questions 1, 2, 4, 5 and 7. Some will answer questions 6 and 9.

ASSESSMENT ACTIVITY 2
Give the children a copy each of page 38 to complete individually.

ANSWERS
Look for a clear description of a fair test in which all the children have rested for the same amount of time before their pulse was taken. A stopwatch or other timer should be mentioned. Look for repetition of the test to check the results. Look for an awareness in the prediction that the pulse rate may vary from person to person, like other features of the body.

LOOKING FOR LEVELS
All the children should show some awareness of fair testing. Most children will clearly describe a fair test in which all the children have rested for the same amount of time before their pulse is taken, and mention a stopwatch or other timer. Some children will also plan to repeat the test to check the results. Most of the children will make a prediction; some may suggest that the pulse will vary from person to person, like other features of the body.

PLENARY
You may wish to go through the answers to the tests with the children.

 # Food groups

◼ The foods in this table have a star rating for the substances they contain.

Food	Materials for growth (protein)	Fats and oils	Sugar and starch (carbohydrates)
Bread	★	★	★ ★
Butter	★	★ ★ ★ ★ ★	–
Jam	★	–	★ ★ ★ ★ ★
Milk	★	★	★
Cheddar cheese	★ ★ ★ ★ ★	★ ★ ★ ★ ★	–
Peanuts	★ ★ ★	★ ★ ★ ★ ★	★
Spaghetti	★	★	★ ★ ★ ★ ★
Lamb	★ ★	★ ★ ★ ★	–
Rice	★	★	★ ★ ★ ★ ★
Chicken	★ ★ ★	★	–
Potatoes	★	–	★ ★
Fish	★ ★	★	–
Bananas	★	–	★ ★
Lentils	★ ★ ★	–	★ ★ ★ ★

1. Which foods are richest in starch and sugar?

_____

2. Which foods are richest in fats and oils?

_____

3. Which foods are richest in materials for growth?

_____

4. Which food has small amounts of all three substances?

_____

5. Think of **5** foods which you like to eat. Write them into the table below.

Foods for growth	Foods rich in fats and oils	Foods rich in starch

Digestion – 1

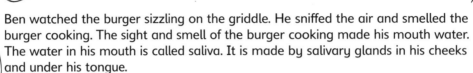

◼ Read what happened to Ben's burger, then answer the questions.

Ben watched the burger sizzling on the griddle. He sniffed the air and smelled the burger cooking. The sight and smell of the burger cooking made his mouth water. The water in his mouth is called saliva. It is made by salivary glands in his cheeks and under his tongue.

When the burger was ready, Ben could hardly wait to eat it. He bit into it with his chisel-shaped front teeth. They are called his incisors. His fang-like canine teeth tore at the bread. When Ben started chewing, he used his premolar and molar teeth at the back of his mouth.

Ben rolled the chewed food to the back of his mouth with his tongue. He swallowed and the chewed food then moved down a tube called the gullet. At the end of the gullet, the food entered Ben's stomach. There the food mixed with a liquid and the muscles in the stomach wall churned up the mixture. Some of the burger broke into smaller pieces. After Ben had eaten his burger, his stomach kept churning it up for some time.

The churned-up burger looked more like soup and the stomach then squirted it into a tube that led to the small intestine. As the food moved along, liquids from the pancreas and liver mixed with it. They helped to dissolve the solid parts of the burger. Some parts of the burger could not be dissolved. They were made of fibre and passed along the small intestine. Other substances in the burger that would provide energy or materials for growth did dissolve. They were taken from the small intestine into the blood and passed around the body.

Undigested food, including the fibre, eventually passed into Ben's large intestine and then into the rectum. Later, the undigested food would pass through the anus when Ben went to the toilet.

1. What two things made Ben's mouth water? _____

2. Where is the water in the mouth made? _____

3. Which teeth bit into the burger and which teeth chewed it up? _____

_____

4. Where did the food go after it left the mouth? _____

5. What happened to the food in the stomach? _____

6. What did the liquids from the pancreas and liver do? _____

7. Where did the dissolved food go after it had left the digestive system? _____

_____

8. What went into the large intestine? _____

Illustration © Robin Lawrie

Digestion – 2

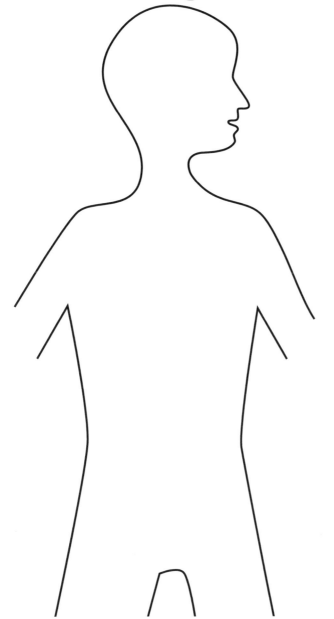

A

B

C

D

E

F

G

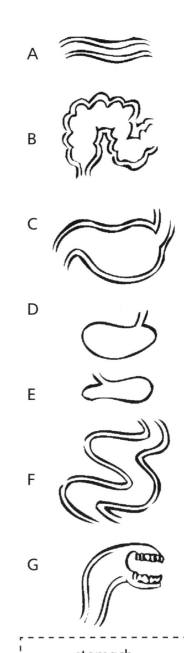

1. Cut out the outline of the body and stick it in the middle of an A4 sheet of paper.

2. Colour in parts A, C, F and G pink. Colour in part B purple, part D brown and part E red.

3. Cut out the body parts. Look at the display in the classroom, then put the parts in the correct places inside the body outline. Check your work with your teacher before you stick the parts in place.

4. Cut out the labels, stick them on the sheet and draw a line from each label to the correct part of the digestive system.

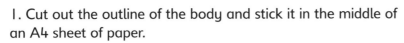

stomach

mouth

colon

pancreas

gullet

liver

small intestine

Illustration © Theresa Tibbetts c/o Beehive Illustration

Digestion – 3

■ Read the information below about the action of each part of the digestive system.

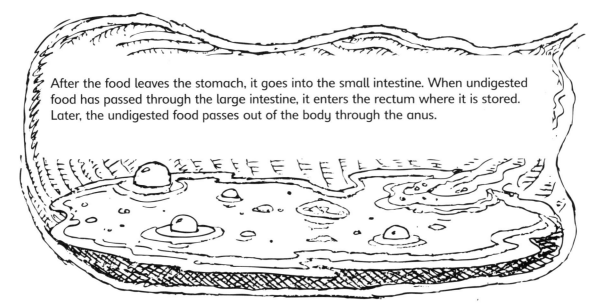

After the food leaves the stomach, it goes into the small intestine. When undigested food has passed through the large intestine, it enters the rectum where it is stored. Later, the undigested food passes out of the body through the anus.

■ Cut out the 'action box' for each part and stick it next to the correct part of the body on your diagram of the digestive system.

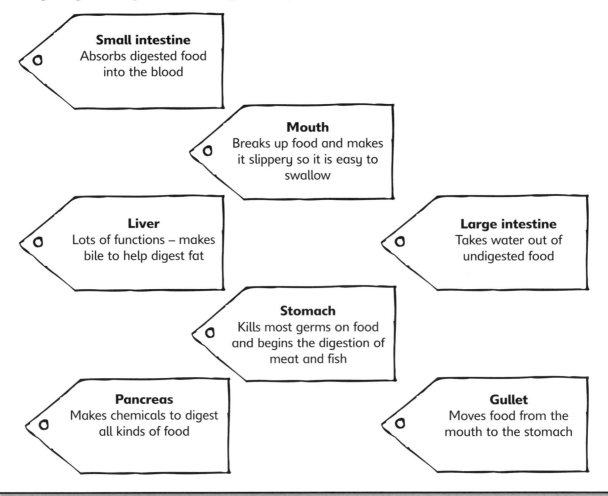

Small intestine
Absorbs digested food into the blood

Mouth
Breaks up food and makes it slippery so it is easy to swallow

Liver
Lots of functions – makes bile to help digest fat

Large intestine
Takes water out of undigested food

Stomach
Kills most germs on food and begins the digestion of meat and fish

Pancreas
Makes chemicals to digest all kinds of food

Gullet
Moves food from the mouth to the stomach

Illustration © Robin Lawrie

Breathing

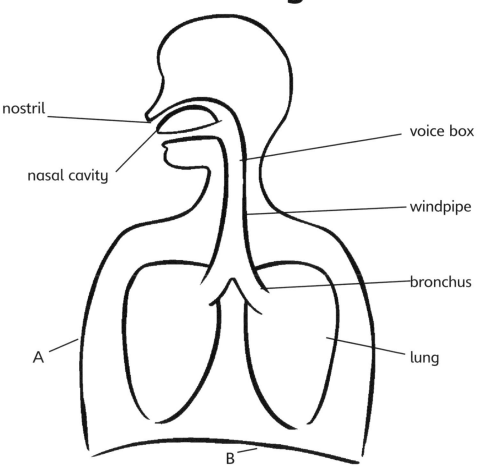

nostril

nasal cavity

voice box

windpipe

bronchus

A

lung

B

◼ Answer these questions:

1. What is A? _____

2. How does it move when you breathe in? _____

3. How does it move when you breathe out? _____

4. What is B? _____

5. How does it move when you breathe in? _____

6. How does it move when you breathe out? _____

7. Imagine you are a tiny speck of dust in the air near someone's nose. Write down, in order, the places you would go to when the person breathes in.

_____

_____

PHOTOCOPIABLE

The heart – 1

The heartbeat is made by the sounds of the heart valves closing. The valves close to stop blood flowing the wrong way. There are two heart sounds. The louder 'lub' sound is made when the larger valves close. The quieter 'dup' sound is made when the smaller valves close. The large valves close first, followed by the smaller valves, so the heartbeat sound is 'lub-dup'.

1. Look at the first two heart pictures and label one as making the 'lub' sound and the other as making the 'dup' sound.

2. Cut out all of these hearts and stick them in the top right-hand corner of 36 pages of your science book. Write 'lub' or 'dup' next to each one and flick your book to see the heart beat.

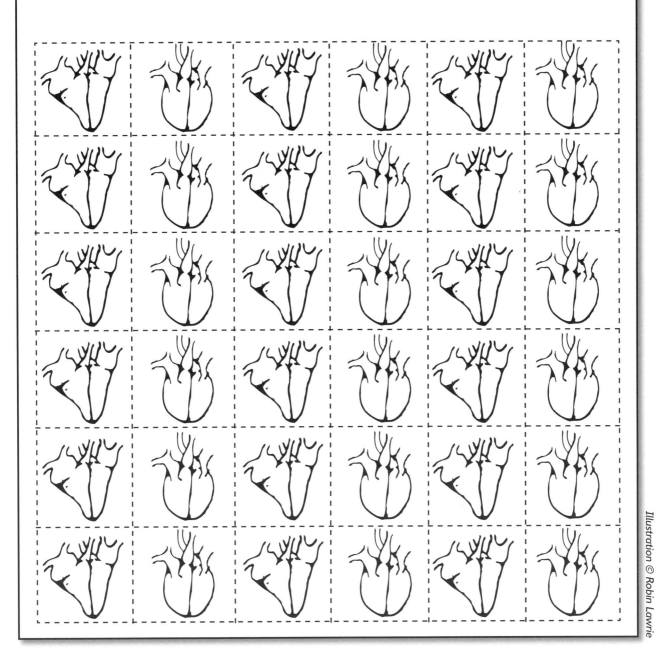

Illustration © Robin Lawrie

■ S C H O L A S T I C

The heart – 2

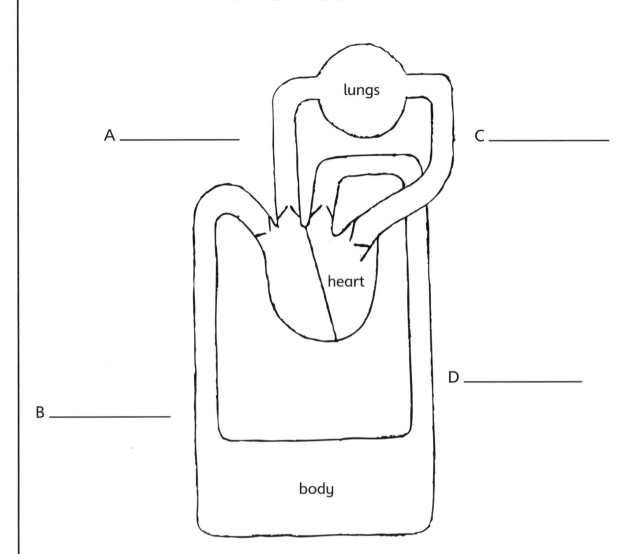

This diagram shows the path of the blood around the body. The two blood vessels, which are close together above the centre of the heart, carry blood away from it. The other two blood vessels, connected to the heart, carry blood towards it.

1. Draw a red line to show the path of the blood from the heart to the lungs.
2. Draw a blue line to show the path of the blood from the lungs to the heart.
3. Draw green line to show the path of the blood from the heart to the body.
4. Draw a yellow line to show the path of the blood from the body to the heart.
5. The blood flows through all the organs of the body. Name any two organs in addition to the heart and lungs.
6. Which blood vessels are arteries and which are veins? Look at A, B, C and D, then write 'artery' or 'vein' next to each letter.

Illustration © Robin Lawrie

PHOTOCOPIABLE

Things to avoid – 1

DRUGS

Medicines are drugs that are given by doctors to treat illnesses. They have been **tested** and are given in **safe doses** to prevent harm to your body. Other types of drugs, sometimes called **recreational drugs**, are not recommended by a doctor or chemist. They have often not been tested, so there is no safe dose (except avoiding them altogether). Sadly, many deaths are caused by these types of drugs each year. Even drugs that have been tested should never be taken unless a doctor has prescribed them for you.

Many drugs are **addictive**, and when addicts stop taking them they suffer from **withdrawal symptoms** such as fevers and cramps. Many people who rely on these drugs lose their jobs and so have to find other ways to pay for their expensive drug habit (such as stealing). Drugs can cause **damage** to the **liver**, the **brain** and other organs. Diseases can spread through the sharing of infected needles.
Does taking drugs seem like a good idea to you?

SOLVENTS

When people talk about 'solvents', they often mean the liquid that keeps glue runny. Glue dries because the liquid part **evaporates** (turns to a gas). The gas is what people call the 'fumes' or 'vapour'. The fumes from some glues cause a kind of dizziness when breathed in. This is hardly surprising because they are **toxic** (poisonous) and also allow less oxygen to reach the lungs. Some people become **addicted** to sniffing these fumes which can sadly cause **brain damage** and **liver failure** and many children die young because of this habit.

In Britain, it is illegal for shops to sell glues containing harmful solvents to children under the age of sixteen.
Do you think this is a good idea?

ALCOHOL

Alcohol is found in many drinks that are sold in pubs, such as wine and beer. It is a type of **drug** that is legal for people over the age of 18. Alcohol causes problems because it is **addictive** and people who are addicted to alcohol are called **alcoholics**. Taking large quantities of alcohol causes damage to many organs, including the liver and brain. One of the most worrying things about alcohol is the way it changes behaviour. Some hospitals have found that over half of the **accidents** they deal with are linked to alcohol and the police say that over 80% of **violent incidents** in the home and on the streets are connected with alcohol. Accidents are more common after drinking alcohol because of the way it affects co-ordination: drinkers are more clumsy and slower to react. **Driving** after drinking alcohol is particularly dangerous – **why do you think this is?**

SUNBURN

High up around the Earth is a layer of gas called the **ozone layer**. This gas does an important job: it stops some of the invisible (ultraviolet) rays from the Sun reaching the Earth. **Ultraviolet (UV)** rays can harm the skin. UV rays pass through the top layer of our skin and damage the cells underneath. As well as causing sunburn, overexposure to the Sun (being out too long without protecting your skin) can cause the skin to **age** more quickly.

Most worrying, though, has been the huge recent increase in the number of cases of **skin cancer** reported each year. The bad news is that the ozone layer is getting thinner and already has large holes in it, so more harmful rays are getting through. The good news is that we now know more about avoiding cancer.

Here are some top tips for sun-seekers:
● Avoid the Sun during the hottest part of the day (11am–3pm), but if you can't...
● Cover all exposed skin with a high factor (20+) suncream
● Wear a hat to protect your nose and neck
● Wear a long-sleeved shirt
● Get a doctor to check any moles or unusual spots if they start to itch or bleed – the doctor won't mind and it is far better to be safe than sorry.

Everyone loves having a tan, but be sensible. Don't forget that the tan will wear off after a few weeks, but the effects of too much sunlight will stay with you for far longer.

Illustration © Robin Lawrie

SCHOLASTIC

Things to avoid – 2

LOUD MUSIC

We lose the sensitivity of our hearing as we grow older (but this doesn't mean your teacher can't hear you whispering). Listening to very loud music damages the way our ears work. Listening to loud music through headphones for a long period of time reduces the sensitivity of the ears and can lead to early **deafness**. Workers who use noisy machinery, such as pneumatic drills, wear **ear defenders** to protect their hearing. Some people suffer from a distressing problem later in life when they can 'hear' a sound that isn't really there. This problem is called **tinnitus**. Take care of your hearing – avoid loud music near the speakers at discos or on headphones.

Loudness is measured in **decibels (dB)**. The sound level at which you can only just hear a sound is 0dB. Passing lorries produce a sound of about 90dB and a jumbo jet makes about 120dB (if you are standing close to it). The sound level in discos is usually around 110dB.

Hearing range (the range of different notes you can hear) is measured in **hertz (Hz)**. The higher the frequency of a sound (in hertz), the more high-pitched the note will sound. Humans can hear between 20Hz and 20 000Hz. Cats can hear between 20Hz and 70 000Hz. Porpoises can hear between 50Hz and more than 130 000Hz.

SMOKING

Sadly, smoking claims many thousands of lives each year. It greatly increases the likelihood of dying through a blood clot in the brain (a stroke), heart disease or lung cancer. Smoking not only leads to an early death, it also reduces the quality of life for smokers. Here's why:

- Our lungs produce **mucus** all the time to trap dust and germs. Cigarette smoke **irritates** our lungs and makes them produce extra mucus, which clogs up the airways (cough cough).
- Delicate hairs called **cilia** line our airways and sweep the mucus towards the mouth. Cigarette smoke paralyses the cilia and **coughing** destroys them. The mucus settles in the airways, making breathing wheezy and giving germs time to breed (ouch, my chest).
- Germs **inflame** the lining of the airways, making them even **narrower** (hold on while I catch my breath). Smoking if you already have **asthma** would be extremely dangerous.
- The tiny **air sacs** at the end of each delicate branch of our lungs are torn apart by constant coughing, leading to **emphysema** (which is very bad news).
- The thousands of chemicals contained in cigarettes produce a sticky **tar** that settles inside the lungs, irritating the lining and harming the cells around it. This increases the risk of **cancer.**
- **Nicotine** is the **addictive** drug in cigarettes that makes smokers want to keep smoking. Giving up smoking is difficult because of this drug.
- Mothers who smoke when they are **pregnant** can cause problems for their unborn children: chemicals in the mother's blood pass on to the child. (And you thought smoking was illegal until you were sixteen!)
- Smoking is expensive, and makes your clothes and breath smell.

Enough facts to be going on with? Think about it. Top athletes and footballers don't smoke – what does that tell you? You are bound to have friends who try smoking when they are older to 'look cool' – it takes character to say 'no'. What will you do? Why not share some facts with them?

Illustration © Robin Lawrie

Things to avoid – 3

Topic	Why I should
Avoid drugs!	
Avoid solvents!	
Avoid sunburn!	
Avoid alcohol!	
Avoid loud music!	
Avoid cigarettes!	

Assessment – 1

1. Identify two foods for growth in this diagram and colour them in red.
2. Identify two foods that provide energy for activity and colour them in blue.
3. Write a name label next to each food you have coloured in.

4. On this diagram of the body, draw the heart in the correct position.

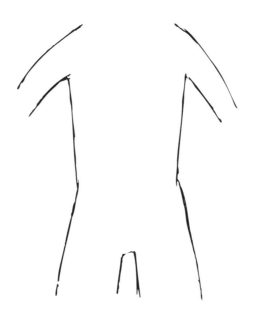

5. Where would you find your pulse? _____

6. What makes the throbbing of the pulse? _____

7. What is the pulse rate? _____

8. How does your pulse rate change as you start to exercise? _____

9. Why does your pulse rate change? _____

Illustration © Robin Lawrie

PHOTOCOPIABLE

Assessment – 2

Paul has four friends: Abigail, Alex, Dean and Laura. He wants to see if their hearts all beat at the same rate.

What could he do to find out?

Predict what you think Paul will find out.

_____

_____

_____

Why do you think that will happen?

_____

_____

_____

■ SCHOLASTIC

CHAPTER 2   Life cycles

Lesson	Objectives	Main activity	Group activities	Plenary	Outcomes
Lesson 1 What plants do we eat?	• To know that flowers produce fruits and that fruits contain seeds. • To learn about plants that humans use as food. • To know that flowering plants have life cycles.	Revise the main parts of a plant. Establish that fruits develop from flowers and that the fruit contains seeds.	Answer questions on the parts of different plants that we eat. Make a detailed drawing of a section of a fruit.	Reinforce knowledge of plant parts and the plant life cycle.	• Know that flowers produce fruits and that fruits contain seeds. • Recognise the parts of plants that humans eat. • Know the main stages in the life cycle of a flowering plant.
Lesson 2 Seeds	• To know that seeds must be dispersed to help new plants grow.	Use an interactive visual aid to explore seed dispersal.	Design a model seed. Comprehension work on the seed dispersal.	Evaluate the designs for a model windblown seed.	• Know the reasons for and the basic methods of seed dispersal.
Lesson 3 Seed germination	• To know the factors that affect the germination of seeds. • To practise and develop investigative skills.	Discuss how to set up experiments on growing seeds in different conditions.	Devise an experiment. Set up the experiment.	Discuss different approaches to similar experiments.	• Know the factors that affect the germination of seeds. • Have developed their investigative skills.
Lesson 4 Seed observations	• To develop observational and recording skills.	Observe and measure the germinated plants. Record results.		Make predictions based on the observed results so far.	• Understand the purpose of accurate observation. • Understand the need for careful recording.
Lesson 5 Successful growth	• To identify a link between environment and seed germination. • To identify patterns and draw conclusions.	Observe and measure the final results. Record findings.		Look for patterns in the class experiments.	• Can identify patterns from their observations. • Can determine whether a test is fair.
Lesson 6 Buzz's adventure	• To know that insects are attracted to flowers. • To know the main parts of an insect-pollinated flower.	Read a 'radio play' about a worker bee visiting a flower for the first time.	Label a flower picture and answer questions on bees. Write additional text for the play.	Listen to the children's further speeches for the play.	• Can name the main parts of an insect-pollinated flower. • Knows about the activities of a worker bee.
Lesson 7 Pollen poaching	• To observe the structure of an insect-pollinated flower. • To recognise flowers that attract insects. • To observe the role of insects in pollination.	Discuss and plan a trip to collect pollen and observe flowers.	Find some insect-pollinated flowers, watch insects, make observational drawings of flowers and collect pollen.	Look at and describe the pollen samples collected.	• Have observed the structure of an insect-pollinated flower. • Know some flowers that attract insects. • Have observed how insects pollinate plants.
Lesson 8 Plant parts	• To know that seeds develop in the ovary. • To know the functions of pollen, the stamen and the stigma in fertilisation. • To know the role of insects in the process of pollination.	Interactive lesson with role play on insect pollination	Sort sentences to describe insect pollination. Design and make a model or collage of an insect-pollinated flower.	Review the group activities.	• Know how fertilisation of a flower takes place. • Know that seeds develop in the ovary. • Know that insects can pollinate flowers. • Know that certain insects and flowers are mutually dependent.
Enrichment Lesson 9 Pollination	• To know that some plants are wind-pollinated. • To know that the fruits of grasses play an important part in our diet.	Discuss wind pollination and the importance of cereals in our diet.	Answer questions on wind-pollinated flowers. Identify cereals in processed foods as seeds of particular plants.	Look at the causes of hay fever and information on other wind-pollinated plants.	• Know that some plants are pollinated by the wind. • Know that the fruits of some grasses play an important part in our diet. • Can represent simple information in a table..
Lesson 10 Plant life cycles	• To know that flowering plants have life cycles. • To extend knowledge of plants that humans use in processed foods.	Identify the plant ingredients in processed foods as plant parts.		Test knowledge of the plant life cycle.	• Develop the concept of a life cycle in relation to a flowering plant. • Know the parts of some plants that are used in processed foods.
Lesson 11 Growing cabbages	• To develop an understanding of life cycles. • To know the life cycle of a butterfly.	Use a letter from an incompetent gardener to discuss insect life cycles.	Answer questions on insect life cycles. Write a critical letter to the incompetent gardener.	Discuss ideas for natural crop protection.	• Have an extended understanding of life cycles. • Know the life cycle of a butterfly.

Lesson	Objectives	Main activity	Group activities	Plenary	Outcomes
Lesson 12 Animal life cycles	• To revise plant and animal life cycles.. • To understand the meaning of the term 'mammal'.	Compare the life cycles of a plant and a thrush with that of a cat.	Answer questions on the mammalian life cycle.	Discuss the graphs of gestation periods and information on other mammals.	• Have consolidated their knowledge of life cycles. • Know that mammals' young are fed on milk from the mother.
Lesson 13 Comparing life cycles	• To compare the life cycles of different animals. • To develop knowledge of some other life cycles.	Discuss the similarities and differences between the life cycles of a cat and a thrush. Describe another life cycle. Make another comparison.		Discuss the life cycles of other animals.	• Know the similarities and differences between some animal life cycles. • Find out about some other animal life cycles.
Enrichment Lesson 14 Human life cycles	• To know the stages of the human life cycle.	Brainstorm the stages in human life and how these form a life cycle.	Draw a diagram of the human life cycle. Research and compare life cycles..	Discuss how advances over the past 1000 years have changed features of the human life cycle.	• Know the key stages in the human life cycle.
Lesson 15 Growth	• To be aware that human bodies vary and that this is natural. • To know that humans have 'growth spurt'. • To know that the body parts change in proportion from birth to adulthood.	Investigate the distribution of heights in the class.	Plot and interpret graphs showing changes in height with time. Consider the changes in body proportions with time.	Use collected data to support the idea of natural variation. Introduce the idea of the 'growth spurt'.	• Is aware that human bodies vary and that this natural. • Can identify the time of the 'growth spurt'. • Can describe how some parts of the body change in proportion from birth to adulthood.
Lesson 16 Changes in the body	• To know about the changes that take place in the body at puberty.	Discuss the changes in boys and girls at puberty.	Match captions to diagrams showing the changes at puberty. Answer questions on the changes at puberty.	The children try to define words related to puberty and reproduction. Introduce a 'question box' for problems.	• Recognise the changes that take place at puberty. • Understand that these changes take place at different times in different people. • Can name some parts of the reproductive system.
Enrichment Lesson 17 The reproductive system	• To know about the structure of the reproductive organs. • To know that changes in the body leading to sexual maturity begin at puberty.	Use large diagrams to consider the reproductive organs of the human male and female, and explain the function of each part.	Match the names of parts with their functions and place them on a diagram. Model sperm and egg cells and try to explain the differences between them.	A quick test on the changes that occur at puberty.	• Can describe the functions of the parts of the male and female reproductive organs. • Know that the changes that bring about sexual maturity begin at puberty.
Enrichment Lesson 18 Life before birth	• To know how fertilisation occurs. • To know how the growing foetus develops and how the baby is born.	Explain fertilisation and the subsequent stages of development up to birth.	Match and sequence pictures of a developing baby, with captions. Draw life-sized pictures of a developing baby.	Relate this lesson to earlier work by discussing the dangers of smoking during pregnancy.	• Can describe the growth of the foetus. • Understand the birth process.
Enrichment Lesson 19 Looking after a baby	• To know about the changes in lifestyle during pregnancy and the care required in parenting. • To develop listening, questioning skills. • To recognise stages in their own development.	The mother of a small child gives an account of the pregnancy and the care required by the baby after birth. The children make notes and arrange and describe photographs of their own early life.		Discuss the responsibility and pressures of parenthood.	• Understand that a pregnant woman needs to take special care of her health. • Understand that being a parent is a demanding task that requires many skills.
Lesson 20 Song thrush survival	• To know that if living things fail to reproduce they become extinct.	Use a game to learn about the life cycle of the song thrush and threats to its survival.	Make a poster to explain why the song thrush may become extinct. Make a charter of ways to help conserve the thrush.	Discuss ideas to help the song thrush and information on other endangered British birds.	• Know that if living things fail to reproduce they become extinct. • Know that living things are face extinction due to environmental change.

Assessment	Objectives	Activity 1	Activity 2
Lesson 21 Life cycles	To assess the children's knowledge of the life cycle of plants. To assess the children's knowledge of some animal life cycles.	Label a flower picture. Answer questions on methods of pollination and seed dispersal.	Answer questions on the life cycles of a butterfly and song thrush, and the value of several animal species to the gardener.

SC1 SCIENTIFIC ENQUIRY

What do seeds need?

LEARNING OBJECTIVES AND OUTCOMES
● To devise and control an appropriate investigation.
● Measure the germination rate of seeds by selecting and controlling a different set of conditions (light, moisture, temperature).
● To know the conditions required for successful seed germination.

ACTIVITY
The children devise a seed germination experiment selecting appropriately from a range of different resources. They observe and record their results.

LESSON LINKS
This Sc1 activity forms an integral part of Lesson 4, Seed observations.

Lesson 1 ▸ What plants do we eat?

Objective
● To know that flowers produce fruits and that fruits contain seeds.
● To learn about plants that humans use as foods.
● To know that flowering plants have life cycles.

Vocabulary
seed, flower, fruit, seed catalogue

RESOURCES ⊙
Main activity: An apple, orange, tomato and cucumber, plus a collection of fruits from other plants that the children will not identify as 'fruits' (such as acorns in cups or a conker in its prickly shell); a knife; five long strips of card with Blu-Tack® on the back (see Preparation); an A3 version of photocopiable page 73 (also 'What plants do we eat?' (red), available on the CD-ROM).
Group activities: 1 Seed catalogues or gardening books (one per pair or group of three children) containing pictures of vegetables; photocopiable page 73. **2** Drawing materials, hand lenses.
ICT link: 'Labelled flower' diagram on the CD-ROM.

PREPARATION
Cut the fruit into sections to reveal the seeds. Rub some orange juice on the apple to prevent the cut surface from browning. On each of the five long strips of card, write one of the following sentences: *Seeds are planted in the ground. Stems and leaves grow up above the ground. Flowers grow on the stems. Fruits are formed from the flowers. Seeds grow within the fruits.*

BACKGROUND
Although flowering plants vary widely in appearance, they are all built to the same basic plan. The children will recognise roots, stems, leaves and flowers from earlier school work. However, their concept of a 'fruit' will probably refer only to the varieties they have seen in shops: apples, oranges, plums, cherries and so on. In botanical terms, the fruit is the ovary that contains the maturing fertilised seeds of the plant. All flowering plants produce fruits. The children will have eaten fruits that they thought of as 'vegetables': tomatoes, runner beans, mange tout and so on.

Many children grow up in an environment that is some distance from the source of the food they eat. They may even be unaware that potatoes grow underground! This lesson will help the children to consolidate their knowledge of the sources of plant food and give them an overview of the life cycle of flowering plants that will put the rest of this unit into context.

STARTER
Tell the children that they are going to think about the food we grow to eat.

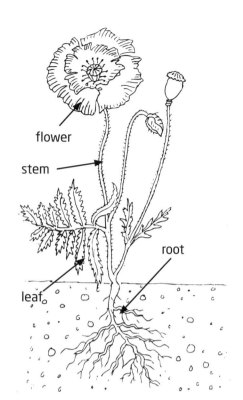

flower

stem

root

leaf

Ask: *Do you know anyone who has an allotment or ever grows food to eat?* Ask any child who says 'Yes' to tell the class what was grown.

MAIN ACTIVITY

Tell the children that they are going to think about the parts of the plant that they eat. Show the children the diagram of the plant (opposite; also on the CD-ROM). Together complete the annotation of the different parts: foot, stem, leaf, and flower. Now point to the fruit and ask: *What do you think we call this seed container?* Show the children the sections of apple, orange, cucumber and tomato that you have prepared, and point out the seeds. Elicit or reveal the answer that the seed container is called a 'fruit'. Label the 'fruit' on the diagram. Emphasise that all flowering plants produce fruits.

Show the children some familiar seed containers that they might not have previously identified as fruits (see Resources). Keep one example back to use for assessment. In each case, ask the children to identify the seeds; stress that the whole seed container is a fruit, then ask: *Where does the fruit come from?* Establish that it was produced from the flower.

Now display the enlarged version of page 73. Look at the first section. Ask: *Which part of these plants do we eat?* Elicit the correct answers in a discussion, and write the name of the appropriate plant part for the first few entries: Lettuce *leaves,* Potato *roots,* Tomato *fruit,* Celery *stem,* Cauliflower *flower.*

GROUP ACTIVITIES

1 Give each child a copy of photocopiable page 73, but encourage the children to work together in pairs to discuss or look for the answers. Identify the secondary sources of information (seed catalogues and books) that they can use to resolve difficulties.
2 Ask each child to make a detailed, enlarged drawing of one of the sections of fruit that were shown to the class (apple, orange, cucumber and so on). Make sure each child has access to a hand lens to encourage detailed observation.

ASSESSMENT

During the plenary session, show the children one further example of a seed container. Establish that they know it is a fruit which contains seeds and has developed from a flower.

PLENARY

Discuss the answers to the photocopiable worksheets. Show the class the children's drawings. Display the five sentences that describe the life cycle of a flowering plant in random order, and ask the children to help you arrange them in the order in which they happen. Display the children's pictures.

OUTCOMES
● Know that flowers produce fruits and that fruits contain seeds.
● Recognise the parts of some plants that humans use as foods.
● Know the main stages in the life cycle of a flowering plant.

LINKS
Art and design: making things.

Differentiation
Group activity 1
To support children, give them 'What plants do we eat?' (green) from the CD-ROM, a simplified version of the core sheet. To extend children, give them 'What plants do we eat?' (blue), which asks them to identify plants which they can then categorise according to the part eaten.

Lesson 2 ▪ Seeds

Vocabulary
dispersal, germinate, sown, reproduce

RESOURCES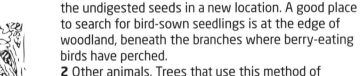
Main activity: The five life cycle sentences from Lesson 1 on card; a large poster of a woodland (see diagram below, also on the CD-ROM); large pictures (from other sources) of a song thrush, a squirrel, a mouse, and, the fruits or seeds shown on photocopiable page 74 (also 'Seeds' (red) available on the CD-ROM), each mounted on card with Blu-Tack® on the back.
Group activities: 1 A selection of art materials, including various papers, drinking straws, glue, scissors, adhesive tape, felt-tipped pens, and a quantity of something very light to act as seeds (such as milk bottle tops, plastic 'unit' cubes or dried bean seeds). **2** Photocopiable page 74.
ICT link: 'Woodland' diagram on the CD-ROM.

PREPARATION
Display the five life cycle sentences from Lesson 1 in a circular sequence. Prepare a poster based on the diagram shown, and display it where it will be clearly visible and accessible. Fasten the six pictures of fruits or seeds to different trees on the poster.

BACKGROUND
For plants to thrive, they need to have access to light, moisture and nutrients. Competition from other plants, including the parent, can delay growth or suffocate the emerging plant. Therefore, if seeds are transported and germinate away from the parent plant, they have a greater chance of survival and success. This is the reason why seeds are dispersed. This lesson focuses on three methods of seed dispersal:
1 Birds. The hawthorn, rowan and elder are examples of trees that rely on birds for seed distribution. The birds eat the attractive fruits and defecate the undigested seeds in a new location. A good place to search for bird-sown seedlings is at the edge of woodland, beneath the branches where berry-eating birds have perched.

2 Other animals. Trees that use this method of dispersal include the oak and beech. The tree produces large numbers of heavy seeds that fall to the ground around the parent tree. These seeds are a valuable winter food supply for woodland animals such as the squirrel, who find and hoard the seeds (often storing them in small holes in the ground). Uneaten seeds may eventually germinate in a new location, some distance from the parent tree.
3. The wind. The seeds of the sycamore and ash will be easiest to find. Both have large appendages that help them to spin away from their parent tree in the wind.

STARTER
Using the five life cycle sentences on flowering plants from Lesson 1, draw the children's attention to the fact that the life cycle begins with seeds being sown and ends with the production of new seeds.

MAIN ACTIVITY
Tell the children that they are going to find out about how seeds are naturally sown in the ground. Explain that you are just going to talk about tree seeds, but that the seeds of other plants are sown in the same way. Refer to the woodland poster. Remove one seed picture from a tree and fasten it to the ground below. Ask: *Why won't this seed grow if it falls here?*

Establish that the parent plant will shade the seed and deprive the infant plant of light and water. Put the seed back on the tree.

Introduce the term 'seed dispersal'. If the plant is to survive and reproduce, it needs to make sure that its seeds are spread out to reach better sites for growing. Use the poster and the seed and animal pictures to demonstrate dispersal by birds, animals and the wind. Show how one seed of each dispersal type is moved to a suitable location and germinates. On the poster, draw a few leaves above the successful seed in its new location. The other seeds are eaten by animals or dropped in an inappropriate location. After demonstration of each method of dispersal, write the terms 'seed dispersal', 'bird-sown seeds', 'animal-dispersed seeds' and 'wind-blown seeds' on the board or flip chart. At the end of the session, ask questions to check that the children understand these terms.

GROUP ACTIVITIES

1 Working in pairs, challenge the children to design and make a model fruit that will carry the 'seed' (a small weight) as far as possible using wind power. Discuss and agree on methods to make the test fair. Decisions will need to be taken about: the range and size of materials that can be used; the weight of the seed; and the method for testing the 'fruits' (including how the fruits will be released and how much time will be allowed for them to blow). Before the test, bring the children back together to discuss their designs. Ask them to predict which 'fruit' will go furthest.
2 Give each child a copy of page 74 to complete individually.

ICT LINK
Display 'Seeds' (red) from the CD-ROM on an interactive whiteboard and complete as a class activity. Write the answers in before the lesson; cover them up using the 'filled box' tool; use the eraser to reveal the answers.

ASSESSMENT
Ask questions to check that the children understand both the reasons for and the methods of seed dispersal.

PLENARY
Discuss the results of Group activity 1. Ask children to explain why some seeds travelled a long distance and why others were less successful.

OUTCOME
● Know the reasons for and the basic methods of seed dispersal.

Lesson 3 ▪ Seed germination

Objective
● To know the factors that affect the germination of seeds.
● To practise and develop investigative skills.

Vocabulary
seedlings, conditions, variable, constant.

RESOURCES
Main activity: The forest poster from Lesson 2; a large copy of the diagram (on page 45, also on the CD-ROM).
Group activities: 1 Paper; writing materials. **2** A variety of large seeds (such as runner beans, dwarf beans, nasturtiums); a variety of pairs of small flowerpots, some identical clear plastic containers and sheets of absorbent paper; a variety of peat-free composts; some garden soil from a single location; some small trowels or similar implements; containers for measuring small amounts of water; black paper; junk materials; elastic bands; labels.
ICT link: 'Seed germination' diagram on the CD-ROM.

PREPARATION
On the board, write the words 'conditions' and 'germinate'. Prepare a large diagram of how to germinate seeds without soil (see diagram). Organise the

classroom so that the flowerpots can be filled with the minimum of mess. Make sure that all the resources are easy to see and access.

BACKGROUND

The main purpose of this lesson is not to grow plants successfully but to devise a scientific experiment. The children are invited to choose from a range of materials in order to test their skill in experimental design. There is a risk of over-managing this kind of experience: if you limit the range of resources and provide just one size of flowerpot, one kind of seed, one kind of seed compost and so on, you may restrict the children's understanding of the process of scientific enquiry; they will all use the same pot, the same seeds and the same compost because that is all there is!

The best seeds to use are runner beans, dwarf beans and nasturtiums. All prefer warm conditions and are easy to obtain and handle. Let the children choose from these. For the growing medium, you could use a variety of seed composts bought from a garden centre. Try to use peat-free composts, since the RSPB are unhappy about the effects of peat extraction on bird habitats. Some groups could use garden soil dug from a single location. Other groups could grow the seeds between the side of a clear plastic container and a coiled sheet of absorbent paper, as shown in the diagram. Watering the experiments fairly will need your support and encouragement. Insist that the children measure and record all that they do. They should revisit the experiment over a period of three or four weeks and record their results. Lessons 4 and 5 outline the development of this investigation.

At the end of the experiment, the children may have some healthy plants. These could be used to create a small class garden. An old car tyre on a corner of the playground could be used to plant the seedlings in. After the summer holidays the plants will have nearly completed their life cycle and you will have the seeds for another class.

STARTER

Tell the children that they are going to think about the conditions that are needed for seeds to germinate. Check that they remember the meaning of the word 'germinate'. Remind them of the lesson on seed dispersal. Point to the forest poster and ask: *Why were the fruits or seeds transported to a new place to grow? Why didn't they grow next to the parent tree?* Elicit the answer: 'The seed needed light and water'. If the answer 'warmth' is not forthcoming, ask the following: *When you have walked past other people's gardens or allotments, have you noticed any other things that might help seeds to grow quickly?* Look for the answer 'greenhouse' or 'cold frame' to establish that gardeners often use the additional warmth of the solar energy trapped under glass to help plants to grow. Reinforce the idea that the three things needed for seeds to germinate are warmth, light and moisture. Write these three words on the board or flip chart.

MAIN ACTIVITY

Ask the children to work in pairs, designing an experiment to prove that seeds need the right conditions in order to germinate. Their experiment should test one factor: warmth, moisture or light. Through questioning, make sure they understand that their test samples need to have the same number of seeds, type of seed, container, soil, depth of planting and so on – establish that there should be only one variant. Write appropriate sentences on the board or flip chart as a guide for Group activity 2, stressing the word 'same' – for example: *We are going to use two sets of the same kind of seed.*

Show the children one experimental design as an example. Ask: *Is soil necessary for seeds to germinate?* Show them the prepared diagram to demonstrate that it is possible to germinate the seeds without soil.

Let the children form pairs and decide which of the three criteria they are testing. Indicate the resources that can be used in the experiment.

Differentiation
Differentiation
Group activity 2
Support children by encouraging them to refer to the writing on the board to help them with the written element of this task. Children who finish quickly could design flowerpot sleeves or notices to explain the purpose of their experiment.

GROUP ACTIVITIES
1 Ask the children to discuss with their partner how they are going to do the experiment, select the materials they need to carry it out and then set it up. Make sure they label each flowerpot with their names.
2 The children should then write down a title for their experiment and an account of how it is organised. Ask them to highlight the word 'same' each time they write it.

ASSESSMENT
During the group work, ask children why it is important to have only one factor that changes in the experiment.

PLENARY
Draw the children's attention to the different approaches used in similar experiments. Remember to stress the importance of not disturbing the experiments. Finally, ask the children which sample of seeds will be the first to germinate and why.

OUTCOMES
● Know the factors that affect the germination of seeds.
● Have developed their investigative skills.

LINKS
Lessons 4 and 5: germination of seeds.

Lesson 4 ▪ Seed observations

Objective
● To develop observational and recording skills.

Vocabulary
seedlings, conditions, variable, constant.

RESOURCES
The growing seeds from Lesson 3; rulers; hand lenses; paper; drawing and writing materials; digital camera (optional).

MAIN ACTIVITY
A week after Lesson 4, remind the children that they are trying to find out how warmth, light and moisture affect the germination of seeds. Select one pot containing germinated seeds. *Look at these seedlings. By next week they may have grown. Next week, how will we remember what the seedlings were like at this time?* Stress the importance of looking carefully at any seeds that have germinated and making careful drawings. Now ask: *How will we know how much these seeds have grown next week?* Stress the importance of making careful measurements. *What parts of the plant could be measured?* List the parts that could be measured on the board, for example the length and width of the largest leaf. Ask the children to make detailed drawings and measurements of their germinated seeds.

ASSESSMENT
As they work, ask children: *Why do we need to look so carefully at our experiments? Why do we need to record carefully what has happened?*

Differentiation
Group activity 2
Some children may find accurate drawing a difficult task. If you have access to a digital camera, this could be used to monitor their experiment.

PLENARY
Ask the children, from their observations, to predict: *Which seedlings will have grown the tallest next week? Which seeds will still not have germinated next week?* Ask them to give reasons for their predictions. Continue the experiments for another week.

OUTCOMES
● Understand the purpose of accurate observation.
● Understand the need for careful recording.

Lesson 5 ▪ Successful growth

Objective
● To identify a link between the environment and seed germination.
● To identify patterns and draw conclusions.

RESOURCES
The children's seed experiments from Lesson 3; plates or trays on which to empty the contents of 'failed' pots; paper towels; soap and a bowl for hand-washing.

MAIN ACTIVITY
A week after Lesson 4, many of the seeds will have germinated and grown well in the warm, light and moist conditions. There may be limited growth in a cool or dry environment. Plants that have been deprived of light may be weak and 'leggy'. Tell the children that this is the end of the experiment and the time to look carefully at all their seedlings. Encourage them to examine seeds that have not germinated. Make sure that they are aware of hygiene issues: they must wash their hands after handling soil or compost. Discuss with the children, and list on the board or flip chart, the things they need to do in order to complete the experiment: draw and measure both successful and unsuccessful seedlings; record their plant measurements; look at their pictures and measurements and decide what they have found out from the experiment; record their conclusions.

ASSESSMENT
As the children complete the work, ask them to state and explain their conclusions.

PLENARY
Invite some pairs of children to show their seedlings and tell the rest of the class their conclusions. Ask the children to listen carefully and decide whether the conclusions were fair. Ask children who conducted similar experiments if their conclusions were similar. There may be some general patterns – for example, the seeds in cool conditions or in dry conditions may have poor germination rates.

OUTCOMES
● Can identify patterns from their observations.
● Can determine whether a test is fair.

Lesson 6 ▪ Buzz's adventure

Objective
● To know that insects are attracted to flowers.
● To know the main parts of an insect-pollinated flower.

Vocabulary
worker bee, hive, stigma, stamen, pollen, nectar

RESOURCES ◉
Main activity: Large pictures of a bee and a cross-section of a flower (see Preparation); Blu-Tack® ; one copy per pair of photocopiable page 75 (also 'Buzz's adventure' (red) available on the CD-ROM).
Group activities: 1 Copies of the questions at the bottom of photocopiable page 75 (one copy per child). **2** Details of this activity on a board or flipchart.

PREPARATION ◉
There are two characters in the play 'Buzz's adventure'. Practise reading the playscript using two voices, or with another adult or a confident child reading one of the parts. Display a foxglove cross-section on an interactive whiteboard or flipchart. (You could use 'Assessment – 1' from the CD-ROM, using the zoom-in tool to make it larger.) Make an enlarged copy of one of the bee pictures on page 75, paste it onto card, cut it out and stick some Blu-Tack® on the back.

Differentiation

Group activity 1

Support children reading through the text of page 75 with them. Ask them to highlight on the text the names of flower parts and write these in the appropriate places on the diagram. They could then draw a worker bee and colour in parts of the diagram.

Group activity 2

Extend children by asking them to write a continuation of the play in which Buzz returns to the hive and meets GCB; others could use secondary sources of information to find out more about honey bees.

BACKGROUND

Flowers are the organs of plant reproduction. This lesson and Lessons 8 and 9 deal with the basic structure of insect-pollinated flowers, introducing the vocabulary 'petals', 'stamen', 'stigma', 'ovary', 'pollen' and 'nectar'. The functions of these parts are explained in more detail in subsequent lessons. This lesson concentrates on introducing all of the terms except *ovary*.

Pollen is an essential element in the reproductive process of plants. It is also a protein-rich food for insects. Pollen is produced in the stamens. It has to be transferred to the stigma, which connects to the ovary where fertilised seeds develop. Once attached to the stigma, the pollen grain puts out a long tube that reaches into the ovary at the base of the flower. Nectar is a sugar-based solution produced in a small gland near the ovary. Petals and nectar play no direct part in the reproductive process: their function is to attract insects. A great variety of insects are attracted to flowers and play a role in the transfer of pollen. The honey bee is used as an example in this lesson because most children will be familiar with it.

Worker bees are female. They collect food, store honey and care for developing eggs. When they visit flowers, they collect pollen in tiny sacs on their rear legs. Pollen also clings to the hairs on their bodies, and as a result is transferred between the stamens and stigmas of different flowers. The other members of a hive are the queen bee and the drones. The queen bee lays all the eggs, which have been fertilised by a male drone. Nectar is an essential food supply for bees. Worker bees will regurgitate excess nectar in the hive, where in a few days it is converted into honey. It is important to stress that insects depend on flowers and flowers depend on insects.

STARTER

Tell the children that during the next few lessons, they will learn how flowers develop into fruits and seeds. Then ask: *Have you ever eaten honey? Where does honey come from?* Ask the children what they know about bees. Explain that the rest of this lesson is concerned with worker bees - the kind of honey bee that they are most likely to see.

MAIN ACTIVITY

Give each pair of children a copy of page 75. Read the introduction to the play and ask questions to make sure that the children understand the context. Explain that bees do not really communicate over a long distance: once a worker bee finds food, she goes back to the hive and gives detailed instructions about where to find it - by dancing! Read the play aloud while the children follow the text.

Now ask two confident children to re-read the parts. Show the children the cut-out 'worker bee' and ask a third child to move the bee to a suitable part of the flower picture as the story develops. Ask the other children to listen to the play and watch the bee. Tell them to put up their hand during the reading if they think the bee is in the wrong place on the picture. Warn the readers that you will interrupt them if you see a hand raised.

If the play progresses well, with only a few interruptions, move on to the group work. If there are lots of interruptions, help the children to find a sensible solution and go through the reading in the same way for a final time. If necessary, take over moving the bee to the appropriate places.

GROUP ACTIVITIES

1 The children can work individually through the exercise at the bottom of page 75.

2 The children can draw a worker bee (as shown on page 75) and a large speech bubble, then write what Buzz might have said about her adventure to the other worker bees back at the hive.

ASSESSMENT

In the plenary session, draw the children's attention to the large foxglove picture and ask them to name each part of the flower as you point to it. Ask them why insects need flowers.

PLENARY

Ask children who completed Group activity 2 to read out what Buzz said on her return to the hive. If time allows, listen to a performance of the 'continued play'. Display the children's work.

OUTCOMES

● Can name the main parts of an insect-pollinated flower.
● Knows about the activities of a worker bee.

Lesson 7 ▪ Pollen poaching

Objective
● To observe the structure of an insect-pollinated flower.
● To recognise flowers that attract insects.
● To observe the role of insects in pollination.

Vocabulary
pollen, stamens, pollination

RESOURCES

Main activity: The foxglove picture from Lesson 6; scissors; card and clear sticky tape (see Preparation).
Group activity: Each child will need a clipboard; a pencil; a copy of photocopiable page 76 (also 'Pollen poaching' (red), available on the CD-ROM) and a 'pollen poaching tool' (see Preparation below); some spare pencils and 'pollen poaching tools' may be needed.

PREPARATION

You will need to identify a safe area outside, but near to the classroom, where there are a number of insect-pollinated flowers for the children to study. If the location is not part of your school site, you will need to arrange additional adult supervision in accordance with your school or LEA policy.

The diagram (left) shows a 'pollen poaching tool'. Use a rectangle of thin scrap card about 10cm × 5cm. Fold it and cut out a narrow rectangle along the fold, then stretch a piece of clear sticky tape across the aperture: you have made a sticky microscope slide. Make a few spare 'pollen poaching tools' and take them with you, in case any children drop or spoil their own.

Try the activity yourself. Don't put too much pressure on the flower when you remove the pollen, or you'll 'poach' more than the pollen. If possible, ask some parents, or other adult volunteers to join you in the outdoor lesson. Make sure that you are following your school's safety procedures.

BACKGROUND

The purpose of this lesson is to consolidate the knowledge of flower parts introduced in Lesson 6. The children will be taken out of school to look for insects that are involved in pollinating flowers; to collect a sample of pollen; and to make a detailed drawing of an insect-pollinated flower. The information the children collect will be used in Lesson 8.

STARTER

Remind the children of the foxglove activity from Lesson 6. Use questions to recap on the names of the flower parts, what attracts insects to the flowers, and why the insects collect pollen and nectar.

MAIN ACTIVITY

Tell the children that they are going on a short outside visit, and that they are going to become 'pollen poachers'. Ask them what a poacher is. (A 'nature thief' might be an appropriate definition.) *How did Buzz the worker bee collect pollen in the previous lesson?* (She scraped the pollen into sacs on her back legs, and some stuck to the hairs on her body.) Demonstrate to

Differentiation
Try to provide extra adult
support for the outdoor
activity. With encouragement,
children will produce excellent
results. Many children will
make very detailed drawings if
they have enthusiastic
support.

the children how to make and use the 'pollen poaching tool', and let them make one each. Show the children a copy of page 76. Tell them that they are going to:
1. Make a pollen poaching tool.
2. Walk together to a site where there are some insect-pollinated flowers.
3. With a partner, watch one area of flowers to see which insects visit them.
4. Individually, make a detailed drawing of a flower with petals, a stigma and stamens. It is important for the next lesson that both children in each pair draw a similar flower.
5. Press the sticky surface of their 'pollen poaching tool' gently onto the stamens of the same flower as they have drawn to poach some pollen.

Give each child a copy of page 76, a clipboard and a pencil. They should attach the 'pollen poaching tool' to the clipboard sticky side up. Take them on the outdoor activity.

GROUP ACTIVITY
Photocopiable page 76 will help to remind the children of the structure of the activity once they are outside the classroom.

ASSESSMENT
On returning to the classroom, sit the children in a circle. Ask them to describe the insects they saw visiting the flowers. *What parts of the flower did the insects visit? What do you think the insects were collecting?* Then ask: *Why do you think it is 'poaching' if we take pollen from flowers?* (Because the plants and insects need pollen and we don't!)

PLENARY
Ask the children to look carefully at their 'pollen poaching tools'. Ask: *Who has poached a lot of pollen?* Ask a successful pair to describe what is on their pollen poaching tool. Finally, ask everyone to show their drawings. Collect the drawings and the pollen poaching tools for the next lesson.

OUTCOMES
- Have observed the structure of an insect-pollinated flower.
- Know some flowers that attract insects.
- Have observed how insects pollinate plants.

LINKS
Lesson 8: the functions of the reproductive parts of a flower.

Lesson 8 ◻ Plant parts

Objective
- To know that seeds develop in the ovary.
- To know the functions of pollen, the stamen and the stigma in fertilisation.
- To know the role of insects in the process of pollination.

Vocabulary
pollen, stamens, pollination

RESOURCES
Main activity: A card with the word 'ovary' on it, Blu-Tack® ; the pictures of a foxglove and a bee, from Lesson 6; the children's drawings of flowers and 'pollen poaching tools', from Lesson 7.
Group activities: 1 Eight strips of card; each strip with one of the following sentences written on it: 'Pollen is made in the stamen of a flower.', 'Colourful petals attract insects to the flower.', 'The insect feeds on pollen and nectar.', 'Some pollen sticks to the body of the insect.', 'The insect carries the pollen.', 'Pollen rubs off the insect's body onto the stigma.', 'A tube grows from the stigma to the ovary.', 'Fertile seeds grow in the ovary.'; Blu-Tack® ; paper; writing materials. **2** A well-organised collection of art materials: bright-coloured paper, junk materials, cardboard packaging, paints, paintbrushes, felt-tipped pens, glue and so on.

Differentiation
Group activity 1
Support children by giving
them a copy of the sentences,
each on a separate strip. They
could sort the sentences into
a sensible order, then paste
them together.
Group activity 2
Extend children by asking
them to mount their writing
from Group activity 1
alongside their flower.

PREPARATION

Look carefully at the children's drawings of flowers from Lesson 7. Make a note of particularly clear pictures of similar species of flower. Sit the class in a circle with the board or flip chart close behind you. Place the children's flower pictures and 'pollen poaching tools' in the middle of the circle.

BACKGROUND

Two forms of pollination by insect are described in this lesson:
1 Self-pollination. This is where pollen is transferred between the stamen and stigma of the same flower, or between flowers on the same plant.
2 Cross-pollination. This is where pollen is moved from the stamen of one plant to the stigma of another plant of the same species.

The Main activity builds on the knowledge and experience of the children, using a visual method to explain pollination. Some children may be puzzled by the nature of the process. They may ask difficult questions such as: *Can the pollen of buttercups be used by bean plants?* The answer is that this does not happen: the plant 'recognises' that the pollen has come from the wrong sort of plant. However, if the children have grown runner beans in a previous lesson, you could tell them: *If you grow a red-flowered runner bean close to a white-flowered runner bean, the seeds the plants produce may grow into plants whose flowers are not the same colour as those of the parent plant. This will show that pollen has been transported from one plant to the other, and the two strains of runner bean have 'crossbred'.*

STARTER

Remind the children of their outdoor work in the previous lesson. Hold up a 'pollen poaching tool' and ask: *What did you collect on these sticky things in the last lesson?* (Pollen.) Pointing to the foxglove picture, ask: *On which part of the flower will the insect find the pollen?* (The stamen.) *What will the flower develop in to?* (A fruit with seeds.)

MAIN ACTIVITY

1 The ovary. Tell the children that they are going to find out what happens to a flower before it develops into a fruit. Encourage them to work out where on the flower the fruit is produced by asking questions based on their observation. Name the part of the flower where the fruit develops as the 'ovary'. Blu-Tack® the word 'ovary' to the foxglove picture.
2 Self-pollination. Using the foxglove picture, explain that before a fruit can develop, pollen has to move across from the stamen to the stigma. Restrict the context to a single plant. Explain that the stamen is the 'male' part of the flower and the stigma is the 'female' part. Establish through questioning that the pollen is transferred on the bodies of insects.
3 The stigma. Refer again to the foxglove picture. Explain that once the pollen is in contact with the stigma, it becomes attached to it. A tube develops from the stigma to the ovary. Draw this tube on the picture. The male reproductive cells in pollen grains will fuse with the female reproductive cells in the ovary – a process called 'fertilisation' – to produce fertile seeds. Write 'fertilisation' on the board or flip chart. At this point, the fruit begins to develop. The flower's purpose is complete and the petals, stigma and stamen will begin to shrivel up.
4 Cross-pollination. Tell the children that there is another way that pollen can go from a stamen to a stigma. Find a pair of similar flowers drawn by two different children in the previous lesson. Ask them to stand up and hold their work on opposite sides of the class circle. Using one of the children's pollen poaching tools and the cut-out worker bee, talk through the reproductive process of the plant with the class. Use the sentences listed in Resources as your script. Holding the bee, 'carry' the pollen across the class circle from one flower to the other. Redirect the children's attention to the foxglove picture and remind them of the roles of the stigma and ovary.

Stress that this kind of fertilisation can only take place between plants of the same species: a buttercup can't fertilise a rose.

Finally, select another pair of similar flowers drawn by different children. Repeat the process, with a third child reading the eight sentences while a fourth child carries the bee and pollen from one flower to another. Direct the attention of the class to the foxglove picture at the appropriate moment.

GROUP ACTIVITIES

1 Display the eight sentences on strips of card in random order. Ask the children to discuss, in pairs, a sensible order for these sentences and to write them down in that order.

2 Ask the groups to create a model or collage of an insect-pollinated flower.

ASSESSMENT

During the plenary session, ask: *Does the insect need the flower, or do the flowers need the insect?* (Both need each other.) Ask the children to explain their answer.

PLENARY

Look at and display the flowers created in Group activity 2. Ask their creators to name some of the flower parts. Discuss the various answers to Group activity 1. Use the sentence strips to make the possible versions clear to the children.

OUTCOMES

● Know that fertilisation of a flower takes place when pollen is transferred to the stigma.
● Know that seeds develop in the ovary.
● Know that insects can pollinate flowers.
● Know that certain insects and certain flowers are mutually dependent.

ENRICHMENT
Lesson 9 ▪ Pollination

Objective
● To know that some plants are pollinated by the wind.
● To know that the fruits from grasses play an important part in our diet.

Vocabulary
pollinated, cereal, wheat, maize, barley, oats, rye

RESOURCES 💿
Main activity: The eight sentence strips from Lesson 8; a cereal flakes box; the wrapper from a loaf of bread; empty processed food containers (one per pair of children); flipchart or interactive whiteboard; an enlarged version of photocopiable page 77 (also 'Pollination' (red), available on the CD-ROM); a few examples of wild or dried grasses, complete with flowers or seeds (one per pair of children); if possible, some ears of wheat; a picture of sweetcorn.
Group activities 1 and 2: Copies of photocopiable page 77; art materials.

PREPARATION 💿
Prepare a copy of the table on page 77 and display it on a flipchart or display 'Pollination' (red) on an interactive whiteboard.
Inform carers of children with pollen allergies of this activity.

BACKGROUND
Many kinds of plant are pollinated by the wind. As insects play no part in this process, there is no need for the plant to develop petals or nectar in order to attract them. Wind-pollinated plants tend to have inconspicuous flowers; the children may not have realised that they have flowers at all.

For pollen to move from the stamen to the stigma, these organs need to be on the outside of the plant. The stigma will be unencumbered by petals and will often be 'feathery' in form, allowing the wind to pass through the structure. This increases the chance of the stigma catching passing pollen grains. The pollen of these plants is finer and lighter than that of insect-pollinated plants.

One large group of wind-pollinated plants is grasses. Children will be familiar with mown surfaces such as lawns and football pitches. The regular mowing nearly always prevents the grass from producing flowers and seeds. Grasses from hedgerows and field margins, which go through their life cycle undisturbed, are attractive examples of wind-pollinated plants. Some specially cultivated grasses play an important part in our diet: wheat and oats are common ingredients of processed foods such as bread and cereals.

STARTER

Tell the children that they are going to learn about a group of plants that produce very important fruits and are not pollinated by insects. Ask: *What do I mean by 'pollinated by insects'?* (Insects transfer pollen from the stamen to the stigma.) Use the sentence strips from Lesson 8, placed in random order, to revise the process of insect pollination.

MAIN ACTIVITY

Ask: *How many of you have eaten some grass for breakfast?* Display a box of cornflakes and explain that breakfast cereals are made from the fruits of some grass plants. Establish that cornflakes are made from the fruit of the maize plant: 'sweetcorn' or 'corn on the cob'. Show the children a picture of 'sweetcorn' (from a seed catalogue). Now show them the wrapper from a loaf of bread. Establish that bread is made from the fruits of a grass (known as wheat) that have been ground into flour. Elicit or state the generic name for grass plants like wheat and maize: 'cereal'.

Give out a set of empty processed food containers so that each pair of children has one. Display the following table:

Processed food	Wheat of flour	Maize (corn)	Barley	Oats	Rye

Explain that several kinds of cereal are used in processed foods: wheat (or flour), maize (corn), barley, oats, and rye. Ask the children to look at the ingredients used in the processed food, and to raise their hands if they can see any cereals mentioned. Explain that, for example, 'corn syrup' is made from maize. Ask a few children to read out the cereal ingredients and add the details to the table. Ask questions based on the data to check that the children understand the tabular form.

Now display the enlarged version of photocopiable page 77 and look at the table. Remind the children of their work on insect-pollinated plants. *Does the insect-pollinated plant have flowers?* Write 'Yes' in the appropriate cell; with the children's help, complete each cell in the 'Insect-pollinated flower' column. Now ask the children what they think should be put in each cell in the 'Grasses and cereals' column. Write in the correct answers: grasses and cereals have flowers, pollen, a stigma, stamen and ovary, and fruits; but the plants do not have petals or scent, nor do they welcome insects. Explain that if farmers see lots of insects on a cereal crop, they often kill them with an insecticide spray to stop them damaging the crop.

Explain that we can only eat the fruits of grasses if the seeds have been fertilised, which means that the pollen has to travel from the stamen of one plant to the stigma of another. Using the examples of wild or dried grasses ask: *How does pollen get moved from the stamen of one plant to the stigma of another?* (By the wind). Wave the dried grasses dramatically, and remind the children how these are blown by the wind and the pollen is spread. Point to the flowers on the grasses. *Why are these light and feathery?* (To let the wind through.) *Why are there no petals?* (They don't need to attract insects.)

Differentiation
Group activity 1
To support children in Group activity 1, give them 'Pollination' (green), which includes fewer questions than the core sheet. Children who finish the Group activities quickly could use secondary sources to find out about other wind-pollinated plants, and how cereals are grown and harvested.

GROUP ACTIVITIES

1 Give the children a copy each of photocopiable page 77 and ask them to complete it individually.

2 Ask the children to make a detailed labelled drawing of one of the examples of dried or wild grasses.

ICT LINK

Children could use a spreadsheet to create their table in Group activity 1.

ASSESSMENT

After the group work, ask the children to explain two different ways that plants can be pollinated, and why some breakfast foods are called 'cereals'.

PLENARY

Ask any children who used secondary sources to tell the class about other wind-pollinated plants and how cereals are grown and harvested.

Tell the children that many other plants are wind-pollinated. The stinging nettle and the birch tree are two examples that they may be familiar with.

OUTCOMES

- Know that some plants are pollinated by the wind.
- Know that the fruits of some grasses play an important part in our diet.
- Can represent simple information in a tabular form.

LINKS

Unit 1, Lessons 1, 2 and 3: looking at foods and cereals.

Lesson 10 ▪ Plant life cycles

Objective
- To know that flowering plants have life cycles.
- To revise and extend knowledge of plants that humans use in processed foods.

RESOURCES

The five sentences on card from Lesson 1, Blu-Tack® ; a collection of containers for processed foods, each with an 'Ingredients' label; a large, blank, ruled table on the board or flipchart with three columns headed 'Processed food', 'Ingredients that we are sure come from plants' and 'Part of plant'; copies of this table; children's dictionaries.

MAIN ACTIVITY

Display the card sentence strips randomly, attached to a vertical surface. Remind the children of Lesson 1 'What plants do we eat?'. Ask them to help you arrange the sentences in the order in which they happen. Rearrange the sentences into a circular pattern and discuss the term 'Life cycle'.

Show the children the processed food containers and identify the 'Ingredients' lists. Show them the prepared table, then select a processed food container and complete a table entry – for example, the food *Baked beans* might have the ingredients *Beans, Tomatoes, Onion Powder, Sugar* and *Maize*; the corresponding plant parts would be *Seeds, Fruit, Roots, Stem* and *Seeds*. Ask the children to work in pairs, selecting one processed food container at a time and completing the table.

DIFFERENTIATION

Support children by giving them a sheet with several lists of plant-derived ingredients from processed foods. They could read the lists, then match each set of ingredients to the appropriate processed food container.

ASSESSMENT

Test the children's understanding with a simple game. Display the five plant life cycle sentences in the correct circular pattern, then ask the children to shut their eyes. Remove a sentence. Ask the children to open their eyes and tell you what sentence has been removed.

PLENARY
Discuss the children's answers in the table. Some ingredients (such as sugar) may originate from more than one type of plant. Whenever possible, stress the relationship between *flowers, fruits* and *seeds.*

OUTCOMES
- Develop the concept of a life cycle in relation to a flowering plant.
- Know the parts of some plants that are used in processed foods.

Lesson 11 ◗ Growing cabbages

Objective
- To develop an understanding of life cycles.
- To know the life cycle of a butterfly.

Vocabulary
butterfly, caterpillar, larva, pupa, pupate, chrysalis, insecticide, parasite, ichneumon fly

RESOURCES ◉
Main activity: The five sentences from Lesson 1, on card; an A3 copy of photocopiable page 78 (also 'Growing cabbages' (red) available on the CD-ROM); the 'reader's letter' (see Preparation); four cards with the words 'adult', 'caterpillar' or 'larva', 'egg', and 'pupa', with Blu-Tack® on the back of each card.
Group activities: 1 Photocopiable page 78 (one copy per child). **2** Paper; writing materials.
ICT link: 'Growing cabbages' interactive and 'Butterfly life cycle' diagram on the CD-ROM.

PREPARATION
Attach the five sentences on strips of card, from Lesson 1 to the board, in random order. Make a large copy of the 'reader's letter' on page 56. Cover the final two paragraphs of the reply on the copy of page 78.

BACKGROUND
The focus of this lesson is the life cycle of a cabbage white butterfly. The life cycle of a parasitic insect, the ichneumon fly, is also discussed.

The cabbage white is one of the most common species of butterfly. There are two varieties: the large white and the small white. Females of both varieties can lay up to 200 eggs on plants such as cabbages and broccoli. The eggs hatch in about a week. The larval or caterpillar stage of both species, which lasts about a month, can cause great damage to crops. The caterpillars are well-camouflaged against the green crop. They are not attacked by birds – probably because they taste bad.

The caterpillars go through several changes of skin (moults) in their rapid growth. They eat greedily in order to store enough food for their pupa or chrysalis stage. The pupa stage lasts two to three weeks, unless it is over-wintering. The adult butterfly that emerges feeds on pollen and nectar. It does not grow; its purpose is to mate and reproduce.

The ichneumon fly (pronounced *ick-new-mon*) is a parasite. It lays its eggs in the bodies of living caterpillars. The flies hatch and feed inside the caterpillar until they are ready to pupate and form yellow cocoons. The caterpillar dies at this stage. Organic gardeners attract ichneumon flies to the vicinity of their *brassica* crops by planting flowers nearby. Insecticides can destroy this beneficial predator, so exposing the crops to caterpillars.

STARTER
Ask the children to help you put the sentences on the plant life cycle in the correct order. Rearrange them in a circular form on the board, and draw arrows between them to convey the idea of a cyclical pattern. Then ask the children: *What do we call this pattern?* (A life cycle.) Tell the children that

Differentiation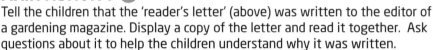

Group activity 1
● Support children by giving them 'Growing cabbages' (green) from the CD-ROM, which includes fewer questions than the core sheet.
    To extend children, give them 'Growing cabbages' (blue), which includes open-ended questioning.

Dear Editor,
    Please can you give me some advice? A few months ago, I planted about eighty cabbages in part of my garden. My family likes to eat fresh cabbage now and again. They grew well for a few weeks, then something started nibbling the leaves. I saw some tiny green caterpillars, so I sprayed the whole garden with insecticide to kill them.
    Then we went on holiday for a few weeks. When we came back, there were no leaves left on the cabbage plants. I pulled up all the stalks that were left and threw them in the dustbin.

they are going to learn about animal life cycles.

MAIN ACTIVITY

Tell the children that the 'reader's letter' (above) was written to the editor of a gardening magazine. Display a copy of the letter and read it together. Ask questions about it to help the children understand why it was written.

Now display an enlarged version of the 'editor's reply' (page 78, 'Growing cabbages (red)) on a flip chart or interactive whiteboard. Read through this with the children as far as the final two paragraphs (which you have covered up); save these for later. Ask questions to develop the children's understanding of the text, focusing on the life cycle of the butterfly.

Uncover the rest of the editor's reply and look at the pictures in the corners. In turn, hold up the cards with the words 'adult', 'caterpillar' or 'larva', 'egg' and 'pupa' and ask the children to help you place each under the correct picture. Draw arrows to indicate the life cycle (see diagram below).

Read the final paragraphs of the editor's reply. Ask questions to help the children see that the ichneumon fly and butterfly life cycles are similar.

Finally, draw the children's attention to the foolish behaviour of the gardener. Ask: *What do you think of the gardener?*

GROUP ACTIVITIES

1 Give out copies of page 78 and ask the children to work through it .
2 Point out that the editor probably thought the gardener was quite stupid. The children can write a different reply that is far less polite. It could begin: *Dear Reader, I am amazed at how stupid you are...*

ICT LINK

The children could complete 'Growing cabbages' interactive from the CD-ROM.

ASSESSMENT

During the plenary session, ask the children to tell you: the four stages in the life cycle of a butterfly an ichneumon fly.

PLENARY

Ask the children for some ideas to help the gardener protect next year's crop. Ask children who have consulted secondary sources to share the information they have found.

OUTCOMES
- Have an extended understanding of life cycles.
- Know the life cycle of a butterfly.

LINKS
PSHE: how gardening involves responsible care for the environment.

Lesson 12 ▸ Animal life cycles

Objective
- To revise the life cycles of the butterfly, thrush and green plant.
- To understand the meaning of the term 'mammal'.
- To know that mammals have life cycles.

Vocabulary
embryo, independent, mammal, gestation, pregnant

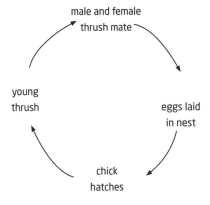

RESOURCES 💿
Main activity: Two flipchart diagrams (see Preparation); two sets of sentence strips (see Main activity), each with Blu-Tack® fastened to the back; a large version of the 'gestation table' from page photocopiable page 79.
Group activity: Copies of photocopiable page 79 (also 'Animal life cycles' (red) available on the CD-ROM).
ICT link: 'Animal life cycles' interactive from the CD-ROM.

PREPARATION
Prepare the two diagrams below on a flipchart. Entitle two other flipchart pages 'Life cycle of a plant' and 'Life cycle of a cat'. Prepare the sentence strips (see Main activity).

BACKGROUND
This lesson is designed to revise the life cycles covered in this unit, and to introduce the life cycles of mammals. Mammals are characterised by the mammary glands of the adult female, which are used to nourish the infant immediately after birth. This represents a closer level of parental care than is found anywhere else in the animal kingdom. Most mammals give birth to a living baby which can survive outside the mother's body.

STARTER
Tell the children that they are going to think about several life cycles, including that of a cat. Ask if any of them have seen a cat with kittens.

MAIN ACTIVITY
Using the flipchart, show the children a circular life cycle pattern for the thrush (see diagram left). Show the same information in a linear form, as in the diagram overleaf. Ask the children to help you show the life cycle for the butterfly in the same form. Write 'Male and female butterfly mate', 'Egg', 'Caterpillar or larva', 'Chrysalis' and 'Butterfly' on the table. Make sure the children understand that in this form, all life cycles of sexually reproducing animals will begin and end with similar words.

Display a flipchart sheet headed 'Life cycle of a plant'. Beneath the heading, write the words: 'Pollen is moved from male stamen to female stigma.' Now display to the children the following card sentence strips in random order: 'The ovary is fertilised.', 'Seeds grow in the ovary, which becomes a fruit.', 'The seeds are dispersed.', 'The seed germinates.', 'Stems and leaves develop.', 'Flowers grow.' Ask the children to help you arrange the sentences on the chart into the correct order.

Show a flipchart sheet entitled 'Life cycle of a cat'. At the top and bottom of the chart, write the same sentence: 'Male and female cat mate'. Now display the following sentence strips in random order: 'An egg is fertilised and develops into an embryo inside the mother.', 'The embryo develops into a kitten inside the mother.', 'The kitten is born.', 'The kitten feeds on its mother's milk.', 'The kitten feeds independently.', 'The kitten develops into an adult cat.' Arrange the sentences in their correct order.

Thrush	Butterfly
Male and female adult thrush mate.	
Eggs incubate in nest	
Chick hatches and grows in nest.	
Young thrush.	
Adult thrush.	

Ask the children to think of some ways in which the life cycle of a cat differs from that of a butterfly or thrush. Draw their attention to two facts: the kitten develops inside the mother, and the new-born kitten feeds on its mother's milk. Tell the children that species of animals that feed on their mother's milk are called 'mammals', and that nearly all mammals give birth to 'live' young. Ask: *Do you know the names of any other animals that are mammals?* Confirm the answers with comments such as: *Yes, a dog has live young.* Make sure that the children identify humans as mammals.

Tell the children that it takes about 65 days from when the female cat's egg is fertilised until the kitten is born. Show them an enlarged version of the 'gestation table' from page 79. Ask: *What do you think the word 'gestation' means?*

GROUP ACTIVITY
Let the children work individually through photocopiable page 79.

ICT LINK ⊙
Children can use the 'Animal life cycles' interactive from the CD-ROM, to sort sentences into the correct order to show the life cycle of a cat.

ASSESSMENT
Ask the children to tell you two differences between the life cycle of a thrush and that of most mammals.

PLENARY
Ask any children who have used secondary sources to tell you about the gestation periods of other mammals. Explain that some mammals (such as the duck-billed platypus) do not have live young, and that others (such as the kangaroo) have very tiny young who need to be carried in a pouch.

OUTCOMES
● Have consolidated their knowledge of life cycles.
● Know that a mammal is a class of animal whose young are fed on milk from the mother.

Differentiation ⊙
Group activity 1
To support children, give them 'Animal life cycles' (green) from the CD-ROM, which asks them just to put sentences about the life cycle of a cat in the correct order. To extend children, give them 'Animal life cycles' (blue), which also asks them to create a bar chart of given animal gestation periods and to investigate the gestation periods of other mammals.

Lesson 13 ▪ Comparing life cycles

Objective
● To compare the life cycles of different animals.
● To develop knowledge of some other life cycles.

RESOURCES
The sentence strips and flipchart sheet 'Life cycle of a cat' from Lesson 12; a flipchart or board with a table as shown on page 59; writing materials; paper; rulers; secondary sources of information on various animal life cycles.

MAIN ACTIVITY
Use the sentence strips and the appropriate flipchart sheet from Lesson 12 to revise the life cycle of a cat.

Discuss the similarities and differences between the life cycles of a cat and a song thrush, and list the suggestions on the table. The differences will be more obvious than the similarities, and will demand more space. Similarities may include: 'The chick in the egg and the kitten inside the mother are both kept warm.', 'The chick and the kitten both need feeding and protecting by the adults.'

Show the children the secondary sources of information on other animal

Similarities between the life cycles of a cat and a thrush	Differences between the life cycles of a cat and a thrush
Male and female adults need to mate to produce offspring.	The thrush chick grows in an egg in a nest. The baby kitten grows inside the mother.

life cycles, and discuss the life cycle of one other creature (such as a frog). Write a set of sentences on the board or flip chart to describe this life cycle. Start with: 'Adult male and female frog mate.'

Ask the children to make a table to show the similarities and differences between the life cycles of the thrush and the butterfly, or the cat and the butterfly. They can use the secondary sources to investigate the life cycle of another animal, and write a set of sentences to describe that life cycle.

ASSESSMENT
At the end of the lesson, ask the children to describe the similarities between the life cycles of the song thrush and the butterfly, or the cat and the butterfly.

PLENARY
Listen to the children's descriptions of other life cycles.

OUTCOMES
● Know the similarities and differences between some animal life cycles.
● Find out about some other animal life cycles.

ENRICHMENT
Lesson 14 ▪ Human life cycles

Objective
● To know the stages of the human life cycle.

Vocabulary
life cycle, fertilisation, fuse, birth, infancy, childhood, adolescence, puberty, adulthood, reproduction, lifespan, mammals

RESOURCES
Group activities: 1 A3 paper (one sheet per pair); colouring pencils. **2** A3 paper (one sheet per pair); textbooks containing references to the life cycles of non-human animals; the *Encarta*® CD-ROM (Microsoft) or similar.

BACKGROUND
A life cycle is the name we give to the key stages of an animal's life. The fact that the death of an individual does not lead to the eventual extinction of the species is the essence of the life cycle. Dying individuals are replaced by new individuals born into the population, and these in turn reach sexual maturity and are able to produce young before they die. The key stages in the human life cycle are fertilisation (the joining or fusing of an egg and a sperm cell), birth (about 9 months from fertilisation), infancy (lasting up to 1 year from birth), childhood (from 1 to 12 years), adolescence (from 11 to 18), adulthood (from adolescence to old age) and ultimately death. The lifespan of an individual is the number of years he or she lives for. In most models, death is not included in illustrations of the life cycle.

STARTER
Ask the children: *What season are we in? How do you know?* They may refer to the temperature outside or the state of the trees. Ask questions such as: *In which season do the trees shed their leaves and disperse their seeds?* (Autumn.) *When are the trees bare except for the closed buds?* (Winter.) Explain that the world we live in is full of patterns of life, such as the changes in plants brought on by the seasons. The life of animals also follows a pattern known as a 'life cycle'. Humans share certain stages in their life cycle with other mammals.

MAIN ACTIVITY

Tell the children that they are going to look at the life cycle of humans. Ask them to help you sort through the most important stages in our lives. Brainstorm their ideas on the board or flip chart: write the words 'The human life cycle' in the middle, and add their suggestions for stages in a circle around it. Start at a random point and deliberately put the stages in the wrong order. The main stages you should aim to include are fertilisation, birth, infancy, childhood, adolescence and adulthood. If the children suggest death, give acknowledgement to this, but explain that it isn't usually included in pictures of the life cycle. Explain that fertilisation is when the sperm and egg cell fuse (join) inside the mother, and this moment marks the start of life; and that adolescence is the time when the body develops to become sexually mature, which means that it changes physically to prepare it for reproduction (having children).

GROUP ACTIVITIES

1 Give each pair of children a sheet of A3 paper and ask them to draw the human life cycle by copying the stages you have listed and arranging them in the correct order. Next, they can try to write down an age range corresponding to each stage, then illustrate their life cycle diagram with a picture of each stage. The illustration below shows a typical answer.
2 The pairs should now try to find out about the life cycle of another animal by referring to textbooks and the *Encarta* ® CD-ROM. They should record and illustrate this life cycle on another sheet of A3 paper. Encourage them to note similarities and differences between this life cycle and that of a human. For example, they could look at the life cycles of butterflies or frogs, which have a stage of metamorphosis. Many insects have a life cycle that goes egg – larva – pupa – adult – egg. Many animals (such as spiders and crabs) have distinct stages of growth when they shed their outer case, leaving behind the old case as a 'ghost'.

ASSESSMENT

Check the children's understanding of the human life cycle from their diagrams. Are the stages in the correct order? Is the correct approximate age range given for each stage?

PLENARY

Ask the children to suggest how parts of the human life cycle have been changed by advances over the last thousand years or so. (We live longer because of better medical care; we tend to have children later in life; children are reaching puberty at a younger age, probably due to improvements in diet and lifestyle.)

OUTCOME

● Know the key stages in the human life cycle.

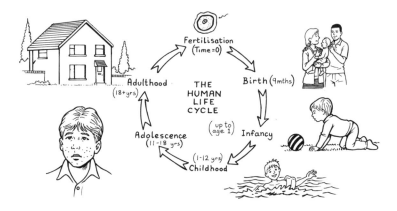

Lesson 15 ▫ Growth

Objective
● To be aware that human bodies vary and that this is natural.
● To know hat humans have a 'growth spurt'.
● To know hat the body parts change in proportion from birth to adulthood.

Vocabulary
height, growth, average, proportions

RESOURCES
Main activity: Metre and half-metre rulers; Plasticine®; paper; pencils; graph paper.
Group activities: 1 and **2** Photocopiable page 80 (also 'Growth' (red) available on the CD-ROM); paper; pencils; graph paper.
ICT link: Graphing tool and diagram 'Growth', from the CD-ROM.

BACKGROUND
You may wish to approach the sensitive topic of puberty through PSHE. This unit approaches growth and development from the scientific perspective, looking at the mechanisms of these changes and introducing the structure of the reproductive organs. This lesson starts by linking the concept of change to the human life cycle (see diagram on the CD-ROM).

There are a large number of facts in this topic and the content will generate a great deal of interest! It is important that the children build up their factual knowledge sequentially as a basis for later work on reproduction; thus there are two full lesson plans for this topic. In this lesson the notion of variation as being natural is reinforced, to reassure the children that they may not all change at the same time, at the same rate, or to the same extent. This is developed into a projection of the growth of 9 to 15-year-olds, based on the measurements of a large number of people. Once the children are comfortable with the idea of a 'growth spurt', they can consider briefly how the proportions of the body change. This activity involves the children using data about their heights. If this is a particularly sensitive issue with your class, use a group of plants of equal age (such as broad bean seedlings). By introducing general change due to growth from a scientific perspective, this lesson prepares pupils for more specific work on puberty in Lesson 16.

STARTER
Tell the children that they are going to look at growth. When we look at any group of living things which are the same age, such as a litter of puppies or a tray full of seedlings, we can see that there is some variation in size. This is also true of the class. Explain that when scientists study the size of individuals in a group, they measure them, divide the measurements into size groups and make a graph.

Differentiation
Group activity 1
Support children by giving them 'Growth chart' (green) from the CD-ROM, which includes a pre-prepared blank graph. To extend children, ask them to return to the class height data and divide it into girls' heights and boys' heights. Alternatively, they could measure the heights of different bean plants and calculate the average height and/or graph the heights as they did for the class. *Do plants show a similar distribution of heights?*
Group activity 2
To support children, ask them to make Plasticine® models of the four bodies to compare.
Extend children by asking them to speculate on how they would look if they still had the proportions of a baby.

MAIN ACTIVITY
In pairs, let the children measure and record each other's height. Bring the class together and find the heights of the tallest and shortest children. Divide the range into five or six size groups. (For example, if the range is 126-146cm, use groups of 126-130cm, 131-135cm, 136-140cm, 141-145cm and 146-150cm. Ask the children to rearrange the class data into these groups and draw a bar graph of them. The children should see that there are a few individuals at the edges of the range, but most are in the middle. Say that as they grow, some individuals will move from the edges of the range towards the middle or vice versa. Introduce the Group activities: looking at how people grow between the ages of 9 and 15, and how body shape changes with age.

GROUP ACTIVITIES
1 The children should use the data on photocopiable page 80 to plot a graph of the heights of girls and boys aged 9-15, with age on the x-axis, height on the y-axis. Select a graph scale appropriate to the children's ability. The height scale may be 0-180cm or 130-180cm; using the smaller scale will show the height differences more clearly. The children should comment that

the girls grow faster than the boys from 11 to 13, then the boys grow faster than the girls from 14 to 15. Some children could use the graphing tool on the CD-ROM to prepare their graph.

2 The children should describe the changes in the sequence of pictures at the bottom of page 80. The answers are: the head becomes proportionally smaller, the face becomes proportionally larger, the body becomes proportionally smaller, the legs and arms become proportionally longer.

ASSESSMENT

Look for accurately plotted points on the graph and clear lines connecting them. Look for clear descriptions of the changes in the proportions of the body.

PLENARY

Discuss how the proportions of our bodies change as we grow. Stress that there is variation in any group of people, and that this is natural. Describe the period of rapid growth that the children are entering as a 'growth spurt'. Highlight that although there is variation, certain changes happen to everyone as they grow into an adult.

OUTCOMES

● Is aware that human bodies vary and that this is natural.
● Can identify the time of the 'growth spurt'.
● Can describe how some parts of the body change in proportion from birth to adulthood.

Lesson 16 ◘ Changes in the body

Objective
● To know about the changes that take place in the body at puberty.

Vocabulary
development, waist, puberty, breast, nipple, pubic hair, testicles, penis, scrotum, vulva, ovary, uterus, genitals

RESOURCES ◉
Main activities: Pictures of an adult male and female (possibly in swimwear), to show differences in body shape.
Group activities: 1 Photocopiable page 81 (also 'Changes in the body – 1' (red) available on the CD-ROM); pencils. **2** Photocopiable page 82 (also 'Changes in the body – 2' (red) available on the CD-ROM); pencils.
ICT link: 'Changes in the body' interactive from the CD-ROM.

BACKGROUND
The activities in this lesson should be done by all the children at the same time. This lesson builds on Lesson 15, looking at further changes in the external appearance of the body due to puberty, briefly considering the changes inside the body related to reproduction, and considering the changes in attitudes that develop. The children should be made aware that they are about to enter 'puberty'; a time of many developmental changes – both external and internal.

STARTER
Tell the children that 'growth' (physical enlargement) occurs in humans from birth until they are about 20 years old. After that, a person's body will stay about the same size until old age, unless too little or too much food is eaten. In old age, a person's body may become slightly smaller. Between the ages of 8 and 17 in girls and 10 and 18 in boys, there are also particular changes or developments to the body in order to prepare it for reproduction (the ability to create new people). These changes affect the body shape, the condition of the hair and skin, and the development of the reproductive organs. This period of change is called 'puberty'.

MAIN ACTIVITY 1

Remind the children of the changes in body shape they studied in Lesson 15. Say that during puberty there are further changes, and that these are different for boys and for girls. Show the pictures of a man and a woman. Point out that the man's shoulders are broader, while the hips are broader in the woman. Highlight the woman's breast development and relate this to feeding a baby. You may add that the female reproductive organs that produce a baby are hidden inside the woman's body. Her external genitals are hidden between her legs and are called the vulva. The male's reproductive organs are partly visible on the outside of the body. The external male genitals are the penis and the scrotum, which contains two testicles. During puberty, the size of the male genitals increases.

At puberty, both boys and girls grow hair under their arms and between their legs. The hair between the legs is called pubic hair. In boys, the hair on the face also starts to grow longer and thicker; the boy may have to shave to remove it. Both boys' and girls' skin produces more oil and this may lead to spots developing. Also when boys go through puberty, their voice-box grows and makes deeper sounds. In the early part of this process, the voice may produce both squeaky and deep sounds and is said to be 'breaking'. This can be embarrassing if the boy needs to speak.

GROUP ACTIVITY 1

Give the children a copy each of page 81 and let them work through it.

MAIN ACTIVITY 2

Remind the children about some boys being embarrassed when their voices break. Broaden this idea to many children being embarrassed or concerned as their bodies start changing. Say that a common fear is to worry whether you are developing normally, and that this is natural.

People also have to cope with changes taking place inside the body. In boys, the testicles start to produce sperm. These are essential for reproduction. The sperm may be released (in a liquid called semen) through the penis at night when the boy is asleep. When this happens, the boy is said to have had a 'wet dream'.

A girl's body contains two ovaries which produce eggs for reproduction. During puberty, the ovaries start to release eggs. When an egg is released, another part of the girl's reproductive system called the uterus or womb develops a thick wall of blood, ready to help a baby develop. If there is no baby, the wall then breaks down and the blood passes out of the reproductive system. When this occurs, the girl is said to be 'having a period'. This can be quite uncomfortable. The releasing of the egg and the development and breaking-up of the womb wall occurs every month, so the girl will experience a monthly period. At this time, she wears a sanitary towel to absorb the blood. These may be available in the girls' toilets or from the school nurse.

The testicles and ovaries also make chemicals known as hormones, which flow around the body in the blood. They cause the body to develop the features of men and women. They can also affect the way that people behave. Boys, for example, commonly become more interested in girls, and vice versa. Girls' hormones can also affect their mood, and may make the girl feel upset or bad-tempered just before the monthly period.

GROUP ACTIVITY 2

Give each child a copy of page 82 to work through.

ICT LINK 💿

Children can use the 'Changes in the body' interactive to label a male and female body, to show the changes that take place during puberty.

ASSESSMENT
Look for accuracy in the children's answers. Discuss the work in the Group activities and assess how fluently the children use the new vocabulary.

PLENARY
Share a 'question and answer' session in which you say some words related to puberty and reproduction and the children give you definitions. Start a question box where the children can put questions about puberty-related problems, written anonymously, to the school 'agony aunt' (a teacher or school nurse). Later, invite the nurse or teacher to read out some of the questions and give their replies.

OUTCOMES
- Recognise the changes that take place at puberty.
- Understand that these changes take place at different times in different people.
- Can name some parts of the reproductive system.

ENRICHMENT
Lesson 17 ◼ The reproductive system

Objective
- To know about the structure of the reproductive organs.
- To know that changes in the body leading to sexual maturity begin at puberty.

Vocabulary
extinct, reproduce, penis, testes, sperm, egg, fertilised, ovary, vagina, oviduct, uterus/womb, puberty, periods, menstruate

RESOURCES ◉
Main activity: Enlarged copies of photocopiable pages 83 and 84 (also 'The reproductive system – 1' (red) and 'The reproductive system – 2' (red) available on the CD-ROM); a 3D model of a human torso (if possible).
Group activities: 1 Copies of photocopiable pages 83 and 84; A4 paper; scissors; adhesive; pencils. **2** Plasticine®. (*Human Body*, CD-ROM (Dorling Kindersley) or similar will be useful for extension work.)

BACKGROUND
The next couple of lessons develop the children's understanding of life cycles further by looking specifically at reproduction in humans and the changes that take place at puberty. This lesson is guaranteed to cause a few smirks and blushes. The range of vocabulary with which the children will be familiar will vary greatly. It is worth sticking to terms that will be used consistently, but in some cases there is more than one correct name for an organ (for example, 'uterus' and 'womb').

In order for a new human being to form, an **egg (ovum)** made in the ovary of the mother has to join with a **sperm cell** made in the **testes (testicles)** of the father. When this happens, we say that the egg has been **fertilised**. Humans reproduce using internal fertilisation. This means that the egg and the sperm cell have to join together inside the mother's body. The reproductive organs of humans are designed to bring the egg and sperm together, and to enable the mother's body to provide care for the growing baby.

The testes of the male are outside the body (so that they are cooler – this helps them to make sperm cells). The **penis** of the male becomes stiff and erect in order to enter the **vagina** of the female during **sexual intercourse**, when sperm made in the testes are released through the penis into the vagina.

The female has two **ovaries** that make eggs. The eggs are carried down tubes called **oviducts** (also known as **fallopian tubes**) to the **uterus (womb)**. If the egg becomes fertilised, it will be nourished and protected here as it completes its development into a baby. At birth, the baby passes out of the mother through the vagina (which is also known as the 'birth canal').

During **puberty**, male and female bodies start to become sexually mature

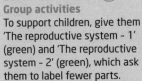

Differentiation

Group activities

To support children, give them 'The reproductive system - 1' (green) and 'The reproductive system - 2' (green), which ask them to label fewer parts.

To extend children, give them 'The reproductive system - 1' (blue) and 'The reproductive system - 2' (blue), which include extension questions.

(able to participate in reproduction). The testes of boys start producing sperm, and girls start to **menstruate** (or have **periods**). Periods occur about once every 28 days, when the lining of the uterus is shed together with the unfertilised egg. The lining is then renewed, ready for a new fertilised egg.

STARTER

Gather the class in a horseshoe shape so that they are all facing you. The first part of the lesson will be a discussion, and it is perhaps best if the children are not too aware of their peers. Remind them of the work they have previously done on life cycles. Explain that over the next few lessons, you are going to look specifically at the part of the life cycle that prevents living things from becoming extinct. *Which part of the life cycle is this?* (Fertilisation.)

MAIN ACTIVITY

Explain to the children that the next few lessons will be about reproduction in humans, and that you will start by looking at the reproductive organs.

Ask the class whether they know why the female body has to be different from the male body. Hopefully this will lead on to the idea that the female body needs to be able to provide for a growing baby. Now say that the female can produce **egg cells**. If the egg (ovum) becomes fertilised, it can grow into a baby. *Do you know where the eggs are made? Where are sperm cells made? What does 'fertilised' mean? How does this happen? Where does the developing baby grow?* Refer to enlarged diagrams of the male and female reproductive organs, and talk through the function of each part. Guide the children towards an understanding that **sperm cells** are made by the male, and that one sperm cell needs to join with the egg cell inside the female to **fertilise** it. The baby develops in the **uterus (womb)** of the mother.

A fun way of getting the children familiar with the names of the different parts is to hold up unlabelled diagrams of the reproductive organs and ask them (as a class) to shout out the correct name for each part as you point to it. The security of a group response makes the children far less self-conscious - though it may surprise anyone passing in the corridor!

Remind children that the time when humans change to become sexually mature (able to parent children) is called **puberty**.

GROUP ACTIVITIES

1 Give the children one copy per pair of pages 83 and 84 (you may find that they are more comfortable working in same-sex pairs) and A4 paper. Ask them to cut out the labels and diagrams, match the correct name of each part of the reproductive system with the job that it does, then stick the labels in place around each diagram (with label lines) on an A4 sheet.

2 Ask the children to look at the diagrams of the sperm and egg cells and try to work out why they are so different. (The sperm cells have a tail to help them swim to the egg. The egg cells are large to store food that provides for the developing baby over the first few days.) Ask them to make a Plasticine model of each cell, using the scale suggested on page 83.

ASSESSMENT

Try to talk to each pair. Can they confidently explain, in simple terms, the function of each part of the male and female reproductive systems?

PLENARY

To consolidate the vocabulary used and link it to the idea that sexual maturity begins at adolescence, ask the children to say whether the following changes happen in males or females at puberty: the testes make sperm; periods start; an egg is released from the ovaries once every 28 days; the penis grows larger; the body gets bigger; breasts start to grow.

OUTCOMES
● Can describe the functions of the parts that make up the male and female reproductive organs.
● Know that the changes that bring about sexual maturity begin at puberty.

LINKS
PSHE: understanding periods; responsible relationships.

ENRICHMENT
Lesson 18 ◗ Life before birth

Objective
● To know how fertilisation occurs.
● To know how the growing foetus develops and how the baby is born.

Vocabulary
uterus (womb), fallopian tubes (oviducts), fertilisation, zygote, pregnancy, embryo, foetus, umbilical cord, placenta, amniotic sac, premature

RESOURCES
Main activity: A ruler; a large diagram of the female reproductive system (from photocopiable page 83); a diagram of a baby in the womb, showing the key features (foetus, umbilical cord, placenta, uterus, amniotic sac).
Group activities: 1 Photocopiable page 85 (also 'Life before birth' (red) available on the CD-ROM); A4 paper; scissors; adhesive. **2** Paper; colouring pencils; sugar paper.
ICT link: 'Life before birth' interactive on the CD-OM.

PREPARATION
3D models of the unborn child at each stage of its development, as well as useful posters, are available from Philip Harris Education, Novara House, Excelsior Road, Ashby Park, Ashby de la Zouch, Leicestershire LE65 1NG. If you can obtain these, or other similar examples, they will make an invaluable contribution to your lesson and emphasise the 'Wow!' factor of the topic.

BACKGROUND
This lesson touches on a fascinating subject, and the children will probably be bursting with wonderful (and weird) questions to ask you. The 'Did you know?' section below is added in anticipation of a few of these questions!

Hundreds of millions of sperm cells are released by the male during intercourse, and they begin their journey through the **uterus (womb)** and up the **fallopian tubes (oviducts)** of the female. Here, they might just meet an **egg** on its journey down from one of the **ovaries**, swept along by millions of tiny waving hairs called cilia. Only one sperm cell can succeed in penetrating the egg (in *very* rare cases, two can – but the baby does not develop healthily); when it does so, it triggers a lightning-fast reaction preventing any others from doing the same. This is **fertilisation**: the fusing together of a sperm cell and an egg cell. The combined genetic material from the two cells (the fertilised egg) is now called the **zygote** – the first stage in its development into a young human being. The zygote passes into the womb and may be successful in settling into the lining. This is called **implantation**, and is the true beginning of **pregnancy**; it triggers many dramatic changes in the body of the mother.

In its earliest stages of development, the growing individual is called an **embryo** – up to the point at which the organs are fully developed (which happens after only nine weeks) and it begins to show a recognisably human form. It is now called a **foetus**. While it is developing, the growing baby receives **oxygen** and **nutrients** from the mother's blood, which also carries away carbon dioxide and other **waste** (including urea, which is usually filtered out by our kidneys and forms part of our urine – the mother's body has to do this for the baby). This exchange of materials happens in the **placenta**, which is rooted to the mother's womb. The materials are then carried along the umbilical cord to and from the body of the baby. While the baby is growing, it is protected within a fluid-filled bag called the **amniotic sac** (which acts similarly to airbags in cars, protecting the baby from bumps).

Pregnancies usually last 39 weeks, though **premature** babies born up to three months before this date are now routinely cared for in Special Care Baby Units and have a good chance of survival. When the 'waters break' (the amniotic sac tears, releasing fluid), powerful **contractions** of the abdomen increase in intensity until the baby is forced down the birth canal and out of the body. In some cases (particularly if the baby is stressed), the baby may be withdrawn by surgery through an incision made in the abdomen of the mother - this is called a **Caesarean** birth.

Did you know?
● The mother and baby have separate blood systems - the baby's blood vessels are very delicate and would soon rupture if the mother's blood, which is at a much higher pressure, entered them.
● The mother doesn't just 'eat for two', she breathes for two and removes waste for two. The growing baby even strips calcium from her bones to make up the supply it needs for its own growing bones!
● Giving birth is probably more painful and hazardous for humans than for any other animal, due to the large skulls of human babies (if you are a mother reading this, I'm sure it didn't need pointing out to you).
● The umbilical cord has no pain receptors; it doesn't hurt the baby or mother when it is cut.
● Identical twins form from one egg, fertilised by one sperm cell. The egg has then, for some reason, divided to make two zygotes - each with identical genetic information.
● Non-identical twins are formed from two separate eggs that have been fertilised by different sperm cells and have then implanted in the womb.

STARTER
Gather the children together. Revise some of the ideas from the previous lesson - in particular, the changes that occur at puberty and how this prepares the male and female bodies for reproduction.

MAIN ACTIVITY
Describe in simple terms how sperm cells are released inside the body of the female during intercourse, and go on to describe the journey the sperm cells have to make. The distance they have to cover is comparable to a swimmer setting off from Blackpool across the Irish Sea to Dublin! Ask: *How are sperm cells designed for swimming?* (They have a moving tail.)
    Explain the meaning of the word 'fertilisation', and go on to put the key events of the baby's life in order, using the text on page 85. Use a ruler to demonstrate the size at each stage.

GROUP ACTIVITIES
1 Working in pairs, the children should cut out the pictures and boxes of text from page 85, match them and arrange them in sequence before sticking them on a sheet of A4 paper.
2 Using the illustrations and measurements given on page 85, the children should work in their table groups to draw life-sized pictures of the developing baby at each stage. These can be coloured, cut out and stuck onto a large sheet of sugar paper, with an appropriate caption for each stage.

ICT LINK 💿
Use 'Life before birth' interactive from the CD-ROM on an interactive whiteboard as a class activity as part of the Plenary.

ASSESSMENT
Read through page 85 as a class. Check that the children have grasped the main developmental stages of the baby. Write these stages on the board and see whether the children can place them in order confidently: A. birth; B.

attachment to lining of womb; C. fertilisation; D. zygote; E. embryo; F. foetus. (Correct order: C, D, B, E, F, A.)

PLENARY

Link this lesson to previous work on healthy lifestyles by asking: *Why is it a bad idea for pregnant mothers to smoke?* (The amount of oxygen received by the baby from the mother's blood is reduced, and the levels of nicotine and other toxic chemicals received by the baby increase. The health of the child, as well as that of the mother, suffers.)

OUTCOMES
- Can describe the growth of the foetus.
- Understand the birth process.

LINKS
PSHE and citizenship: safety and responsibility.

ENRICHMENT
Lesson 19 ▪ Looking after a baby

Objective
- To know about the changes in lifestyle that are necessary during pregnancy and the skills and care required in parenting.
- To develop skills in listening, note-taking and asking questions.
- To recognise stages in their own development.

RESOURCES

A3 paper or sugar paper; adhesive; colouring pens or pencils; a new mother who is willing to talk to the children about the experience of being pregnant and caring for a baby. The children also need to bring in labelled pictures of themselves at various times from ante-natal scan to two years old. Scans could be photocopied for inclusion in displays. Five photographs of each child at different stages will be enough.

MAIN ACTIVITY

The issue of parenting may be a sensitive one in cases where family splits have occurred, so use your judgement as to the best way to tackle each situation. Ask the children, a week in advance, to request parental permission to bring in pictures of themselves at different stages from scans to their second birthday. Remember that childhood photos will be priceless to the children's parents – so make sure that they are clearly labelled with the child's name, and protected from damage. Invite a parent who has recently had a baby to visit the school, show their child and talk to the children about the pregnancy: the preparation needed leading up to the birth, the birth itself, and the subsequent care of the child.

Start the lesson by asking how the children's families would cope if they had to look after a new-born baby. *What would the baby need? How would their lifestyle have to change?* Introduce the mother and baby. Emphasise that you are fortunate in having this visitor, as she is going through the experience of being a mother to a new child. Explain to the children that you want them to make rough notes while your visitor speaks (make sure you share the questions in advance with the mother, so that she feels prepared). Ask questions such as:
- What the pregnancy itself was like. What special food did the mother have to include in her diet? Did she have to change her lifestyle, for example her exercise routine? What checks were carried out by the health visitor or hospital before the birth?
- What the birth was like. How long did the mother and baby stay in hospital? What special help did the nurses give to help the mother care for the baby?
- How the lifestyle of the mother changed in caring for the baby. How often does the baby cry, sleep, feed, need its nappy changing, need bathing? Has the house had to be rearranged to suit the needs of the baby? What

check-ups is the baby having? When will/did the baby start eating solid food?

Give each child a sheet of A3 paper headed 'Looking after a baby'. Ask them to arrange some photographs of themselves in order of increasing age. Now ask them to write something next to each picture about the care they needed at that stage, and how this might have affected their parents' lives.

ICT LINK
The children could make a power point display of photographs of themselves from being a baby to the present.

ASSESSMENT
From the children's display work, check if they have grasped the main points of the visitor's talk and have arranged the pictures with relevant, informative captions.

PLENARY
Ask one or two of the children to read out their accounts. Ask: *Is being a parent easy? Has it made you think a little differently about your own parents?* If they have younger brothers or sisters, perhaps they can understand why their parents sometimes need a little help around the home. Mention that sometimes girls become pregnant while only in their young teens. *Do you think this is a good thing to happen? How might it be difficult for the girl to cope?* Take care not to sound judgemental – you could be talking about a sister or a parent of one of the children!

OUTCOMES
● Understand that a pregnant mother needs to take special care of her health.
● Understand that being a parent is a demanding task that requires many skills.

Lesson 20 ▪ Song thrush survival

Objective
● To know that if living things fail to reproduce they become extinct.

Vocabulary
extinction, habitat, predators, sparrow hawk, crow, magpie, brood, reproduce

RESOURCES
Main activity: Two enlarged copies of the song thrush survival game; page 86 (also 'Song thrush survival game (red) available on the CD-ROM); pictures (from wildlife identification books) of a song thrush, sparrow hawk, magpie, crow, and squirrel; three large dice.
Group activities: 1 Paper; drawing and writing materials. **2** Paper; writing materials.

PREPARATION
On one copy of the Song thrush survival game, cover up the sentences in italics in the 'Risks' column. You will need to enlarge the photocopiable to use with the class.

BACKGROUND
The song thrush is an indigenous British bird whose population is in steep decline. The four main reasons are:
1 Loss of habitat. The bird nests mainly in hedges and thickets. Increased farm mechanisation has meant an expansion in field sizes and loss of hedgerows and trees.
2 Increased predation. The numbers of domestic cats have increased in the UK in recent decades. The sparrow hawk too has recovered from its post-War decline (an effect of DDT insecticide poisoning). Populations of the

predators of the infant bird (magpies, crows and squirrels) seem well-adapted to current environmental conditions.

3 Reduced food supply. The song thrush is an omnivore. Its diet mainly consists of worms, snails, insects and berries. Surveys show that the young bird is vulnerable to starvation when it leaves its nest. Often this period (early summer) is when the ground is hard. Worms are difficult to locate and seasonal berries are unavailable. It is thought that modern farming methods, insecticides and increased field drainage have reduced the supply of snails at this critical time in the bird's life.

4 Tidier gardens. It has never been easier to tidy the part of the environment that we manage. Tools to trim hedges, mow lawns and strim grass are widely used. There are few berries in the hedgerows, and no home in the garden for the insects that are an essential part of the bird's food chain.

Ways to encourage the song thrush include the following: plant hedges or thickets as nesting sites; allow hedge plants to develop berries for winter thrush food; avoid using insecticides and slug pellets - the thrush is a natural 'pest control'; use organic methods of cultivation that encourage worms and other small animals; allow parts of the environment to be naturally untidy.

STARTER

Ask the children to define 'an endangered species'. Ask them to tell you about some endangered species they know about and why these species are in danger of extinction. Expect some exotic answers: the tiger, the blue whale and so on.

MAIN ACTIVITY

Tell the children that they are going to look at the life cycle of the song thrush, an endangered British bird. Show them a picture of a song thrush.

Now say that you are going to play a game with two teams: you versus the class. Display the first sheet with the risks in italics covered. Using the information in the first column discuss the different stages in the life cycle of the bird. Explain the dangers faced by a song thrush at different stages of its life cycle. Show the children pictures of the predators of the bird: magpie, crow, sparrow hawk. Explain that life for all creatures is a lottery, and that a song thrush will often try to incubate two broods of three or four eggs in a year so that some will survive.

Explain the rules of the game (see page 86): the winning team is the one with the most surviving birds at the end. After each throw, teams can use the blank columns to record the progress of their game with symbols. For example, if the teacher throws a 1 on their first turn, the eggs from their first brood are all lost; if the children throw a 4, their first brood of eggs survive and move on to the chick stage; the teacher now throws for their second brood.

When the first game has finished, play again, this time displaying the second version and discussing the new risks (those in italics). They are mostly caused by human activity. Ask children to explain why few or no birds survived the second game. *What will happen to the song thrush if no young birds survive to become adults?* Emphasise the answer: *They will become extinct because they cannot reproduce.*

Ask the children for suggestions to reduce the risk to the song thrush. List their ideas on the board or flip chart for use in Group activity 1.

GROUP ACTIVITIES

1 Invite the children to make a poster to show other children in the school why the song thrush may become extinct.

2 They can make a scroll or charter to explain what could be done to help the song thrush.

ASSESSMENT

At the end of the game, ask the whole class: *What happens to a species if it cannot reproduce itself?*

PLENARY

Look at the results of the Group activities. Listen to any additional information on other birds.

OUTCOMES

- Know that if living things fail to reproduce they become extinct.
- Know that living things in our immediate environment are facing extinction through environmental change.
- Know that we can all do something to promote conservation.

LINKS

PSHE: responsibility towards the environment.

Lesson 21 ▪ Assessment

Objective
- To assess the children's knowledge of the life cycle of plants.
- To assess the children's knowledge of some animal life cycles.

RESOURCES

The sentence strips from Lesson 12, photocopiable pages 87 and 88 (also 'Assessment - 1' (red) and 'Assessment - 2' (red) available on the CD-ROM); pencils.

PREPARATION

Make one copy per child of each assessment sheet.

STARTER

Display the sentence strips referring to cats from Lesson 12 in random order, and ask the children to rearrange them beneath the sentence 'Male and female cat mate' on the board or flipchart.

ASSESSMENT ACTIVITY 1

Give out copies of photocopiable page 87 and let the children work through it individually.

ANSWERS

1b. Stamen; 1c. Petal; 1d. Ovary; 1e. The plant needs to be pollinated for fruits and seeds to be produced, and the insects help to do this; 2. Colourful petals and scent (or nectar); 3a: Ash: wind; 3b. Holly: birds; 3c. Oak: animals; 4. To have better access to moisture and light; 5. Most seeds may be eaten or fail to germinate because of lack of light, moisture, warmth or soil.

LOOKING FOR LEVELS

All the children should be able to answer questions 1, 2 and 3. Most children will complete the remainder of the sheet.

ASSESSMENT ACTIVITY 2

Give out copies of photocopiable page 88 and let the children work through it individually.

ANSWERS

1. Male and female butterflies mate; The female lays eggs on a cabbage leaf; The eggs hatch into caterpillars or larvae; The caterpillar pupates into a chrysalis; A butterfly emerges from the chrysalis.
2. The male and female thrush mate; The female lays eggs in an nest; The eggs are incubated; Chicks hatch from the eggs; Chicks live in the nest, fed

by the adults, until they are ready to fly; The young thrushes leave the nest; Male and female thrushes mate.

3a. The removal of hedges; 3b. The use of pellets or pesticides to kill slugs and snails and/or the draining of fields, leaving no moist ground for slugs and snails; 3c. There is less insect food for the song thrush; 3d. There are more predators of the song thrush.

4. Ichneumon flies and song thrushes eat garden pests, so that people can grow crops organically without using pesticides.

LOOKING FOR LEVELS

This sheet is more demanding than page 87. All the children should be able to answer questions 1 and 2. Some children should provide cogent answers to questions 3 and 4.

ICT LINK 💿

Display 'Assessment - 1' (red) and 'Assessment - 2' (red) on an interactive whiteboard. Use the drawing tools to complete the activities as a class, as part of the Plenary.

PLENARY

Discuss the answers to both sheets. Page 87 could be marked with the children at the end of the session. A discussion about the range of acceptable answers to the questions on both sheets will be informative for the teacher and the children.

What plants do we eat?

1. A gardener listed in a table all the seeds that were needed to grow plants in the garden. When each plant has grown, at least one part of it can be eaten.
Next to each plant, write down the name of the part that we eat. If you are not sure of the answer, look for a picture of the plant in a seed catalogue.

Plant	Part eaten	Plant	Part eaten
Lettuce		Melon	
Potato		Sweetcorn	
Celery		Turnip	
Tomato		Runner or French bean	
Cauliflower		Broccoli	
Cabbage		Brussels sprout	
Carrot		Parsnip	
Beetroot		Courgette	
Cucumber		Radish	
Leek		Onion	

2. Look carefully in the seed catalogue for the names of plants you don't think you have eaten, but could eat. List three of these plants and the parts that you think you would eat.

Plants I don't think I've eaten	Parts of the plant I would eat

3. A healthy diet contains a mixture of foods. Look at the plants listed in question 1 and any others you have seen in the seed catalogue. Now choose your favourite food plants to fill these spaces.

Parts of the plant I eat	Favourite plant
Root	
Stem	
Flower	
Fruit	
Seed	

Illustration © Robin Lawrie

Seeds

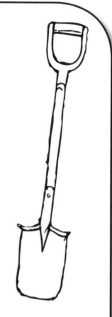

Tree	Fruit or seed
Oak	Has an acorn, often found in a cup.
Sycamore	Has double-winged keys.
Holly	The red fruits are near the stalk of a prickly leaf.
Rowan	Red fruits surrounded by feathery leaves.
Ash	Has long, narrow, wing-shaped keys.
Horse chestnut	A shiny, heavy 'conker' in a prickly shell.

1. Look at how the fruits and seeds of each tree are described in the table above. Find the picture below that fits each description and write the name of the tree below it.

2. Think about the three ways that each seed could be dispersed: birds, other animals or the wind. Below each seed picture, write how the seed would be dispersed.

3. Draw a cartoon creature beside each seed: a squirrel or badger next to the animal-dispersed seeds or a blackbird or song thrush next to the bird-sown seeds. Write a 'W' next to the wind-blown seeds.

Tree _____
Dispersed _____

Tree _____
Dispersed _____

Tree _____
Dispersed _____

Tree _____
Dispersed _____

Tree _____
Dispersed _____

Tree _____
Dispersed _____

Illustration © Robin Lawrie

Buzz's adventure

Read this play with your partner, one of you reading the part of Buzz and the other the part of GCB.

Buzz, a young worker bee, is on her first ever flight from the beehive. Buzz knows what pollen is but not where to find it. GCB is another worker bee. She is directing other bees outside the hive to their destination by radio. Of course this does not happen, but use your imagination!

Buzz: Buzz to Ground Control for Bees. Over!

GCB: I hear you, Buzz. Please call me 'GCB'. Over!

Buzz: Thanks GCB. I've a small problem. Over!

GCB: What's the problem, Buzz? Over.

Buzz: This is the first time I've flown out of the hive. I'm meant to be looking for flowers, but I don't know what flowers look like. Over.

GCB: Oh, Buzz, flowers are easy to spot! Look down into the fields. Flowers try to attract insects like us. Look for spots of bright colour near the ground. Over.

Buzz: I can see lots of bright purple spots in the field below me. I'm flying down to investigate. Over.

GCB: If the purple things are flowers Buzz, they'll probably have a sweet scent as you get close to them. Over. (There is a short pause as Buzz flies closer to the flower).

Buzz: I'm hovering over the purple thing now GCB. There is a sweet scent so it must be a flower! Where will I find the pollen? Is it on the purple bits? Over.

GCB: No, the purple bits are the petals. They're just to attract you and other insects to the flower – and it's worked! Over.

Buzz: Where is the pollen then? Over.

GCB: If you look carefully, you will see small stick-like things in the centre of the flower. There is often one stalk in the centre that is very different from the others. It's called the stigma. Can you see it? Over.

Buzz: Yes, I'm going down to the stigma now. (Pause.) I'm looking at the stigma now but there's no pollen on it (Pause). Where is the pollen? Over.

GCB: You won't find much pollen on the stigma. Pollen is produced in the other stalks inside the flower. They're called stamens. Take a look at the stamens now. Look closely and tell me what you see. Over.

Buzz: (Pause). Oh yes! The stamens have got loads of pollen on them. There are some little sacs at the end of the stamens that are bursting with the stuff. I'll get to work straight away. Over.

GCB: Start filling the pouches on your back legs Buzz. Then I'll tell you where to find a real treat! Over.

Buzz: Hey GCB, this is good fun! The pollen is sticking to all the hairs on my body and the sacs on my legs are quite full. I will need to visit a few more flowers to fill them though (Pause). Can I have my treat now? Over.

GCB: Well done, Buzz! If you want your treat, look right inside the flower, into the space between the stamens and the stigma. Push between them and tell me what you find deep inside the flower. Over.

Buzz: Grunt! (She pushes down between the stamens and the stigma). All the pollen is brushing off my body (Pause). Hey, there's a lovely sugary liquid in here. I know what this is, I've tasted it in the hive. It's nectar!

GCB: You're right! It's nectar. Drink as much as you possibly can. When you get back to the hive you can regurgitate some nectar and other worker bees can turn it into honey!

Buzz: Glug... glug... glug... Hey GCB, I'm full to the brim! I'm going to fly back to the hive now. Thanks for your help. Over!

GCB: No problem, Buzz. Over and out!

1. Can you work out the names of the parts of the flower that Buzz visited? Label the diagram with the names petal, stigma and stamen.

2. Where on the flower did Buzz discover pollen and nectar? Label those parts.

Answer these questions in full sentences.

3. How did Buzz know the correct direction to fly from the hive?

4. What are the two things that might attract an insect to a flower?

5. Why do bees collect pollen and take it back to their hive?

6. Where on the bee's body does the pollen go?

7. What is honey made from?

Illustration © Robin Lawrie

Pollen poaching

◼ Clip your 'pollen poaching tool' here. Make sure the sticky side faces upwards!

1. With a partner, look at the flowers that you think will attract insects. Watch carefully and quietly for a few minutes.

   (a) Which insects visited the flowers?

   (b) What did the insects do?

2. With your partner, choose two similar flowers. Each draw a detailed picture of your flower in the space below.

3. When you have made a good drawing of your flower, use your pollen poaching tool to get some pollen from it. Be gentle – don't damage the flower!

Illustration © Robin Lawrie

◼ S C H O L A S T I C

Pollination

1. Complete this table by writing 'Yes' or 'No' in each cell.

Does the plant have...	Insect-pollinated flower	Grasses and cereals
flowers?		
pollen?		
stigma?		
stamen?		
ovary?		
fruit?		
petals?		
scent?		
Does the plant welcome insects?		

■ Answer these questions in sentences.

2. How does the pollen from the stamen of one grass plant travel to the stigma of another?

_____

3. Why does an insect-pollinated plant need petals and scent?

_____

4. Why don't cereals and grasses need petals or scent?

_____

5. If a farmer saw lots of insects on a cereal crop, why might he or she use an insecticide?

_____

6. Why do the stigmas on grasses and cereals often have a feathery pattern on the tallest part of the flower?

_____

7. Think about the food that some insects get from insect-pollinated plants. As well as pollen, can you think of something else that **will not** be found in grasses and cereals? (Clue: it is the main ingredient of honey)

_____

8. Some people suffer from 'hay fever'. It makes them sneeze and their eyes water. What do you think causes hay fever? (Clue: a hay field is full of flowering grasses)

_____

Illustration © Robin Lawrie

PHOTOCOPIABLE

Growing cabbages

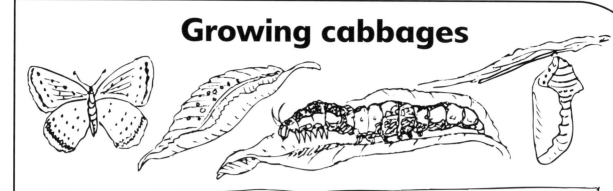

Dear Reader,

Thanks for telling us your problem. We are glad you are growing your own fresh food, but we think you have made a few mistakes.

Firstly, we think you are growing far too many cabbages! All those cabbages will be ready to eat at the same time. You'll need a big family to eat all eighty!

The tiny green caterpillars you saw were probably from the Cabbage White butterfly. The female butterfly was attracted to your cabbages by their smell. If you had planted fewer cabbages and put some onions or garlic alongside them, the female might not have smelled your plants.

When the male and female butterflies mate, the female usually lays her cone-shaped yellow eggs underneath the cabbage leaves. After a short time, the eggs hatch out and tiny caterpillars begin to feed on the cabbage leaves. They grow quite quickly and spend most of the time underneath these leaves, where enemies can't find them and your spray won't reach them.

While you were on holiday, the caterpillars ate your cabbages and grew bigger, shedding their skin several times until they were ready to pupate. Then, they crawled away to a safe, cool, dry place where they fastened themselves to a stalk with a silken thread. After a few days, the shrivelled dry skin of each caterpillar dropped off, leaving the pupa or chrysalis. At the moment, inside each dry silky shell, a butterfly is developing. In two or three weeks, adult butterflies will emerge. They will then fly off to feed on pollen and nectar.

When you sprayed your garden with insecticide, you probably missed the caterpillars but killed one of their deadly enemies. The ichneumon fly lays eggs in the bodies of caterpillars. Each egg hatches into a tiny larva that eats the caterpillar slowly from the inside. As the larva pupates, the caterpillar dies. If you grow flowers near your cabbages, you will encourage more ichneumon flies in that part of your garden and they will deal with the caterpillars.

It was sad that you pulled your damaged cabbages up. If you had left them in the ground, many would have grown new leaves. – *The Editor*

◼ On a separate piece of paper, write sentences to answer these questions.

1. Which butterfly lays the eggs: the male or the female?
2. How does the butterfly find the cabbage plants?
3. What do the butterfly's eggs hatch into?
4. What happens to the caterpillar's skin as it grows bigger?
5. What does the caterpillar eventually change into?
6. What comes out of the chrysalis?
7. What do butterflies feed on?
8. Write down three sensible things the gardener could do next year to make sure the cabbages are not so badly damaged.
9. Copy or cut out the drawings on this sheet and arrange them in a life cycle pattern. Stick them down on another piece of paper.

Illustration © Robin Lawrie

Animal life cycles

1. These sentences tell you about the life cycle of a cat. Write them in the correct order.

The kitten develops into a cat.
The embryo develops into a kitten inside the mother.
The kitten feeds on its mother's milk.
The kitten is born.
An egg is fertilised and develops into an embryo inside the mother.
The kitten feeds independently.

The first sentence is written for you:

Male and female cat mate.

_____

_____

_____

_____

_____

_____

Animal	Days
Cat	65
Human	280
Lion	105
Fox	55
Giraffe	435
Gorilla	260
Camel	365
Rabbit	28
Guinea pig	63
Cow	280

Here is a **gestation** table.
The time of gestation is the number of days between the fertilisation of the egg and the live birth. **Pregnancy** has a similar meaning to 'gestation'.

2. How many days does it take for a fox to grow inside its mother?

_____

3. Which animal is inside its mother for the same number of days as a human?

_____

4. Which animal is pregnant for the longest time?

_____

5. Which animal will give birth the shortest number of days from fertilisation?

_____

Growth

The height of a large number of people aged between 9 and 15 were measured. From this, a typical height for girls and a typical height for boys were found for each year group. The results are shown in this table:

Age	Height of girls (cm)	Height of boys (cm)
9	133	136
10	139	140
11	145	144
12	152	150
13	158	153
14	160	163
15	161	168

■ On graph paper, draw one line graph showing both these sets of results. Draw the girls' line in red and the boys' line in blue.

Who grows faster, girls or boys? Why do you think that happens?

The diagram below shows the human body at four different ages. All the bodies have been made the same size, so you can see how the **proportions** of the body (the amount of the total each part takes up) have changed. Describe the changes which you can see, in the proportions of each body part, as a person grows.

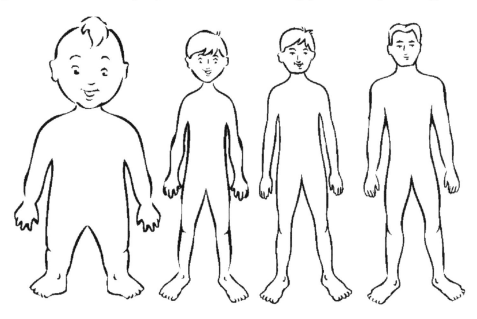

Illustration © Theresa Tibbetts c/o Beehive Illustration

■SCHOLASTIC

Changes in the body – 1

■ These pictures show the bodies of a boy and girl who are about to start puberty. The statements at the bottom of this sheet describe the changes that will happen when one or both go through puberty. Cut out the pictures and stick them onto a large piece of paper. Cut out the statements and use them to label the pictures.

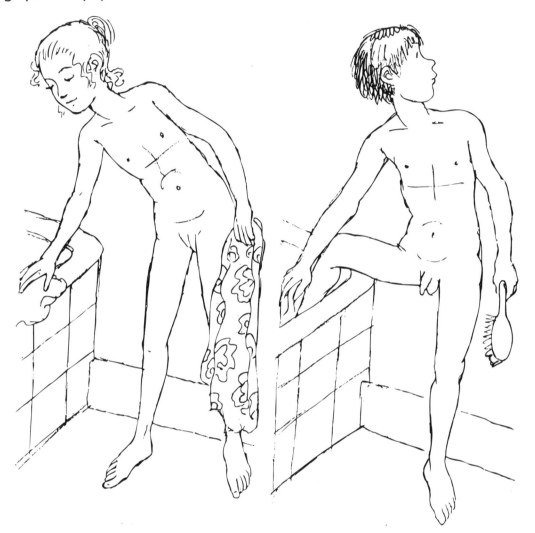

skin and hair become more oily	breasts and nipples grow
hips grow wider than shoulders	waist develops
shoulders grow wider than hips	skin may become spotty
testicles and penis grow	hair grows in armpits
hair grows between the legs	hair grows on face

Illustration © Robin Lawrie

Changes in the body – 2

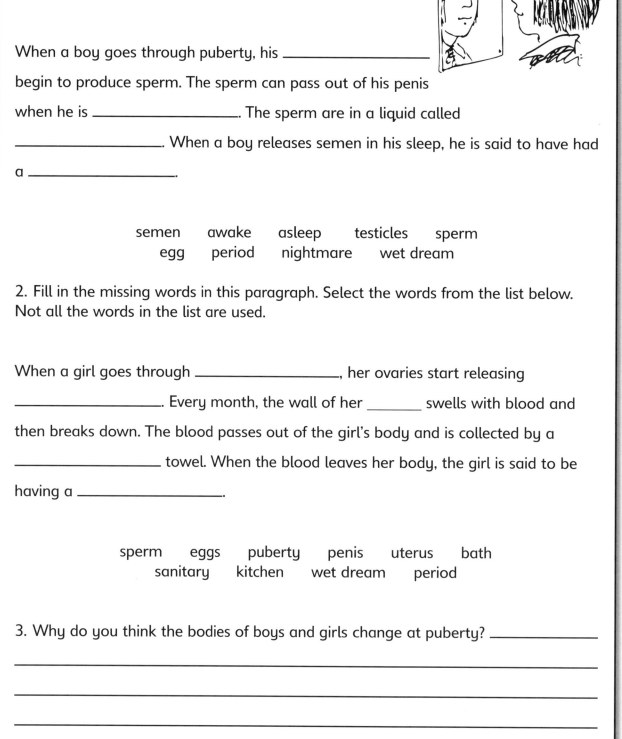

1. Fill in the missing words in this paragraph. Select the words from the list below. Not all the words in the list are used.

When a boy goes through puberty, his _____

begin to produce sperm. The sperm can pass out of his penis

when he is _____. The sperm are in a liquid called

_____. When a boy releases semen in his sleep, he is said to have had

a _____.

semen   awake   asleep   testicles   sperm
egg   period   nightmare   wet dream

2. Fill in the missing words in this paragraph. Select the words from the list below. Not all the words in the list are used.

When a girl goes through _____, her ovaries start releasing

_____. Every month, the wall of her _____ swells with blood and

then breaks down. The blood passes out of the girl's body and is collected by a

_____ towel. When the blood leaves her body, the girl is said to be

having a _____.

sperm   eggs   puberty   penis   uterus   bath
sanitary   kitchen   wet dream   period

3. Why do you think the bodies of boys and girls change at puberty? _____

_____

_____

_____

_____

Illustration © Robin Lawrie

■SCHOLASTIC

The reproductive system – 1

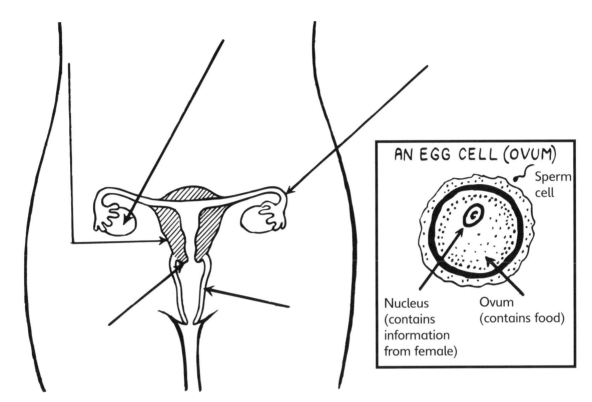

AN EGG CELL (OVUM)

Sperm cell

Nucleus (contains information from female)

Ovum (contains food)

1. Cut out the labels below and match the name of each part with its function. Cut out the diagram. Put the labels around the diagram on a sheet of paper. Check with your teacher that they are in the right places, then stick them down.

2. Draw a coloured line to show the route the egg (ovum) takes on its journey from the ovary to the uterus.

3. Under the labelled diagram, write down why you think the ovum (egg cell) is so much larger than the sperm cells that try to fertilise it.

labels

| uterus | ovary | oviduct (fallopian tube) | vagina | cervix |

functions

Releases an egg (ovum) into the oviduct once every 28 days.	A special sac that provides nutrients and protection for the fertilised egg as it develops. If the female is not pregnant, the lining is shed once every 28 days during her period.
The penis releases sperm here during intercourse. The baby is born through this tube.	
The narrow entrance to the uterus through which the sperm have to travel.	The tube down which the egg is moved after it is released from the ovary. Sperm may reach and fertilise the egg here on its journey to the uterus.

Illustration © Tony O'Donnell/Sarah Wimperis

The reproductive system – 2

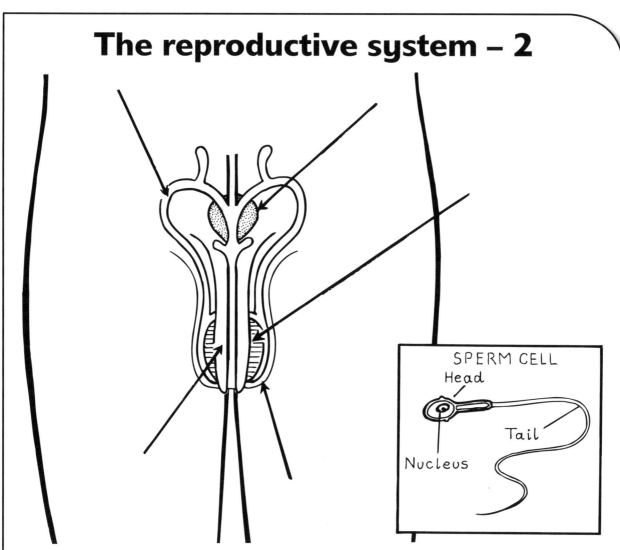

1. Cut out the labels below and match the name of each part with its function. Cut out the diagram.

2. Put the labels around the diagram on a sheet of paper. Check with your teacher that they are in the right places, then stick them down.

3. Under the labelled diagram, write down why you think each sperm cell has a tail.

labels				
testes	penis	prostate gland	sperm tube	scrotum

functions	
Becomes erect as blood rushes into it. During intercourse it enters the vagina of the female and releases sperm.	This and other glands add special chemicals to the sperm cells to make them active before they are released.
Special organs that produce millions of sperm cells.	
The sac that contains the testes.	The tube down which sperm cells travel from the testes.

Illustration © Tony O'Donnell/Sarah Wimperis

Life before birth

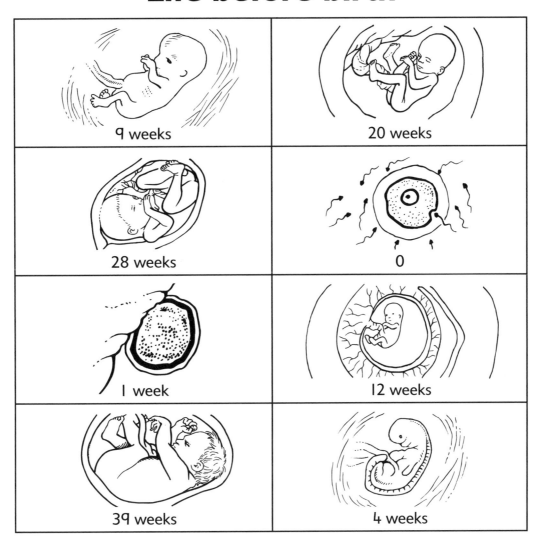

9 weeks

20 weeks

28 weeks

0

1 week

12 weeks

39 weeks

4 weeks

Time = **9 weeks**
The growing baby is about 25mm long and has all of its organs. It is now called a foetus.

Time = **12 weeks**
The foetus is now 56mm long and appears far more like a human baby.

Time = **1 week**
The fertilised egg (called a **zygote**) implants itself in the lining of the uterus. It is smaller than a grain of rice.

Time = **39 weeks**
The baby is ready to be born! It is now about 520mm in length. Happy birthday, baby!

Time = **20 weeks**
The foetus is now 160mm long and is busy exercising its limbs. Its movements can be felt by the mother. (Sorry Mum – were you sleeping?)

Time = **4 weeks**
The zygote has grown to become an **embryo**. It is 6mm long and has some of its most important organs.

Time = **28 weeks**
The growing baby would have a good chance of surviving if it were born now. It is about 370mm long.

Time = **0**
One sperm out of the millions released joins with the egg. This is **fertilisation**.

Illustration © Tony O'Donnell/Sarah Wimperis

PHOTOCOPIABLE

Song thrush survival game

Life cycle stages	Rules – How many dice can you throw?	Risks, predators, loss of habitat, food supplies	First teacher brood	Second teacher brood	First children brood	Second children brood
Eggs in the nest Mother builds nest, about 2m from ground in hedges. Eggs incubated for 13 days until they hatch.	*Throw one dice.* Your 3 eggs will hatch if you avoid the risks.	1 Nest raided by magpies, crows or squirrels. All die. 2 Increase in sparrow hawks. Mother ambushed on nest. All die. 3 Hedges dug up. Nest destroyed. All die. 4 5 6				
Chick in nest Lives in nest for 4 weeks after hatching. Both parents feed it worms and insects.	If you survived the egg stage you will have 3 tiny, blind chicks. *Throw one dice.* All chicks will live if you avoid the risks.	1 Very cold and wet weather. Chicks freeze. All die. 2 All fields sprayed with insecticide. No insect food. One bird dies. 3 4 5 6				
Young bird 4–12 weeks. Its summer diet is snails and insects. In autumn it will eat berries too.	*Throw one dice for each surviving chick.* Any chick that avoids a risk will survive.	1 Hot summer, no snails or worms to eat. Bird dies. 2 Ambushed by predator: kestrel or sparrow hawk. Bird dies. 3 Increase in cat population. Bird caught and dies. 4 Farmers use slug pellets and kill the snails. Bird starves and dies. 5 Farmers kill weeds. Weeds feed insects. No insect food. Bird dies. 6				
Adult Survives winter. Finds mate. Looks for nesting habitat.	*Throw one dice for each surviving young bird.* If it survives it can find a mate.	1 Very cold winter, can't find enough food. Bird dies. 2 Hedges cut, no winter berry food. Bird dies. 3 Gardens too tidy. No insects or snails. Bird dies. 4 5 6				

Each team takes it in turns to throw the dice. Each turn takes you to the next stage in the life cycle.

If you avoid the risks, you survive! Start your second brood when your first brood die, or survive to become adults.

You only have two broods. There are three eggs in each brood.

The team that has the most survivors wins.

Illustration © Robin Lawrie

📖 SCHOLASTIC

Assessment – 1

1a. Look at this picture of a flower cut in half. Write these names of flower parts in the correct places: petal, stamen, stigma, ovary.

1b. In which of these four parts of the flower is pollen produced?

_____

1c. Which part attracts insects to the flower?

_____

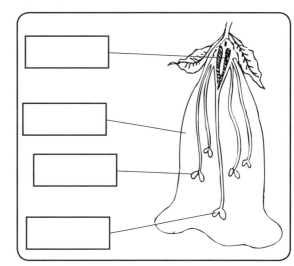

1d. In which part of the flower is a seed produced? _____

_____

1e. Why do these flowers need to attract insects? _____

_____

2. An insect-pollinated flower has two things that a wind-pollinated flower does not need. What are they?

_____

3. The seeds of trees are dispersed in three main ways: by animals, by birds or by the wind.
   Look at these pictures of the fruits and seeds of trees. How are each tree's seed dispersed?

Ash _____

Holly _____

Oak _____

4. Why do plants need to disperse their seeds?_____

_____

5. Why do many types of plant produce a great number of seeds?

_____

 # Assessment – 2

1. Here are some sentences about the life cycle of the Cabbage White butterfly.
◼ Rewrite the sentences in the correct order . The first one has been done for you.

A butterfly emerges from the chrysalis.	Male and female butterflies mate.
The eggs hatch into caterpillars or larvae.	
Male and female butterflies mate.	
The caterpillar pupates into a chrysalis.	
The female lays eggs on a cabbage leaf.	

2. Describe the life cycle of a Song thrush. The first sentence has been written for you. Here are a few words that might help: egg, chick, hatch, food.

The male and female thrush mate.

3. Human beings have changed the environment. There is a danger that these changes may make many creatures extinct. Think about the Song thrush: what it eats, where it lives and so on. Now complete this table.

	The problem for the Song thrush	What's causing the problem?
a	There are fewer places for the thrush to make its nest.	
b	There are not enough slugs and snails around to feed it.	
c		Farmers are using insecticides to kill insects on the crops they grow.
d		Magpies, crows and squirrels seem to do well in the new environment.

4. Why do some people believe that it is important to encourage ichneumon flies and Song thrushes into fields and gardens?

CHAPTER 3 Gases around us

Lesson	Objectives	Main activity	Group activities	Plenary	Outcomes
Lesson 1 Solids and liquids	• To know the characteristic features of the solid and liquid states of matter. • To sort materials as solids and liquids. • To describe the processes of melting and dissolving.	Review the children's knowledge of solids and liquids. Demonstrate melting and dissolving. Sort materials into solids and liquids.		Sort materials as a class, summarising the key features of the solid and liquid states.	• Can distinguish solids and liquids by their properties. • Can give examples of melting and dissolving.
Lesson 2 Air	• To know that air is all around us. • To know that air is a type of material called a gas. • To know that air has mass.	Demonstrate some properties of air using a beach ball, a marble, a feather and a simple 'balloon balance'.	Identify and discuss devices that make use of the air. Use a sheet of paper to demonstrate that air is a material.	Review the group work. Summarise the physical properties of air.	• Know that we are surrounded by air. • Recognise that air is a material. • Can demonstrate the presence of air. • Can describe how the mass of air can be demonstrated.
Lesson 3 Porous materials	• To know that porous materials are composed of solid particles or regions surrounded by gaps. • To know that when porous materials are dry, the gaps are filled with air. • To observe that water can displace the air from the gaps in porous materials.	Demonstrate the presence of air in a porous material by submerging Oasis in water.	Observe and draw the displacement of air from sponge by water. Observe and draw a piece of sponge using a magnifier.	Review the children's drawings. Use these to reinforce the idea of a porous material.	• Can state that porous materials contain many air-filled holes. • Can identify bubbles rising from a submerged piece of material as air that was in the spaces in the material. • Can recognise the need to repeat experiments in order to check observations.
Lesson 4 Soil investigation	• To know that soil contains air. • To use measuring cylinders and jugs to measure volumes of water. • To compare the volumes of air present in different soils.	Demonstrate a water displacement method for determining the volume of air in a soil sample. Discuss the need to repeat measurements for accuracy.	The children use the method to compare soil, sand and gravel samples.	Review the children's results and discuss their implications for gardening.	• Can use measuring cylinders or jugs to measure water volumes. • Can explain the importance of taking care when reading scales, and of repeating measurements in order to check results. • Understand that in order for a comparison to be fair, all variables except the one being tested must be kept the same.
Lesson 5 Types of gas	• To know that there are a variety of useful gases.	Use secondary sources to research the properties and uses of gases. Make a poster about each gas.		Children display their posters and describe their findings.	• Know that a number of gases exist. • Can describe the uses of a variety of gases.
Lesson 6 From liquid to gas	• To know that when a liquid evaporates, it forms a gas.	Demonstrate examples of evaporation. Groups research and write about the operation of 'drying machines' such as hairdryers.		Groups present their findings.	• Recognise that when a liquid evaporates, it forms a gas. • Recognise that rate of evaporation depends on temperature. • Recognise that rate of evaporation depends on air movement. • Can explain how appliances that dry things (e.g. a hairdryer) work.

Lesson	Objectives	Main activity	Group activities	Plenary	Outcomes
Lesson 7 Comparing solids, liquids and gases	• To know that gases do not have a fixed volume as solids and liquids do. • To know that gases are more easily compressed (squashed) than solids and liquids. • To know that gases and liquids can flow and change their shape, but continuous solids have a fixed shape.	Compare and contrast solid, liquid and gas samples. Make carbon dioxide and demonstrate that it is heavier than air.	Role-play molecules in gases, liquids and solids. Make cards summarising the properties of the different states.	Children show and discuss their 'state' cards.	• Know that a gas can be poured and squashed, has no fixed shape or volume, and can spread out into the air when released from its container. • Can describe the different properties of solids, liquids and gases.

Assessment	Objectives	Activity 1	Activity 2
Lesson 8	• To assess the children's knowledge and understanding of gases, the differences between gases, liquids and solids, and changes of state. • To assess the children's ability to explain observations and to draw conclusions from measurements.	Give examples of solids, liquids and gases and describe their properties. Identify the changes of state involved in melting, boiling, evaporating and condensing.	Interpret some simple temperature data in physical terms.

SC1 SCIENTIFIC ENQUIRY

Air in soil

OBJECTIVES AND OUTCOMES
● Make a fair test or comparison by changing one factor and observing or measuring the effect while keeping other factors the same.
● Use simple equipment and materials appropriately and take action to control risks.
● Make systematic observations and measurements.
● Check observations and measurements by repeating them where appropriate.

ACTIVITY
The children devise a test to investigate how much air a range of soil samples contain, ideally using a water displacement method suggested in a previous lesson.

LESSON LINKS
This Sc1 activity forms an integral part of Lesson 4, Soil investigation.

Lesson 1 ⬤ Solids and liquids

Objective
● To know the characteristic features of the solid and liquid states of matter.
● To sort materials as solids and liquids.
● To describe he processes of melting and dissolving.

Vocabulary
solid, liquid, rigid, stiff, pour, flow, shape, fixed, change, melt, dissolve

RESOURCES
Main activity: A wooden brick; a wax candle; sugar lumps; jugs of water; an empty bowl; a spoon.
Group activities: cards (one set per group) with the names of different solid and liquid materials (such as stone, wood, ice, glass, water, paraffin, lava, mercury, milk, blood, written on); cards with solid and liquid properties written on them (rigid, stiff, fixed shape, changes shape, pours, flows).

PREPARATION
Set out the samples where the children will see them as they come into the classroom. Prepare the cards and sort them into sets for each group.

BACKGROUND
The solid state and the liquid state are two of the common states of matter with distinct properties. Solids have a fixed shape. They are stiff or rigid and do not change shape as you pick them up and move them around. You cannot easily push a spoon into a solid - the solid resists the motion of the spoon through it because its particles are held rigidly together by strong bonds. Liquids change shape easily. They take the shape of any container into which they are poured. Liquid particles are easily parted, with a spoon for example. A liquid flows around any object pushed into it.

Melting and dissolving are two processes that can transform a solid into a liquid. Melting takes place when a solid is heated to its melting point. The particles (atoms or molecules) that make up the solid gain enough energy to move freely over each other, breaking the bonds that held them in a rigid structure. When a solid dissolves in a liquid, the presence of the liquid molecules reduces the forces that hold the solid particles together. The particles can separate and enter the liquid state.

STARTER
The children should already be familiar with the differences between solids and liquids. Review their understanding by asking them to identify the samples you have provided as solids or liquids. Can they name any other solids and liquids?

Differentiation
Group activity 1
Support children by asking them to select examples of solids and liquids from the cards.
Group activity 2
Extend children by giving them the cards listing the characteristic properties of solids and liquids. They should select a property, and then select substances from the solid/liquid set that have that property. Are the substances they select all solids or all liquids?

MAIN ACTIVITY
Develop the topic by discussing the characteristic properties of solids and liquids. Are they rigid or can they flow? How easy is it to change their shape? What happens if you try to push something into them? Use the samples to demonstrate the various properties as you talk about them.

Ask the children if it is possible to change a solid into a liquid. Can they think of two ways to do this? Demonstrate melting by lighting the candle and observing the wax. Demonstrate dissolving by stirring a sugar lump into water. Discuss everyday examples of melting and dissolving that the children have experienced (melting ice, sugar in tea, making jelly and so on).

GROUP ACTIVITIES
1 Give the children the cards to sort into solids and liquids.
2 Give each group a blank sheet of A4 paper. Ask them draw up a table with two columns and list as many examples of solids and liquids as they can.
3 Each group should think of one example of melting and one example of dissolving to describe to the class.

ASSESSMENT
Sort the cards as a class, reviewing the properties of each material in turn.

PLENARY
Ask each child to pick a solid and a liquid from the cards, then write one or two sentences about the properties of their chosen materials. Check that they understand that a solid has a fixed shape, but a liquid flows to take up the shape of its container. Ask them to name two ways in which solids can change into liquids.

OUTCOMES
- Can distinguish solids and liquids by their properties.
- Can give examples of melting and dissolving.

Lesson 2 ◖ Air

Objective
- To know that air is all around us.
- To know that air is a type of material called a gas.
- To know that air has mass.

Vocabulary
air, air resistance, deflate, gas, liquid, solid, inflate, weight, state

RESOURCES ◖
Main activity: An inflatable beach ball and ball pump; a feather; a marble; an electric fan; two party balloons; thread; a wire coat-hanger; a digital balance (if available). 'Balloon balance' diagram available on the CD-ROM.
Group activities: 1 Paper; pencils. **2** Blank A4 paper.

PREPARATION
Inflate two party balloons and tie them to either side of a wire coat-hanger with thread. Suspend the coat-hanger from a string. Adjust the positions of the balloons until the coat-hanger balances horizontally (this needs some care). Position the electric fan where the children will feel it blowing air on their faces when they are sitting down at the start of the lesson.

BACKGROUND

There are three common 'states' of matter: solid, liquid and gas. The different properties of matter in these three states can be explained by the arrangement and behaviour of the particles (molecules) from which the matter is composed. The molecular structure of matter is examined further in Lesson 7.

The air is a mixture of gases. In the

gaseous state, matter is so thin we can move through it, pushing it aside with little resistance. Most gases are invisible, though some have a colour and can be seen (for example, the poisonous gas chlorine is green).

Although air is invisible, we can easily detect that it is all around us by its effects. You can feel the movement of air when you blow on the back of your hand. When you blow up balloons or bicycle tyres, you are filling them with air. Air expands to fill the space available to it, and exerts a pressure on the walls of its container. It can be compressed into a smaller volume by increasing the pressure applied by the walls, for example by squashing a ball between your hands. The increased pressure of the air trapped inside the ball makes it feel springy. If you let the air out from an inflated tyre or a balloon, it escapes in a rush – making a steady hiss or a sudden bang.

The Earth is cloaked in a layer of gases called the 'atmosphere'. We call this mixture of gases 'air'. The wind is the movement of air through the atmosphere. The push of the wind flaps washing on a line, carrying away moisture. Air has mass. The air inside a typical classroom has about the same mass as the teacher!

For us, the most important property of air is that 21% of it is the gas oxygen, which almost all living things need for respiration. Most of the rest of the atmosphere (78%) is the relatively unreactive gas nitrogen. The atmosphere also contains water vapour (in varying amounts), carbon dioxide (0.03%), tiny quantities of 'rare' gases such as argon, and pollution products emitted by vehicles, power stations and factories.

STARTER

The children should already be familiar with the differences between solids and liquids from work in Year 4/Primary 5. Ask them what they can feel blowing on their faces from the fan: *Is the sensation caused by a solid, a liquid or something else?* (It is caused by moving air, which is neither a solid nor a liquid.)

Ask them to think of some other ways that they can tell they are surrounded by air. If necessary, prompt them to talk about the sensation of moving through the air on a bicycle, the power of the wind to lift kites and turn windmills, and their need to breathe air in and out of their lungs. Build on the children's ideas to explain that air is not 'nothing', but a special kind of material called a 'gas'. Say that you will demonstrate to them that air flows, is springy, drags on moving objects, and has a mass of its own.

MAIN ACTIVITY

Inflate the beach ball. Explain how you are using the pump to fill the ball with air. Demonstrate how it becomes firmer and more 'bouncy' as you squeeze more air inside it. Discuss the use of a bicycle pump to inflate bicycle tyres, and the effect of getting a puncture.

Drop a marble, then drop a feather. Ask the children to explain why the feather falls more slowly than the marble. If they think it is just because of the weight difference, drop a pin to show that a light object can fall just as fast as a heavier one. Develop the idea that the large feather has to push more air aside than the marble or the pin, and so experiences more air 'resistance'; because it is light, this resistance can be as strong as the effect of gravity. Discuss the application of air resistance to slowing down the fall of a parachutist.

Ask the children whether air has mass (and thus weight). Many children will think that air is weightless, since it does not appear to fall. Explain that, although gases are much lighter than liquids and solids, they are not completely weightless: air settles on the surface of the Earth, which is why the air is 'thinner' at high altitudes. If the air had no mass, it would drift off into space. Show the children the 'balloon balance' and ask them to predict what will happen if you let the air out of one of the balloons. Pinch the neck of one balloon and puncture the pinched-off part with a pin. This will allow

Differentiation

Group activity 1
Support children by asking them to give a simple explanation of one of the items shown on the board, such as how a kite or a sailboat works (the push of the wind). Extend children by encouraging them to tackle a wider range of items involving more properties of gases, such as the spring (pressure) of the air squeezed inside a tyre. As an additional challenge, ask children which items would work on the Moon. They should know or be able to find out that there is no air on the Moon, so any device that uses air in the atmosphere (such as sailboats, kites and planes) will not work. Air-filled items such as tyres and balls will work on the Moon, but they will need to be filled with air (or another gas) brought from the Earth.

Group activity 2
Some children may need prompting to use the paper as a fan; other children will generate a wide range of imaginative ideas.

you to let the air out slowly. When the balloon is deflated, release the balance and let the children see whether their prediction was correct.

If you have a digital balance, you can demonstrate directly that a fully inflated balloon is slightly heavier than a deflated one. (NB You cannot use this method to 'weigh' the air inside the balloon directly, since the buoyancy of the inflated balloon needs to be allowed for.)

GROUP ACTIVITIES

1 List and sketch the following things on the board or flip chart: a kite, a sailboat, a hand-held fan, a car tyre, a windmill, a football, a parachute, a hot air balloon, a sycamore seed, an aeroplane. Ask the children to think about these and discuss in their groups how air helps to make each thing work. Each child should then select an item and write one or more sentences on a sheet of paper to explain how it makes use of the air. Encourage them to write about as many items as they can.
2 Give each group a blank sheet of A4 paper. Ask them to think of as many ways as they can of using the paper to show that air exists. (For example, they might fan themselves with it, let it flutter to the ground, blow it across the table, make a tube and blow through it, make a paper aeroplane, and so on.)

ASSESSMENT

Check that the children understand that air is not 'nothing', but is a material with its own mass that can affect objects within it. The children's writing about the items drawn on the board or flip chart will reveal their level of understanding of the air as a gas.

PLENARY

Ask representatives from each group to read out some of their writing about the items on the board. Ask each group to demonstrate one method of showing the presence of air with the sheet of paper. Use the children's writing and demonstrations to summarise the key learning points: air is all around us; air is a gas; air has mass.

OUTCOMES

- Know that we are surrounded by air.
- Recognise that air is a material.
- Can demonstrate the presence of air.
- Can describe how the mass of air can be demonstrated.

Lesson 3 ▪ Porous materials

Objectives
- To know that porous materials are composed of solid particles or regions surrounded by gaps.
- To know that when porous materials are dry, the gaps are filled with air.
- To observe that water can displace the air from the gaps in porous materials.

Vocabulary
solid, pores, porous, absorb, air bubble, displace

RESOURCES

Main activity: A jar full of marbles; a sand bucket; dry sand; a plastic jug, a piece of dry oasis (from a florist or garden centre); a wooden spoon or ruler; a large clear plastic tank; water.
Group activities: 1 and **2** A water tray; pieces of natural and synthetic sponge; samples of any other porous materials you have (such as oasis, sand, cotton wool, fabrics, foam rubber); magnifying glasses or low-power microscopes (if available); paper; pencils.

PREPARATION

Fill the sand bucket to the brim with dry sand and level off the surface. Stand the bucket in a tray next to a plastic jug full of water. Three-quarters fill the plastic tank with water and stand it where all the children can see it. Lay out pieces of sponge, magnifying glasses, paper and pencils ready for the Group activities.

BACKGROUND
Solids such as metals, glass and the most dense rocks are continuous: there are no pores, gaps, or spaces within the structure of the material. Continuous solids do not contain air, and usually do not absorb water when they are made wet. But many other common materials, such as powders, sand, sponge, foam plastic, paper, card and most fabrics, are porous. A porous material contains many tiny holes or gaps that surround the solid particles or regions that make up the bulk of the material. When a porous material is dry, these pores are filled with air. When it is immersed in water, the air is displaced and rises as bubbles to the water surface as the water soaks into the material.

STARTER
Show the children the bucket full to the brim with sand. Ask whether they think it is possible to get anything else into the bucket. Some children may say that it is not possible, because the bucket is already full. Slowly pour some water on to the surface, so that it is absorbed into the sand without spilling over the edge. Ask the children where the water has gone. Explain that it has 'fitted in' to the spaces between the sand grains. Ask what was in these spaces before the water entered them (air, which is a gas). Ask what happened to the air as the water filled the spaces (it was displaced into the air above the bucket).

Use the jar of marbles to demonstrate what happens when water is poured into a porous material. The children will see the water filling the gaps between the marbles. Explain that the marbles are just like the particles of sand, but on a larger-scale.

MAIN ACTIVITY
Show the children a piece of dry oasis. Explain how it is used by florists to hold water for an arrangement of flowers. Like sand, oasis is a porous material with many holes. Ask the children to try to think of an experiment to prove that the pores in dry oasis are filled with air. The water-filled tank may trigger some ideas. With the children observing, rapidly submerge the oasis in the water tank. Hold it under the surface with a wooden spoon or ruler. Ask the children to describe what they see (a mass of air bubbles streaming upwards from the oasis). Ask what the bubbles are. Explain that they are air bubbles displaced by the water from the pores on the oasis.

Discuss the importance of repeating scientific experiments to confirm that the observed results are reproducible and not a fluke. Repeat the experiment with a second piece of dry oasis.

GROUP ACTIVITIES
1 Ask a child to submerge a piece of sponge in the water tray while the rest of the group observe what happens. They should repeat the test at least once more to confirm what they have seen. Each child should draw a labelled sketch of his or her observations and write a brief account of the experiment.
2 Ask the children in their groups to observe the structure of a piece of sponge through a magnifying glass or low-power microscope. Both natural and synthetic sponges can be studied. The children should sketch what they see and label the pores as 'filled with air'. Encourage them to go on to examine other porous materials.

ASSESSMENT
Check that all the children understand that the gaps in porous materials are not 'empty', but are filled with air. Note whether the most able children can explain how the water displaces the air from the pores as the sponge is submerged.

Differentiation
Group activity 1
The children's attainment will be differentiated by the detail of their drawings, and by the level of understanding expressed in their written accounts. All the children should be able to state that the dry sponge is full of holes and that these are full of air, which is a gas. To extend children, ask them to explain why the air bubbles rise when a porous material is submerged. (Air is lighter than water, so it floats to the surface.)
Group activity 2
Support children by asking them to concentrate on observing and sketching a piece of sponge. Other children will be able to observe and sketch a wider range of porous materials, including Oasis, sand, cotton wool and fabrics. Their sketches should show the different characteristic features of these materials.

PLENARY

Ask representatives from the groups to show their sketches of the different materials and to describe the differences they observed. Use the children's observations and ideas to summarise the key learning point: that some solid materials contain air.

OUTCOMES

● Can state that porous materials contain many air-filled holes.
● Can identify bubbles rising from a submerged piece of solid material as air that was in the spaces in the material.
● Recognise the need to repeat experiments in order to check observations.

Lesson 4 ▪ Soil investigation

Objectives
● To know that soil contains air.
● To use measuring cylinders and jugs to measure volumes of water.
● To compare the volumes of air present in different soils.

Vocabulary
soil, particles, pores, porous, absorb, volume, millilitre, measuring scale

RESOURCES ⊙

Main activity and **Group activity:** A soil sample; buckets of gravel, sand, and garden soil; three empty buckets; trowels and/or spades; stickers or felt-tipped pens; plastic beakers, measuring jugs and cylinders; water, photocopiable page 102 (also 'Soil investigation' (red) available on the CD-ROM), pencils.

PREPARATION

Set out three plastic beakers, a measuring cylinder or jug and a trowel for each group. Make one copy per child of photocopiable page 102.

BACKGROUND

The children learned in the previous lesson that porous materials contain air. Soil is also porous. The presence of air in soil is significant for the various things that live there. The children will have observed how air can be displaced from porous materials by water. In this investigation, they will measure the amount of air in different soil samples by using the displacement technique. When water is poured onto a soil sample, the volume of air displaced is equal to the volume of water absorbed. The children can therefore equate their measurement of the volume of water a sample absorbs to the volume of air it contained initially. Water volumes can be measured with a measuring cylinder calibrated in millilitres.

The volume of air a soil sample contains is a measure of its porosity (how porous it is), which affects the rate at which the soil drains. Sandy soils are more porous, and so drain more quickly, than clay soils. They are therefore less likely to become waterlogged in wet weather.

STARTER

Show the children a soil sample and ask them what living things they might find in it. Ask the children which of these living things need to breathe air. (Small animals, some microbes.) *How do they manage to breathe in the soil?* The children should recall your demonstration in Lesson 2 that porous materials such as sand contain air. *Do you think there is air in soil? How much? Do all soils contain the same amount of air? Can you think of a method for measuring the amount of air in soil?* Try to lead the children towards devising an approach based on displacing the air with water, developing from their observations in the previous lesson.

MAIN ACTIVITY

Demonstrate the method to the children. Two-thirds fill a plastic beaker with gravel from the bucket. Use a sticker or felt-tipped pen to mark the level of the gravel surface. Fill a measuring jug with water. Show the children the scale on the jug, and remind them that water volumes can be measured in millilitres. Note the initial reading on the jug (for example, 1000ml). Slowly pour water from the jug onto the gravel sample until the gravel is saturated (the water level just reaches the gravel surface, and does not fall again). The children will observe air bubbles rising through the water in the beaker as the air is displaced from the gravel. Note the new reading on the jug (for example, 550ml) and explain that the volume of water poured onto the gravel is equal to the difference between the initial and final readings on the jug (1000ml–550ml=450ml). Make sure the children understand that this volume is equal to the volume of air that was in the gravel initially.

Discuss the accuracy of the measurement. Explain the importance of standing the jug on a level surface and putting your eye close to the scale when making a reading. Explain that to check the reliability of a measurement, it is always good practice to repeat it at least once. Empty the wet gravel into an empty bucket and refill the beaker with a dry sample. Discuss the importance of filling the beaker to the same level as before, so that the volumes of the two samples are the same. Repeat the measurement and take an average of the results to obtain a 'best' estimate.

GROUP ACTIVITY
Divide the children into groups and ask them to use this method to compare the volumes of air in three different samples: gravel, sand and garden soil. Each child should record the group's results on a copy of page 102.

ASSESSMENT
Check that the children are taking appropriate care with their measuring. They should be able to explain that in order for their comparisons to be 'fair', they need to use the same volume of dry soil for each test.

PLENARY
Ask representatives from each group to hold up their record sheets and describe their findings. *Which sample held the most water? Which held the least? Are the results consistent between different groups? Can the figures be compared directly, or did the different groups use different amounts of soil for their tests?* The children will probably have found that the gravel held the most water and is therefore the most porous material. The sand is the next most porous material, and the garden soil the least porous. Discuss the use of gravel to make a dry, well-drained surface for garden paths and driveways. *Why do gardeners sometimes dig sand into sticky clay soils?* (To improve the drainage.)

OUTCOMES
● Can use measuring cylinders or jugs to measure water volumes.
● Can explain the importance of taking care when reading scales, and of repeating measurements in order to check results.
● Understand that in order for a comparison to be fair, all variables except the one being tested must be kept the same.

LINKS
Unit 5d, Lesson 7, The Earth and its water.

Lesson 5 ▸ Types of gas

RESOURCES
A selection of secondary sources that the children can use to research the properties and uses of gases: encyclopaedias, CD-ROMs and videos; posters and pamphlets produced by industrial gas companies; a pack of cards (one per group) with the names of different gases: oxygen, nitrogen,

Differentiation
Support children by asking them to find one use for a more familiar gas, such as oxygen. Extend children by asking them to find a range of properties and uses for a number of less familiar gases, such as hydrogen and chlorine.

helium, natural gas, hydrogen, chlorine etc.; large sheets of paper; felt-tipped pens.

MAIN ACTIVITY

Remind the children of the composition of air. Ask them whether they can name any other gases that are not normally present in air. They may be familiar with helium (used in party balloons) and 'natural gas' (mostly methane; used for cooking and heating). Divide the class into groups and give each group a card naming a gas. Ask the groups to use the secondary sources to research the properties and uses of their named gas. Each group should record their findings on a poster.

ASSESSMENT

Ask the children to pick a gas and write one or two sentences about its uses in their science notebooks. Check that they understand that a gas is a material similar to the air, and that different gases have different properties.

PLENARY

Each group should display the poster they have prepared and describe their findings to the rest of the class.

OUTCOMES
- Know that a number of gases exist.
- Can describe the uses of a variety of gases.

Lesson 6 ▪ From liquid to gas

Objectives
- To know that when a liquid evaporates, it forms a gas.

RESOURCES
Perfume; a dish; a battery-powered fan; cotton handkerchiefs; a hairdryer; string; clothes pegs; catalogues and magazines with pictures of hairdryers, tumble dryers and other 'drying machines'.

MAIN ACTIVITY
Demonstrate the evaporation process by putting a little perfume in a dish. Waft the smell towards the children with the fan. Discuss examples of the evaporation of water, including washing drying on the line, puddles disappearing and people drying in the sun after a swim. Wet a handkerchief and hang it on a line. Discuss how the rate of evaporation depends on temperature and air flow. Demonstrate the effect of the hairdryer. Ask groups to find pictures of different 'drying machines' and write about how they work.

ASSESSMENT
Ask the children to explain what happens to the water when something dries out. Check that they understand that the water is not 'vanishing', but is changing into an invisible gas that becomes part of the air.

Differentiation
Support children by asking them to focus on explaining where the water goes when something dries out. Extend children by asking them to discuss the factors that affect the rate of drying, including air flow, surface area and temperature.

PLENARY
Invite a representative from each group to display their pictures and read their writing about a drying machine.

OUTCOMES
- Recognise that when a liquid evaporates, it forms a gas.
- Recognise that rate of evaporation depends on temperature.
- Recognise that rate of evaporation depends on air movements.
- Can explain how appliances that dry things (e.g. a hairdryer) work.

Lesson 7 ▸ Comparing solids, liquids and gases

Objectives
● To know that gases do not have a fixed volume as solids and liquids do.
● To know that gases are more easily compressed (squashed) than solids and liquids.
● To know that gases and liquids can flow and change their shape, but continuous solids have a fixed shape.

Vocabulary
gas, compress, expand, space, flow, pour, rigid, fluid, liquid, solid

RESOURCES
Main activity: An inflatable beach toy and pump; a small candle; a fireproof container such as a biscuit tin; a large plastic lemonade bottle; a small plastic funnel; sodium bicarbonate (baking powder); vinegar; party balloons; a solid wooden brick or ball; plastic beakers.
Group activities: 1 The playground or school hall. **2** Three small plastic lemonade bottles per group, each filled to the brim with sand; water or air and with the tops screwed on tight; A4 sheets of card; felt-tipped pens.

PREPARATION
Partly inflate a party balloon, then hold the neck under a running tap to fill it with water. Tie off the neck. Partly inflate a second balloon with air and tie off the neck. Put two teaspoons of sodium bicarbonate into the large empty lemonade bottle (use the funnel to help). Set out the plastic bottles, cards and pens ready for the Group activities.

BACKGROUND
Some properties of gases can be illustrated with an inflatable beach toy. When you inflate the toy, air from the pump (or your lungs) is squashed inside it. The air expands and changes shape to fill the space available. The inflated toy is squashy and springy. If you pull out the stopper, the air flows out and expands into the surrounding atmosphere. In contrast, liquids and solids occupy (more or less) fixed volumes: they do not expand to fill the space available, and are less compressible than gases. Liquids can be poured, and change shape as they flow. Solids are rigid and do not pour. A solid, such as a brick or a stone, has a fixed shape that does not change as it is moved. An applied force (such as a hammer blow) may change the shape of a solid, but gravity alone is not usually strong enough to do so.

The contrasting properties of gases, liquids and solids can be explained with a simple picture of the tiny particles from which they are made (see illustration below or see diagram 'Particles' from the CD-ROM). These particles (molecules) are much too small to see even with a powerful microscope, but experiments prove that they exist. In a solid, the particles are linked together by strong forces. Individual particles cannot move over each other, so a solid is rigid. In a liquid, the particles have more freedom of movement. Forces hold the particles close together, so the liquid has a fixed volume; but because the particles can tumble over each other (rather like grains of sand), the liquid pours and flows. In a gas, the particles are widely separated and move around almost independently. The wide separation explains why gases are light, have no strength to resist stretching or bending forces, and are easily compressed. The independent motion of particles explains why a gas expands to fill whatever space is available.

STARTER
Pump up the beach toy in front of the children. Remind them that you are filling it with a gas called 'air'. Ask them to consider how the toy would be different if it were filled with a liquid or a solid (it would be much heavier and less squeezy; if it were filled with a solid, it would be hard and rigid).

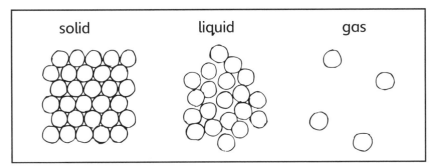

solid   liquid   gas

Differentiation
Group activity 1
This activity should be accessible to all the children.
Group activity 2
Support children by asking them to list at least one characteristic for each state (for example: gases are light, liquids pour, solids have a fixed shape). Extend children by asking them to use the particle model to account for the properties they identify.

MAIN ACTIVITY

Show the children the air-filled and water-filled balloons and the wooden brick. Use these items to compare and contrast the properties of gases, liquids and solids. Write words that describe these properties ('light', 'heavy', 'strong', 'weak', 'rigid', 'fluid') on the board.

Explain that, although you cannot see most gases, it is possible to demonstrate that they can expand, pour and flow. For example, you can feel and hear the air flowing out of an inflated beach toy when you remove the stopper. Explain that you are going to make the gas carbon dioxide by pouring a little vinegar onto some sodium bicarbonate in the lemonade bottle. Pour about an eggcup full of vinegar through the funnel. The children will observe the mixture fizzing and foaming as the gas is produced. Stretch the neck of a party balloon over the open bottleneck: the balloon will be partly inflated by the expanding gas.

Light a candle inside an open biscuit tin. Explain that carbon dioxide is heavier than air, so you can pour it out of the bottle. Remove the balloon and slowly pour the gas from the bottle into the tin (be careful not to pour out the vinegar). The carbon dioxide will extinguish the candle flame. During the experiment, stress the need for safety; tell the children that they should not attempt to repeat school science experiments at home.

GROUP ACTIVITIES

1 Ask the children to imagine that they are the particles in a solid, liquid or a gas. Get each group to describe and act out (perhaps in the playground or school hall) the motion of the particles in the different states. To represent a solid, the children should link arms to form a rigid shape. In the liquid state, they should remain close together but move around, changing places, so that the group flows and changes shape. In the gas state, the children should spread out, rushing around in all directions.

2 Ask each group to prepare a set of three cards that summarise the different properties of solids, liquids and gases. Encourage them to use the descriptive words written on the board, and to examine the three lemonade bottles on their table in order to develop their ideas.

ASSESSMENT

Check that all the children can identify whether a container is filled with a gas, a liquid or a solid. Ask them to describe a difference between a gas and a liquid, between a gas and a solid, and between a liquid and a solid. Ask: *Which state can expand most easily? Which state is often hard and rigid? Which states can pour and flow?*

PLENARY

Ask a representative from each group to talk through the information they have included on one of their 'state' cards. Use the children's ideas to summarise the key learning points.

OUTCOMES

● Know that a gas can be poured and squashed, has no fixed shape or volume, and can spread out into the air when released from its container.
● Can describe the different properties of solids, liquids and gases.

LINKS

Unit 5d, Lesson 2, Condensation.

Lesson 8 ▪ Assessment

Objectives
● To assess the children's knowledge and understanding of gases, the differences between gases, liquids and solids and changes of state.
● To assess the children's ability to explain observations and to draw conclusions from measurements.

RESOURCES ◉
Photocopiable page 103 (also 'Assessment' (red) available on the CD-ROM); pencils; pens.

STARTER
Use a brief 'question and answer' session to review the key learning points of the unit. Draw the children's attention to the posters, charts and experiments displayed around the room to remind them of the investigations they have made. They should recall the following facts:
● We are surrounded by a mixture of gases that we call 'air'. Air has mass.
● Soil and other porous materials contain air. The amount of air in soil can be measured by displacing it with water.
● There are a range of useful gases - for example, carbon dioxide is used in fizzy drinks and helium in balloons.
● Solids, liquids and gases have different properties.

ASSESSMENT ACTIVITY
Use photocopiable page 103 to test the children's knowledge and understanding. Let them complete it individually. You will probably need to review and mark the sheets yourself to get a proper appreciation of each child's attainment. If you wish to give the children a numerical mark, you could award one mark for each correct answer. This gives 12 marks altogether.

ANSWERS
The following are sample answers:
1, 2, 3. Accept any correct examples of gases, liquids and solids and their properties.
4. So that the water surface is level against the scale.
5. He must subtract the second reading from the first reading.
6. He must use the same quantities of soil for each test.

LOOKING FOR LEVELS
All children should be able to give an example of a gas, a liquid and a solid. Most children should be able to describe one or more 'special' properties of each of the three states of matter. Some children will produce accurate sketches of the particle arrangements in each of the three states. Most children should answer questions 4 and 5 correctly. Some children will be able to answer question 6.

PLENARY
Review the question papers with the class, discussing each question and the different answers given by the children in turn.

Soil investigation

Sample 1

Description _____

	Jug readings in millilitres		Volume of water/air in sample
	Start	Finish	Start – finish
Test 1			
Test 2			
Average of test 1 and test 2			

Sample 2

Description _____

	Jug readings in millilitres		Volume of water/air in sample
	Start	Finish	Start – finish
Test 1			
Test 2			
Average of test 1 and test 2			

Sample 3

Description _____

	Jug readings in millilitres		Volume of water/air in sample
	Start	Finish	Start – finish
Test 1			
Test 2			
Average of test 1 and test 2			

Illustration © Robin Lawrie

SCHOLASTIC

Assessment

gas	liquid	solid
	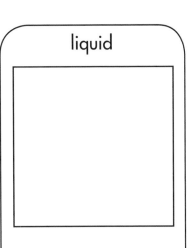	

Imagine that the boxes contain a gas, a liquid and a solid.

In each box, write and draw:

1. An example of a material or substance in that state.
2. One special property of the state (gas, liquid or solid).
3. A sketch of the particles in that material.

Simon performs an experiment to find the amount of air present in two soil samples. This is what he does:

◾ He puts a soil sample in a jar and some water in a measuring jug.

◾ He stands the jug on a level surface and records the amount of water in the jug from the scale.

◾ He pours the water from the jug onto the soil until the water just reaches the soil surface.

◾ He records the new water level in the jug.

4. Why did Simon stand the jug on a level surface before reading the scale?
5. How can Simon use his two readings to find the amount of air in the soil?
6. Simon wants to compare the amounts of air in the soil samples from different places. How can he make sure his comparisons are fair?

CHAPTER 4 Changing state

Lesson	Objectives	Main activity	Group activities	Plenary	Outcomes
Lesson 1 Evaporation	• To conduct an investigation into the factors affecting the rate of evaporation.	Groups devise an experiment to investigate the factors that how fast water evaporates.		Groups display their results as a chart or graph and report their findings to the class.	• Can plan and carry out an investigation and record the results.
Lesson 2 Condensation	• To know that gases can be turned into liquids by cooling. • To know that this process is called condensation. • To know that water vapour is present in the air, but cannot be seen.	Demonstrate examples of condensation on cold items. Observe condensation of water vapour from cut flowers.	Observe condensation on cooled cling film over warm water. Identify places in a house where condensation might occur.	The children report on their observations and knowledge of condensation.	• Recognise that when a gas condenses, a liquid is formed. • Can identify where condensation takes place in the home. • Recognise that water vapour is present in the air, but cannot be seen.
Lesson 3 Boiling	• To know that when a liquid is heated to a certain temperature, it boils. • To know that when a liquid boils, it changes into a gas. • To know that water boils at 100°C.	Record temperature-time data for water heated to boiling point. Observe changes in the water's appearance.	Plot a graph using the data. Interpret the graph to identify significant facts.	Review the information gained and reinforce the concept of boiling point.	• Recognise when a liquid is boiling. • Recognise that the white cloud seen over boiling water is made up of condensed water droplets. • Can interpret data from a graph.
Lesson 4 Melting	• To conduct an investigation into rates of melting. • To know that the freezing/melting temperature of water is 0°C. • To know that the temperature in the classroom is 18–22°C.	Record temperature-time data for an ice-water mixture. Consider factors that might affect the rate of melting.	Investigate (as a class) how the rate of melting depends on the number of ice cubes in a drink.	Review and combine the children's results to produce a class graph.	• Know that ice melts at 0°C. • Know that normal room temperature is 18–22°C. • Can identify one or more factors that affect the rate at which ice melts. • Can carry out an investigation.
Lesson 5 Materials and heat	• To know that heating/ cooling can cause materials to change • To know that some materials are natural and others are manufactured, • To know that many materials are manufactured and processed by methods involving the use of heat.	Demonstrate candle-making. Discuss other manufacturing processes involving heating or cooling. Groups use secondary sources to research these processes and make charts.		Groups display their charts and describe their findings.	• Recognise examples of melting, boiling, freezing, evaporation and condensation. • Recognise a range of natural and manufactured materials. • Can describe processes in the making of materials.
Lesson 6 Water in the environment	• To know where ice, liquid water and water vapour are found in the natural environment. • To know about evaporation and condensation in the water cycle, and freezing and melting in erosion.	Class discussion of water and its changes of state in the natural environment. Groups use secondary sources to research and make posters on topics such as rainfall, glaciers and icebergs.		Groups present their posters and describe their findings to the class.	• Know where water is found as a solid, as a liquid and as a gas in the environment. • Can explain the part played by evaporation and condensation in the water cycle.
Lesson 7 The Earth and its water	• To know that water circulates through the environment.	Discuss the water cycle and how water is distributed on the Earth's surface.	Order sentences to describe the water cycle. Draw a graph to show the distribution of water.	Discuss the graphs. Consider the proportion of fresh water available to humanity.	• Can describe the path of water in the water cycle and the changes that take place.

Assessment	Objectives	Activity 1	Activity 2
Lesson 8	• To assess the children's knowledge and understanding of gases, differences between gases, liquids and solids and changes of state. • To assess the children's ability to explain observations and to draw conclusions from measurements.	Give examples of solids, liquids and gases and describe their properties. Identify the changes of state involved in melting, boiling, evaporating and condensing.	Interpret some simple temperature data in physical terms.

SC1 SCIENTIFIC ENQUIRY

How can we dry the washing quickly?

OBJECTIVES AND OUTCOMES
● Make a fair test or comparison by changing one factor and observing or measuring the effect while keeping other factors the same.
● Make systematic observations and measurements.
● Use a wide range of methods, including diagrams, drawings, tables, bar charts, line graphs and ICT, to communicate data in an appropriate and systematic manner.

ACTIVITY
The children investigate how the number of ice cubes in a drink affects the rate of melting.

LESSON LINKS
This Sc1 activity forms an integral part of Lesson 4, Melting.

Lesson 1 ▪ Evaporation

Objective
● To know that when a liquid evaporates, it forms a gas.
● To conduct an investigation into the factors affecting the rate of evaporation.

Vocabulary
liquid, gas, water vapour, evaporate, rate, temperature

RESOURCES 💿
Starter: A wet shirt in a bowl.
Group activities: Cotton handkerchiefs; paper; string; clothes pegs; various containers; rulers; graph paper; pencils; timers.
ICT link: Graphing tool on the CD-ROM.

PREPARATION
Set out the materials on desks in preparation for practical group work.

BACKGROUND
Wet washing dries because the water trapped in the fabric evaporates into the air. The rate (speed) of evaporation depends on the following factors:
● temperature: the rate of evaporation increases as the temperature rises
● surface area: a large surface area increases the rate of evaporation (this is why washing dries faster when it is spread out rather than crumpled up.
● air flow: moving air carries away water vapour more rapidly than still air.
From the effects of the three factors described we can predict that washing will dry best when it is spread out on a line (to increase the surface area), on a warm, windy day.
    In this lesson children plan and carry out an investigation of the factors that affect the rate of evaporation.

STARTER
Use the wet shirt in the bowl to introduce the topic. Ask the children to describe what must happen for the shirt to dry (the water must evaporate). Discuss how we can dry the shirt in the shortest possible time. With the children's help compile a list of the possible factors that may affect the rate at which the water evaporates. Explain that the children's task is to plan an investigation of the effects of one or more of the factors they have identified on the evaporation rate.

MAIN ACTIVITY
Set the children to work in groups to work on their plans. Emphasise the importance of devising a fair test. Which factor will they investigate? What

Differentiation
Support children by asking them to compare the drying time of a screwed-up wet handkerchief with that of one hung on a line, the drying times of sheets of wet paper placed in the sun and in the shade, or in front of a fan and in still air.

Extend children by asking them to plot graphs of the depth of water over time in open containers left in different locations. They could record the temperature with a thermometer or datalogger and the airflow with an anemometer. For fair comparisons, the exposed surface areas should be the same. The effect of changing the exposed surface area can also be investigated.

will they do? What observations will they make? How will they record their observations? Each group should describe its plan to the class before proceeding to the practical work.

GROUP ACTIVITIES
The children work in groups to carry out their investigations.

ASSESSMENT
Ask the children to explain how they planned their investigations. Did they predict how the drying time would depend on the location? Were their predictions confirmed? Make sure that they understand the importance of changing only one variable at a time when they are investigating the effect of a single factor.

PLENARY
Each group should report their findings to the rest of the class and display them as a chart or graph. Some children could use the graphing tool on the CD-ROM to do this.

OUTCOME
● Can plan and carry out an investigation and record the results.

Lesson 2 ● Condensation

Objective
● To know that gases can be turned into liquids by cooling.
● To know that this process is called condensation.
● To know that water vapour is present in the air, but cannot be seen.

Vocabulary
condense, condensation, water vapour, changing state, liquid, gas

RESOURCES
Main activity: A picture of people or animals with steaming breath; a refrigerator, a small mirror; a pair of spectacles, a can of fizzy drink; cut flowers in a narrow-necked vase, a polythene bag; modelling clay, rubber bands.
Group activities: 1 Plastic bowls; warm water; cling film; ice cubes; paper; pencils. **2** Photocopiable page 116 (also 'Condensation' (red) available on the CD-ROM); pencils.
ICT link: 'Condensation' interactive from the CD-ROM.

PREPARATION
Cool the mirror, spectacles and can of drink in the refrigerator, for half an hour, before the lesson. Make sure there is a good supply of ice cubes available. Set out a plastic bowl and piece of cling film for each group, and a copy of page 116 for each child.

BACKGROUND
Condensation is the process by which a gas changes into a liquid. It is the reverse of evaporation. Children will be familiar with the condensation that takes place on a cold glass or metal surface, when it is brought into a warm room - the surface of a drink can or bottle taken from the fridge becomes wet with condensation. Spectacles 'steam up' with condensation when you come indoors on a cold day. Cool surfaces such as windows and mirrors become covered with water droplets in kitchens and bathrooms, when there is a lot of water vapour in the air.

As a result of the evaporation of water from the soil, lakes, rivers and oceans, water vapour is always present in the atmosphere. Warm air can hold more water vapour than cooler air. This is why condensation is observed when warm air comes into contact with a cooler surface: the air adjacent to the surface is cooled and can no longer hold as much water in the gaseous state. Some of the water vapour condenses into drops of liquid water that form on the cold surface. The same process explains 'steamy breath' on winter days and the formation of clouds: water vapour condenses into clouds of fine water droplets as warm breath comes into contact with cold air. Clouds form in the atmosphere as warm air filled with water vapour rises and cools. The water vapour condenses into water droplets, which eventually fall back to the ground as rain.

STARTER

Show the children a picture of people or animals with steaming breath on a cold day. Explain what is happening: water vapour in the warm breath is condensing into fine drops of liquid water as it comes into contact with cold air. Explain that condensation is a general word used to describe the change from gas to liquid. Ask the children to think of some more examples of condensation they have observed around the home (steamed-up windows, breath clouding on mirrors and so on). Discuss the process of cloud formation: clouds in the atmosphere form in the same way as 'clouds' of breath – by water vapour condensing into droplets.

MAIN ACTIVITY

Demonstrate examples of condensation by taking the three items from the refrigerator. Observe that the spectacles steam up in the warm room (you can breathe on them to increase the amount of condensation), but that as they gradually warm up to room temperature the condensation clears. Study the condensation on the mirror and the drinks can in the same way. Ask the children to predict on which item the condensation will stay the longest. (The drink can – because it is full of cold liquid, it stays cold for longer than the spectacles or the mirror.)

Explain to the children that you can use condensation to demonstrate that cut flowers give out water. Show them the vase of flowers. Seal the stems into the neck with modelling clay, so that water cannot escape from the vase. Cover the flowers with an inverted polythene bag and fix the bag around the neck of the vase with rubber bands. Leave the vase on a window sill overnight. The next day, the children will observe water droplets condensed on the inside surface of the bag. Explain that the flowers take water up their stems and release it as vapour through their petals. Eventually there is so much water vapour in the air inside the bag that it cannot hold any more, and drops of liquid water start to condense.

GROUP ACTIVITIES

1 Sit each group around a plastic bowl. Pour some warm (not hot) water into each bowl, and ask the children to cover the bowl with a sheet of cling film. Put two or three ice cubes onto the centre of the cling film cover. Ask the children to sketch what they observe and explain what is happening, either orally or in writing.

2 Ask the children to find one or more places in the diagram of the house on page 116 where they think condensation might occur. Ask them to draw a simple diagram of what happens and write a few sentences to explain the process.

ICT LINK

Children can use the 'Condensation' interactive from the CD-ROM, to identify areas of a house where condensation is likely to occur.

ASSESSMENT

Use the children's drawings, writing and/or oral explanations to check that they understand condensation as the change of state from a gas to a liquid. Check that they know that the 'steam' on a steamed-up window or mirror is a coating of liquid water droplets, and that clouds form in the atmosphere as the air cools and water vapour condenses.

Differentiation
Group activity 2
To support children, give them 'Condensation' (green) from the CD-ROM, which does not ask them to explain why condensation occurs. To extend children, give them 'Condensation' (blue), which asks them when in the year condensation is most likely to occur and to explain their answer.

PLENARY

Ask a representative from each group to describe their group's observations with the help of their sketches. Ask each group to talk to the class about one example of condensation in the home. Use the children's ideas to summarise the key learning points.

OUTCOMES

- Recognise that when a gas condenses, a liquid is formed.
- Can identify where condensation takes place in the home.
- Recognise that water vapour is present in the air, but cannot be seen.

LINKS

Lesson 7, The Earth and its water.

Lesson 3 ▪ Boiling

Objective
- To know that when a liquid is heated to a certain temperature, it boils.
- To know that when a liquid boils, it changes into a gas.
- To know that water boils at 100°C.

Vocabulary
temperature, boil, liquid, gas, steam, vapour, boiling point

RESOURCES

Main activity: An electric kettle; a stove or hotplate; a Pyrex® saucepan; a small hand mirror; a digital thermometer and probe; a whiteboard or flip-chart and marker pens; a digital timer or clock; a data-logger (optional).
Group activities: 1 and **2** Paper; graph paper; pencils; pens.
ICT link: Graphing tool and 'Water boiling' diagram from the CD-ROM.

PREPARATION

For safety reasons, the children must not boil water or handle containers of boiling water themselves. Boiling a pan of water can be demonstrated in the classroom on a portable hotplate, or on a stove in a teaching kitchen. In both cases, all the children should stay well back. Stand the pan on the stove and position the thermometer display and timer where the children can see them. Set up a data-logger and computer if you have the technology available; this will enable you to generate a graph directly (see example below; also available on the CD-ROM). If not, draw a table on a flipchart or whiteboard in which the temperature of the water can be recorded at one-minute intervals for a ten-minute period.

BACKGROUND

When a liquid boils, it changes its state from liquid to gas at a constant temperature. Boiling is a vigorous process in which bubbles of vapour form inside the liquid, rise to the surface, burst and escape into the atmosphere. The surface of the boiling liquid is agitated by the bursting gas bubbles. The temperature at which a liquid boils is called its 'boiling point'. The boiling point of a liquid depends on the surrounding atmospheric pressure: liquids boil at lower temperatures when the pressure is reduced. For this reason, the standard boiling point of a liquid is the one measured at normal atmospheric pressure at sea level. Under these conditions, the boiling point of water is 100°C. The children need to know this temperature, but they are not expected to know at Key Stage 2 that boiling point varies with pressure. You should not demonstrate the boiling of any liquid other than water in the classroom, as flammable or toxic vapours may be produced.

When a liquid is heated to its boiling point, the temperature does not rise any further as it

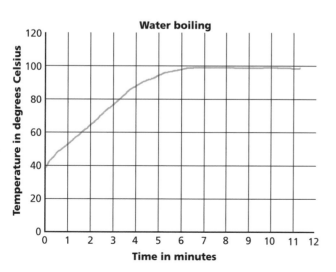

boils, even though heat continues to be supplied. During boiling, the heat energy available is used to overcome the attraction between the particles (molecules) that holds them together in the liquid state, and to separate these particles into the gaseous state.

The gaseous form of water (which is invisible) is called 'steam' or 'water vapour' by scientists. In everyday language, we also use the word 'steam' to refer to the white cloud of suspended water droplets over hot water. As with the word 'weight', the everyday meaning and the scientific meaning are not exactly the same.

STARTER

Ask the children to watch and listen as an electric kettle comes to the boil. Ask them to explain what is happening to the water in the kettle when it reaches boiling point. (It is changing into the gas steam, which emerges from the kettle spout.) Hold a cold mirror near the spout so that the children can see water condensing from the invisible vapour onto the cold surface. Ask the children why the kettle is designed to switch off automatically when the water reaches boiling point. (To prevent it from boiling dry.) *If a kettle were allowed to boil dry, where would all the water have gone?* (Into the atmosphere.)

MAIN ACTIVITY

Show the children the pan of water on the stove. Tell them that you are going to investigate the way its temperature rises as it is brought to the boil. Stir the water with the thermometer probe and draw the children's attention to the temperature display. Remind them that temperatures are measured in degrees Celsius. Appoint a child to act as recorder, and position him or her by the whiteboard with a marker pen. (Alternatively, use a data-logger to record results directly onto the PC screen.) Record the current water temperature (at 0 minutes) and start the clock. At 1 minute, record the temperature again and turn on the stove. Continue recording the temperature at one-minute intervals until the water has been boiling for two or three minutes. Stir the water with the probe before each reading to make sure that the temperature is fairly uniform throughout the pan.

Draw the children's attention to the change in the appearance of the water as it comes to the boil. Explain that the small bubbles that appear as the water is warmed are bubbles of air that had been dissolved in the cold water. Larger bubbles of steam don't start to form until the water boils.

GROUP ACTIVITIES

1 Give each child a sheet of plain paper and a sheet of graph paper. Ask them to draw a table and copy the results recorded on the whiteboard into it. Then explain how they can transfer these results onto a graph (with suitable axes) to show how the temperature of the water changes as time passed. Discuss what axes are appropriate (see example on page 108).
2 Ask each group to locate a particular value from the graph. Values that can be assigned to different groups include:
● the starting temperature of the water
● the time the hotplate was turned on
● the time when the water reached 70°C
● the 'boiling point' temperature of the water
● the time when the water started to boil.

ICT LINK

Use the graphing tool on the CD-ROM to create a graph of results as a class.

ASSESSMENT

Check that the children know that when a liquid boils it changes into a gas, and that the boiling point of water is 100°C. Can a representative from each group indicate in which region of the temperature–time graph the water is boiling?

PLENARY

Ask a representative from each group to display their graph and explain how they located the required temperatures or times. Discuss the boiling process with the help of the graphs, and emphasise the key learning points. As an additional challenge, you could ask children to find out from secondary sources why it is difficult to boil an egg or make a good cup of tea at the top of Mount Everest. (The atmospheric pressure is lower, so water boils at a lower temperature.)

OUTCOMES

- Recognise when a liquid is boiling.
- Recognise that the white cloud seen over boiling water is made up of condensed water droplets.
- Can interpret data from a graph.

Differentiation

Group activity 1
Some children will need considerable guidance in constructing axes for a graph and transferring the data to it from the table. If you used a data-logger, you could print out the graphs that were displayed on the screen for the children to interpret, thus avoiding the difficulties of the children producing their own graphs.

Group activity 2
Ask children who need support to locate the time when the water started to boil. Extend children by asking them individually to locate and label all the significant points.

Lesson 4 ▪ Melting

Objective

- To conduct an investigation into rates of melting.
- To know that the freezing/melting temperature of water is 0°C.
- To know that the temperature in the classroom is normally 18–22°C.

Vocabulary

ice, melt, melting point, temperature, rate of melting, changing state

RESOURCES 💿

Main activity: an ICT temperature sensor linked to a computer; a clear plastic beaker; ice cubes; water; access to a refrigerator.
Group activity: Plastic beakers; digital thermometers; timers (to measure up to 30 minutes); ice cubes; water; ruled or squared A4 paper, pencils.
ICT link: Graphing tool and 'Iced water' diagram on the CD-ROM;

PREPARATION

Set up a temperature sensor and a computer with a screen displaying temperature against time. Select a time interval for the time display, so that a temperature graph is plotted over a 30-minute period on the monitor. Set out plastic beakers, thermometers, timers, paper, pencils and a sheet of ruled or squared A4 paper for each group. Have a supply of ice cubes ready for use.

BACKGROUND

Melting is the process by which a material changes its state from solid to liquid at a constant temperature. Children will be familiar with melting ice, candle wax and chocolate. At normal atmospheric pressure at sea level, ice melts to liquid water at 0°C. Normal room temperature is 18–22°C. Ice straight from the deep-freeze has a temperature of about –20°C. In a warm room, ice gradually heats up until its surface temperature is 0°C. The ice surface then starts to melt to liquid water. The temperature of the ice-water mixture does not rise above 0°C until all the ice has melted. While there is still ice present, the heat transferred from the surroundings goes into breaking the bonds between the water particles (molecules) that hold them rigidly together. When these bonds are broken, the molecules move freely in the liquid state. The rate at which the ice melts depends on the temperature of the surroundings and the properties of the container in which it is held.

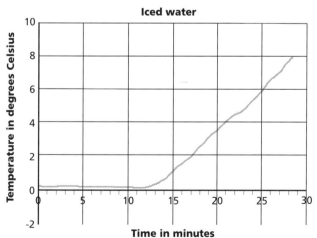

STARTER

Show the children an ice cube in a clear plastic

beaker and discuss the melting process. Ask them to describe any other examples of melting they are familiar with. Explain that they are going to investigate how long an ice cube keeps a drink cold before it melts.

MAIN ACTIVITY

Take a beaker of iced water from the fridge. Start the computer display with the sensor in air. Indicate to the children that the monitor is displaying the temperature of the room. Plunge the sensor into the iced water and observe how the temperature graph falls to, and remains at, 0°C. Stir the mixture every few minutes with the sensor. Explain that this is necessary to keep the temperature uniform (even) throughout the mixture.

Ask the children to predict what will happen to the temperature as time passes. *Will it rise or fall as the ice melts?* (The temperature will stay around 0°C while there is ice in the water. Only when all the ice has melted will the temperature of the water start to rise towards room temperature.) Ask the children to list factors that they think will affect the time taken for the ice to melt in a drink. Prompt them to consider the amount of ice (number of ice cubes), the amount of liquid, the temperature of the room, the insulating properties of the container and the initial temperature of the drink before ice was added. Tell them that they are going to conduct a fair test, in groups, to see how the melting time depends on the number of ice cubes.

GROUP ACTIVITY

Ask each group to prepare a record sheet for their experiment. They will need to record the initial water temperature in °C, the number of ice cubes used and the temperature at one-minute intervals. Each group should have an identical beaker of water at the same (chilled) temperature. Ask the groups to measure and note the water temperature with a thermometer. Explain that all the water samples must start at the same temperature in order for the test to be fair. Take a tray of ice cubes from the fridge. Add one cube to the first group's beaker, two cubes to the second group's, three to the third group's and so on. Ask the children to record the temperature of the ice-water mixture on their record sheet at one-minute intervals, until the ice has melted and the water temperature has started to rise.

ICT LINK 💿

Use the graphing tool on the CD-ROM to create a graph of results as a class.

ASSESSMENT

Check that every child can describe melting as the process in which a solid changes into a liquid, and can give examples such as a melting ice-lolly. Ask them to give the melting temperature of ice and to describe one or more factors that affect the rate at which ice melts.

PLENARY

Ask each group to use their data to determine a melting time for their ice sample. Combine the results to produce a class graph of melting times for different numbers of ice cubes. Discuss how the test was kept fair, so that valid comparisons could be made.

OUTCOMES

- Know that ice melts at 0°C.
- Know that normal room temperature is 18-22°C.
- Can identify one or more factors that affect the rate at which ice melts.
- Can carry out an investigation.

Differentiation

Support children by giving them a prepared record sheet on which to write their results. Other pupils can plot graphs as they go along. Extend children by asking them to label distinct regions on the graph (the time period during which solid ice is present, the period when the water is starting to warm towards room temperature). Children who would like to take the investigation further can investigate the effect of changing other factors – for example, the initial temperature of the water.

Lesson 5 ▪ Materials and heat

Objectives
● To know that heating/cooling can cause materials to melt, boil, evaporate, freeze or condense.
● To know that some materials are natural and others are manufactured.
● To know that many materials are manufactured and processed by methods involving the use of heat.

RESOURCES
A wax candle-making kit; a selection of secondary sources that children can use to research the manufacture and processing of materials (these could include: science encyclopaedias and CD-ROMs; posters, pamphlets and videotapes produced by industrial companies); large sheets of card; felt-tipped pens.

MAIN ACTIVITY
Demonstrate the candle-making process. Explain that you are using heat to melt the wax so that it can be poured into a mould. When it cools, it 'freezes' solid again. Discuss the role of heat in extracting or manufacturing new materials from natural materials, and in processing them. For example, metals are extracted from ores by heating the ores in furnaces. Petrol and paraffin are extracted from crude oil by heating the oil so that the petrol and oil evaporate as gases, then cooling them so that they condense back to liquids. Salt is extracted from sea water by allowing the heat of the Sun to evaporate the water, leaving the salt behind.

Divide the class into groups. Issue each group with a large card to make a wall chart. Ask the groups to use secondary sources to research examples of industrial processes that use melting, freezing, condensation, evaporation or boiling. Materials to study could include metals, glass, plastics, oil and petrol, frozen or dried foods, sea-salt, wines and spirits, scents and cosmetics. Each group should record their findings on a card.

ASSESSMENT
Ask each child to pick a manufactured material and write a few sentences describing the action of heat in its production or processing.

Differentiation
Ask children who need support to find examples of how melting is used to shape or mould materials.
Extend children by asking them to find separate examples of how melting, freezing, evaporation, condensation and boiling are used to change or process materials.

PLENARY
Each group should display the chart they have prepared and describe their findings to the rest of the class.

OUTCOMES
● Recognise examples of melting, boiling, freezing, evaporation and condensation.
● Recognise a range of natural and manufactured materials.
● Can describe processes in the making of materials.

Lesson 6 ▪ Water in the environment

Objective
● To know where ice, liquid water and water vapour are found in the natural environment.
● To know about evaporation and condensation in the water cycle, and about freezing and melting in erosion.

RESOURCES
Secondary sources of information on the water cycle and the role of water in physical processes in the environment; felt-tipped pens; large sheets of paper.

MAIN ACTIVITY
Prompt the children to describe locations where ice, liquid water and water vapour are found in nature. Ask them to describe situations in which natural changes of state take place (such as evaporation from rivers, lakes freezing in winter and glaciers melting in summer). Divide the class into groups. Ask the groups to use secondary sources to research different aspects of water in the environment. Topics might include rainfall, erosion, glaciers, the water cycle, floods and icebergs. Each group should prepare a poster on their topic.

Differentiation

Ask children who need support to describe where ice, liquid water and water vapour occur naturally. Extend children by asking them to describe processes in which changes of state are significant, such as the water cycle, erosion and glaciation.

ASSESSMENT

Ask each child to pick a topic and write one or two paragraphs about it. Check that they understand that water occurs in three states in nature.

PLENARY

Each group should display their poster and describe their findings to the rest of the class.

OUTCOMES

● Know where water is found as a solid, as a liquid and as a gas in the environment.
● Can explain the part played by evaporation and condensation in the water cycle.

LINKS

Enrichment unit: Chapter 5, Water in the environment.

Lesson 7 ◼ The Earth and its water

Objective
● To know that water circulates through the environment.

Vocabulary
evaporate, condense, naturally, water vapour, liquid, solid, gas

RESOURCES 💿

Main activity: Colour pictures of the Earth and another planet, taken from space; six strips of card (see Preparation), Blu-Tack®.
Group activities: 1 Writing and drawing materials, paper. **2** 1cm² squared paper; glue; plain or coloured mounting paper; drawing materials; scissors.
ICT link: Graphing tool and 'Water cycle' diagram on the CD-ROM.

PREPARATION 💿

Display an enlarged copy of the water cycle from the CD-ROM on an interactive whiteboard, or draw a sketch on a flip chart. Prepare six card strips, each with one of the following sentences: 'The heat of the sun evaporates water from the sea.'; 'The air from over the sea moves the water vapour over the land.'; 'Some of the water vapour in the air begins to condense into clouds.'; 'Rain or snow falls.'; 'Water runs into rivers, streams, lakes and ponds.'; 'Eventually the water finds its way back into the sea.'

On a new page, write the following facts about the Earth's surface: 'Three quarters of the Earth's surface is covered with water or ice'; 'less than a quarter is suitable for humans to live on'; '71% of the Earth's surface is covered by water'; '3% of the Earth's surface is covered by ice'.

BACKGROUND

This lesson introduces the children to the water cycle. This is the process that moves water, about the planet. The physical features that are part of this process, such as seas and rivers, will be studied as part of the geography curriculum; considering the distribution and care of this precious resource is relevant to PSHE.

Using the children's own experience of where water naturally occurs, the lesson directs their attention to the three physical states of water: liquid, solid (ice) and gas (water vapour). In the Plenary session, the children are made aware of how limited the planet's fresh water supplies are.

STARTER

Show the children a colour picture of the Earth taken from space. Tell them that this is the only place in our solar system where life is known to survive. Show a colour picture of another planet and ask: *How does the Earth look different from other planets?* (It looks blue, the others do not.) *Why does the Earth look mainly blue when viewed from space?*

Differentiation
Group activity 1
Support children by giving them a copy of the water cycle diagram and the six sentences (in random order). Ask then to cut out the sentences and paste them under the diagram in a sensible order, then number the sentences and annotate the diagram with the numbers.
Group activity 2
Children who complete this activity quickly could find more facts from secondary sources about natural water features: the deepest ocean, the highest waterfall, the longest river and so on.

MAIN ACTIVITY 💿

Ask the children to help you list all the places where water occurs naturally on our planet. They are most likely to focus on water in its liquid state: seas, rivers, ponds, lakes, streams, puddles. Other children may correctly suggest that water is stored naturally in plants and animals. If the children suggest manufactured features such as canals and reservoirs, list these separately.

Remind the children that water can be a solid as well as a liquid. Ask: *What do we call water when it is a solid?* (Ice.) *Where does ice occur naturally?* You should be able to add 'glaciers' and 'polar ice sheets' to the list. Finally, remind the children that water can also be a gas – for example, water evaporates into the air when wet washing is hung out to dry. Water in the atmosphere forms clouds and rain. Add 'air' or 'atmosphere' and 'clouds' to the list of places where water occurs naturally on our planet.

Now talk about the path of water in the water cycle. Show the children a glass of drinking water. *In what way is the water we drink different from the water in the sea?* (Sea water tastes salty) Say that the water we drink is on a journey that starts at the sea and finishes at the sea. Show the children the water cycle diagram on the board. Pointing to different areas of the diagram, elicit answers to questions to make sure the children understand the processes shown. Try to use sentences similar to those on the prepared sentence strips. Draw arrows onto the diagram to show the cyclical pathway, and stress that this pattern is called the 'water cycle'.

Go back to the children's list of places where water occurs naturally and ask questions about them that relate to the water cycle diagram, such as: *How does water get into ponds?* (Rain-water or melted ice runs down into a pond by a stream or river.)

Display facts about the Earth's surface and discuss the meaning of this information. Show the children an example of how one fact could be displayed graphically: you could use the graphing tool on the CD-ROM to do this.

GROUP ACTIVITIES

1 Display the six card sentence strips in random order and fix them with Blu-Tack® to a vertical surface. Ask the children to copy the sentences in a sensible order and make their own diagram to explain the water cycle.
2 Give the children graph-making materials (see Resources). Ask them to make a graph, with linked pictures, to show the other children the facts about the Earth's surface from the board. This will develop their understanding of percentages.

ICT LINK 💿

Use the graphing tool on the CD-ROM to create class graphs.

ASSESSMENT

During the Plenary session, present the water cycle sentence strips and ask the children to help you arrange them in a sensible order.

PLENARY

Look at some of the graphs produced by the children in Group activity 2. Now explain that 98% of the world's water is salty; only 2% is fresh, and much of this is frozen. Discuss the implications of this: very little of the planet's water is immediately fit for us to drink.

OUTCOME

● Can describe the path of water in the water cycle.

LINKS

Geography: seas, rivers, clouds and rainfall.

Lesson 8 ▶ Assessment

Objectives
● To assess the children's knowledge and understanding of gases, differences between gases, liquids and solids and changes of state.
● To assess the children's ability to explain observations and to draw conclusions from measurements.

Vocabulary
evaporate, condense, naturally, water vapour, liquid, solid, gas

RESOURCES
Photocopiable page 117 (also 'Assessment' (red) from the CD-ROM); pencils; pens.

STARTER
Use a brief 'question and answer' session to review the key learning points of the unit. Draw the children's attention to the posters, charts and experiments displayed around the room to remind them of the investigations they have made. They should recall the following facts:
● Melting, boiling, evaporation, freezing and condensation are reversible processes in which materials change from one state to another.
● Ice melts at 0°C. Water boils at 100°C.
● Changes caused by heat are used to manufacture and process materials.

ASSESSMENT ACTIVITY
Give each child a copy of photocopiable page 117. This sheet focuses on interpreting a simple set of measurements to draw conclusions and make predictions, based on knowledge and understanding acquired during the unit. You could award up to four marks for each answer, giving a possible total of 20 marks.

ANSWERS
1.
boiling	liquid ⟶ gas
evaporating	liquid ⟶ gas
condensing	gas ⟶ liquid
freezing	liquid ⟶ solid

2a. Sophie stirs the drink to make sure that the temperature is 'even' or 'constant' throughout the liquid.
2b. Drink B is the one with ice, since an ice-water mixture has a temperature of 0°C.
2c. Beakers A and B, because condensation of water vapour from the air takes place on surfaces that are colder than the surroundings.
2d. The temperature of beaker A will rise; that of beaker B will stay the same (since it still contains ice); that of beaker C will stay the same (since it is at room temperature); that of beaker D will fall.

LOOKING FOR LEVELS
All children should be able to identify the start and end states for both boiling and freezing. Most children will know the start and end states involved in evaporation and condensation.

All the children should give correct answers to questions 2 and 3. Most children should answer question 4 correctly and explain it as above. Some children will predict correctly in their answer to question 5.

PLENARY
Review the question papers with the class, discussing each question and the different answers given by the children in turn.

PHOTOCOPIABLE

Condensation

1. Where in this home might you observe condensation?
2. Draw circles around the labels.
3. Why does water sometimes condense in these places?
   Write on the back of the sheet.

Bedroom windows

Bathroom window

Bottle garden

Bathroom mirror

Freezer

Refrigerator

Kitchen window

Greenhouse

Assessment

1. The following words describe materials, for example water, changing from one state to another. Fill in the blank spaces with the names of the states involved. The first one has been done for you.

melting   solid   ⟶   liquid

boiling   _____   ⟶   _____

evaporating   _____   ⟶   _____

condensing   _____   ⟶   _____

freezing   _____   ⟶   _____

Sophie uses a digital thermometer to measure the temperature of four drinks in beakers. She stirs the drinks carefully before each measurement. Here are her results.

beaker	temperature
A	9°C
B	0°C
C	20°C
D	38°C

The temperature in the classroom in which the beakers are standing is 20°C.

2a. Explain why Sophie stirs each drink before measuring its temperature.

_____

_____

_____

2b. One drink has ice in it. Which drink is it? Explain how you know.

_____

_____

2c. There is condensation on the outside of two of the beakers. Which beakers are these? Explain why there is no condensation on the other two beakers.

_____

_____

_____

2d. Sophie leaves the beakers standing for 10 minutes. There is still some ice in one of the drinks. She repeats her measurements using the same method. Predict how the temperature of each drink will have changed. Will it have risen, fallen or stayed the same? Circle the correct answer for each.

A

        risen   fallen   stayed the same

B

        risen   fallen   stayed the same

C

        risen   fallen   stayed the same

D

        risen   fallen   stayed the same

CHAPTER 5 Water in the environment

Lesson	Objectives	Main activity	Group activities	Plenary	Outcomes
Lesson 1 Water in our homes	• To recognise things in our homes that create or remove water vapour. • To know that water vapour is invisible but surrounds us.	List things in our homes that produce or remove water vapour. Use tables to classify and present this information.		Discuss why excess water is extracted from our homes.	• Know where water vapour is produced in our homes.
Lesson 2 Conditions for drying	• To devise an experiment to show how wet materials can be dried efficiently.	A structured class experiment to test predictions about what factors affect the speed of drying.		Discuss how some products are deliberately kept moist.	• Know what conditions encourage water to become vapour. • Know what conditions encourage wet things to dry.
Lesson 3 Changing water levels	• To know that the amount of water in a habitat varies.	Consider how to use rainwater over a year to prevent a garden pond drying out.	Answer questions on the pond problem. Design a school wildlife pond.	Children report on their wildlife pond designs. Discuss the effectiveness of these.	• Can describe how the amount of water in a habitat varies. • Can explain the purpose of reservoirs and why they are needed.
Lesson 4 Floods and droughts	• To understand the catastrophic effects of floods and drought.	Use secondary sources to find out about and describe the effects of floods and droughts, and how floods can be prevented.		Children share their reports and findings.	• Understand some of the reasons for and effects of major floods and droughts.
Lesson 5 Top tips for saving water	• To know that we use a great amount of water and that water must be conserved.	Consider how much water is used in various activities and products in the home. Discuss ways of saving water.	Complete a sheet of tips for water saving. Make a poster to present ideas for saving water.	Discuss wasteful water-using practices. Discuss the effectiveness of the children's posters.	• Recognise some activities that require a great amount of water. • Can explain the need for water conservation. • Can describe simple ways in which we can conserve water.
Lesson 6 A frog's guide to ponds	• To know that water can be polluted by waste from human activities.	Look at the biological indicators of how polluted an area of water is.	Fill in a table on water pollution indicators. Answer questions on biological indicators of water pollution.	Consider ways to prevent water pollution. Plan the equipment needed to check water pollution in local fresh water.	• Can identify sources of water pollution. • Know how water pollution can be assessed using biological indicators. • Know some of the effects of water pollution. • Know some ways to reduce water pollution.
Lesson 7 A pond survey	• To use pollution indicators to monitor a local pond or stream.	Use observation and knowledge of biological pollution indicators to assess the health of a pond or stream.		The children assess the water quality and explain their decision.	• Can assess water quality in the local environment.
Lesson 8 Air pollution	• To recognise some activities that cause air pollution. • To recognise some effects on the environment of air pollution. • To know some ways in which air pollution can be reduced.	Use role-play to consider the chain of events that cause acid rain and global warming. Consider ways of reducing air pollution.	Make a comic strip to explain the effects of air pollution. Make a poster encouraging people to reduce air pollution.	Discuss the children's ideas for ways to reduce air pollution. Could any of these be implemented in the classroom?	• Recognise some activities that cause air pollution. • Can describe some effects of air pollution on the environment. • Can describe some ways in which air pollution can be reduced.

Lesson	Objectives	Main activity	Group activities	Plenary	Outcomes
Lesson 9 A fisherman's tale	• To know that human activities are affecting fish stocks. • To understand why an indigenous fish species is in danger of extinction. • To know that fish stocks need to be conserved if species are to survive.	Extract scientific information from a play about the dangers facing the wild salmon.	Continue the play with a further scene. Complete a table showing the dangers to the salmon at each stage of its life cycle.	Children perform their scenes. Discuss ways to conserve wild salmon.	• Understand how human activities reduce fish stocks. • Know the life cycle of an important indigenous fish species and understand some of the problems facing it. • Can suggest some ways in which fish stocks can be conserved.

Assessment	Objectives	Activity 1	Activity 2
Lesson 10	• To assess children's knowledge of the water cycle and where water appears in the environment. • To assess the children's knowledge of the effects of human activity on the quality and distribution of water in the environment.	Answer questions on the water cycle and water conservation.	Answer questions about water distribution, water pollution and the causes and consequences of air pollution.

SC1 SCIENTIFIC ENQUIRY

What is the best way to dry wet materials?

LEARNING OBJECTIVES AND OUTCOMES
● To know that water, in its liquid state, can change into water vapour and some of the conditions that encourage this change.
● To recognise some of the conditions that encourage wet articles (washed clothes, swimming costumes, towels etc.) to dry.

ACTIVITY
The children wet identical samples of a material (e.g. paper towels, newspaper etc.) with an equal amount of water

They hang their wet samples in one of a variety of locations (e.g. Outside in either an exposed or sheltered area. Inside, in a warm or cold room.) in an unfolded, folded and screwed up state in order to dry.

They examine by look and feel and record the drying progress of each sample over a period of time

LESSON LINKS
Use this Sc1 activity as an integral part of Lesson 2, Conditions for drying.

Lesson 1 ◗ Water in our homes

Objective
● To recognise things in our homes that create or remove water vapour.
● To know that water vapour is invisible but surrounds us.

RESOURCES 💿
A diagram of the water cycle; a mirror; hairdryer and kettle; a chilled drink.
ICT link: 'Water cycle' diagram on the CD-ROM.

MAIN ACTIVITY 💿
Show the children the water cycle picture. Ask the children how water from the seas gets into rivers and streams. Focus on the role of water vapour. Explain that water vapour is in the air we breathe, but that we cannot see it. *How could we prove that water vapour is in the air we breathe?* Show the children a mirror as a clue. Ask a child to breathe on the mirror and create 'mist'. Explain that the mist is 'condensation': droplets of liquid water formed by cooling water vapour. Ask the children where else they have seen condensed water vapour; list suggestions on the board or flipchart.

Ask the children if they can think of anything in the home that is used to change liquid water into water vapour. Show them a hairdryer and explain that it evaporates the water. Ask them to suggest other household

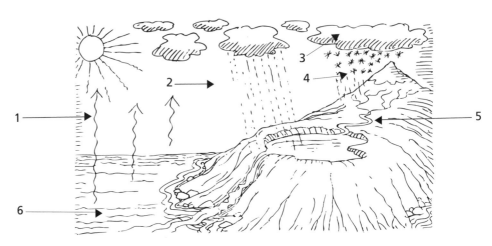

Differentiation
Support children by giving them pre-prepared tables to complete. Extend children by asking them to complete both tables.

Where we see evidence of water vapour	What the evidence is	Things in our home that change liquid water into water vapour	Things in our home that make water vapour while they are doing something else	Things in our home that remove water vapour

appliances that perform a similar task and list these. Now ask them to think of appliances that make water vapour while doing something else. Show a kettle as an example, and explain that steam is condensed water vapour. Ask for other suggestions and list these. Now ask the children if they know of anything at home that removes water vapour. Elicit ideas such as open windows, extractor fans and dehumidifiers. List these and discuss in simple terms how they work: they exchange air that contains lots of water vapour for drier air.

Draw two tables on the board or flipchart (see above). Ask the children to use the lists to complete either of these.

ASSESSMENT
Show the children a chilled drink container and ask them to explain the 'misted' surface

PLENARY
Ask the children why they think water vapour is often removed from our homes. Elicit or explain the idea that water vapour, when it condenses, can damage the materials in our home.

OUTCOME
● Know where water vapour is produced in our homes.

Lesson 2 ● Conditions for drying

Objective
● To devise an experiment to show how wet materials can be dried efficiently.

RESOURCES
Paper towels or serviettes; water; teaspoons; a temporary clothes line and pegs; newspaper; colouring pencils; a flipchart with a table showing the following column headings: 'Where can we put the paper towel to dry', 'Folded', 'Unfolded', 'Screwed-up'; a copy of the table for each child.

MAIN ACTIVITY
Tell the children that in this lesson they are going to devise an experiment on 'drying'. Show them two coloured paper towels: one dry, the other wet. *How can you tell which one is wet?* Discuss differences in appearance and feel. *Why does a wet towel feel colder on your face than a dry one?* Explain that water touches your skin and turns to water vapour, taking heat away from the skin. *Where would you put a wet paper towel to dry it quickly?* List suggestions in the table - one for each group of six children to try. *Do you think it makes any difference to the speed of drying if the towel is folded, unfolded or screwed up? How could you test the difference?* Establish the conditions for a fair test.

Give all the children a copy of the table; ask them to copy all the locations and colour in the cells where they think the towel will dry quickly. Let each group test the three conditions in a particular location (one towel per pair). Revisit the experiment later in the day or the next day. Each pair should put a tick or cross in the appropriate cell on the flipchart to show whether or not

Differentiation
Some children may need support in interpreting the cells in the table.

it is dry. Ask the children to compare the full set of results with their predictions.

ASSESSMENT
After the experiment, ask the children how they would dry a wet towel and swimming costume quickly after swimming. Ask them what has happened to the water in the paper towel.

PLENARY
Some products (such as 'baby wipes') are deliberately kept moist. Discuss how manufacturers keep the moisture in these products.

OUTCOMES
● Know what conditions encourage water to become vapour.
● Know what conditions encourage wet things to dry.

Lesson 3 ◗ Changing water levels

Objective
● To know that the amount of water in a habitat varies.

Vocabulary
flood, drought, reservoir

RESOURCES 💿
Main activity: A water cycle diagram as in Lesson 1; enlarged copies of the pond and barrel diagrams, the 'reader's letter' and the reply from photocopiable page 134 (also 'Changing water levels' (red) available on the CD-ROM); Blu-Tack®.
Group activities: 1 Photocopiable page 134 (also 'Changing water levels' (red) from the CD-ROM); glue; paper; writing materials. **2** Writing and drawing materials.
ICT link: 'Water cycle' diagram on the CD-ROM.

PREPARATION
Write a list of questions on a board or flipchart:
● *Where would we build a new school wildlife pond?*
● *Where would we get the water to fill the pond?*
● *How could we prevent the pond from drying up or being flooded?*
● *How would we prevent the pond from being a hazard to children and wildlife?*

BACKGROUND
Only 2% of the world's water is fresh and can be used for human consumption. The vagaries of the climate mean that often there is too little or too much water in a region at any one time. Droughts and floods can be catastrophic in their effects, and are often reported in the news. This lesson introduces the idea of flood and drought in the context of a garden wildlife pond filled with rain-water.

Inevitably, the children will ask: 'Why doesn't the gardener just fill the pond with water from the tap?' The answer is linked to the concept of 'sustainable development'. There are two good reasons why the gardener should not fill the pond with tap water. Firstly, a huge amount of energy is expended in pumping water to different households. Much of that energy is produced in power stations that consume fossil fuels. The carbon dioxide emissions from burning these fuels contribute to global warming, and so to climate changes that are making droughts and floods more likely to occur. Secondly, 70% more water is used in our homes than was used 30 years ago. More water is being removed from rivers, threatening the wildlife habitats in the vicinity of the river.

Differentiation 💿
Group activity 1
Support children by giving them Changing water levels' (green) from the CD-ROM, which includes fewer questions than the core sheet.
Group activity 2
Extend children by asking them to look in secondary sources for ideas on pond design and construction.

STARTER

Ask the children questions to recap on some of the facts from Lesson 1, using the water cycle diagram. Then point to the area on the diagram where it is raining. Ask: *What would happen to the rivers, streams, lakes and ponds if it kept on raining?* (It would flood.) *And suppose that for some reason it didn't rain for several months. What would happen to the streams, rivers, ponds and lakes then?* (They would dry up.) Explain or confirm the meanings of the words *flood* and *drought.* Write both words on the board or flipchart.

MAIN ACTIVITY

Tell the children that they are going to look at a problem caused by flood and drought. Display the 'reader's letter' and the pond diagram from photocopiable page 134. Don't display the editor's reply: give the children a chance to solve the problem for themselves. Read the letter to the children and ask questions to check that they understand the problem. Then ask: *Why didn't the reader want to fill the pond with water from the tap?* You will need to explain that most tap water is taken out of rivers, streams, lakes and ponds and sent along pipes to our homes. *What will happen to the wildlife living in rivers, streams, ponds and lakes if we take too much water out of them?* (They will lose their habitat.)

Ask the children how they would solve the gardener's problem. At an appropriate moment, show them the editor's answer and read it to them. Cut and drag a hose to link the barrel overflow to the house drain. To check that the children understand the solution, ask: *What is a reservoir?* (A store of water.) *What happens when the reservoir is full?* (It will overflow into a drain.) *The editor has not said how to get the water from the barrel into the pond. How can this be done?* (Use the tap at the bottom of the barrel plus a bucket or pipe.)

Using the questions written on the board (see Preparation), discuss with the children how they would design a new school wildlife pond and where it should be built.

GROUP ACTIVITIES

1 Give the children a copy each of photocopiable page 134 and let them work through it individually.
2 The children can use the list of questions to design a new school wildlife pond.

ASSESSMENT

During the Plenary session, ask the children to explain the purpose of reservoirs and why they are needed.

PLENARY

Ask the children who completed Group activity 2 to show the class their findings. Encourage the class to evaluate the effectiveness of these.

OUTCOMES

- Can describe how the amount of water in a habitat varies.
- Can explain the purpose of reservoirs and why they are needed.

LINKS

Geography: natural and human features of a landscape.

Lesson 4 ▫ Floods and droughts

Objective
● To understand the catastrophic effects of flood and drought.

RESOURCES
The pond picture from Lesson 3; secondary sources (such as newspaper cuttings and magazine articles) on catastrophic floods and droughts; writing materials. Write a list of questions on the board or flipchart: 'Where did the catastrophe happen?', 'What caused it to happen?', 'How many people were affected?', 'What was being done to help the victims?', 'If possible, what might be done to prevent a similar catastrophe from happening?'

MAIN ACTIVITY
Using the pond picture from Lesson 3, remind the children how the gardener solved the problem of 'floods and droughts'. Point to the list of questions (see above). Reading from a secondary source, describe the catastrophic effects of an actual flood or drought. Discuss the answers to the displayed questions with the children.

Give the children copies of news reports or other secondary sources on floods and droughts. Ask them to use the displayed questions to help them write a short report on the flood or drought described earlier. They can also use secondary sources to find out about methods of flood prevention, such as the Thames Barrier, sea defences and flood plains.

ASSESSMENT
During the group work, ask the children to explain the meanings of 'flood' and 'drought'.

PLENARY
Ask some children to read out their reports of catastrophes and to share their information on methods of flood prevention.

Differentiation
Support children by giving them a focused resource sheet on a particular catastrophe to work from.

OUTCOME
● Understand some of the reasons for and effects of major floods and droughts.

Lesson 5 ▫ Top tips for saving water

Objective
● To know that we use a great amount of water and that water must be conserved.

Vocabulary
immersed, conserve, consume, production, recycle

RESOURCES 💿
Main activity: The water cycle and wildlife pond visual aids from Lessons 1 and 3; an A3 copy of photocopiable page 135 (or 'Top tips for saving water' (red) to display on an interactive whiteboard; an empty litre bottle; a 10-litre bucket.
Group activities: 1 Copies of photocopiable page 135 (also 'Top tips for saving water' (red); writing materials. **2** Paper; drawing and writing materials.

PREPARATION
Prepare two separate charts as shown in the Main activity.

BACKGROUND
The consumption of water per person in Britain has increased rapidly over the decades since the 1950s. All the water that we use is abstracted from river systems or artesian sources. Much of the abstracted water is stored temporarily in reservoirs. The children will probably not realise how much water we use (between 300 and 700 litres per family per day), and that water is used in the manufacture and maintenance of most of the products we rely upon.

Excessive abstraction from rivers has caused environmental problems in many parts of Britain. River flows have been reduced and water tables have been lowered. Wildlife habitats for species as diverse as fish, frogs, otters and dragonflies have been depleted. The extra demand for water has put pressure on sewage treatment facilities and has led, as a consequence, to increased river pollution. Finally, the increase in demand for water has meant the construction of additional reservoirs and pipelines, many of which have altered the character of existing natural areas.

STARTER
Ask the children: *Where does water from the tap come from?* Using the water cycle visual aid from Lesson 1, establish that our domestic water is rain-water which has been taken out of the water cycle, cleaned, and piped to our homes. *How do we make sure that we've got enough water to use even when it's not raining?* Use the visual aid of the pond and a barrel from Lesson 3 to establish that water has to be stored in reservoirs to ensure that we always have enough for our needs.

MAIN ACTIVITY
Tell the children that they are going to find out how much water they use at home. Display an empty litre bottle and a 10-litre bucket, both clearly marked with their capacity, to help them judge quantities. On the board or flipchart, display this list of water-consuming activities:

How much water do we use in:
A bowl of washing-up?
A bath?
A shower?
Washing hands in a sink?
A flush of the toilet?
A washing machine load?

The answers are: 10 litres, 70 litres, 30 litres, 3 litres, 10 litres, 90 litres. Write these on the board in order of increasing quantity. Ask the children to guess from this list how much water is used for each activity. Write the correct answer alongside each activity. Check that the children understand how many full buckets of water would be needed in each case.

Now say that lots of water is used to make other things. Display a second list:

How much water is used to:
make a car?
clean and prepare a frozen chicken?
make a kilogram of paper?
make a can of beer?

The answers are: 78,000 litres, 26 litres, 250 litres and 10 litres. Display these in order of increasing quantity. Before asking the children to guess the volume of water used in each product, give them a simple indication of how water is used in the production:

Car: Water is an ingredient in the paint on a car, and used to cool and clean the metal, glass and plastic from which the car is made.
Frozen chicken: Dead chickens are immersed in boiling water to loosen their feathers, and their meat is cleaned with water before they are frozen.
Paper: The tiny particles that make paper are floated and kept separate by water until the paper is made.
Beer: Barley and hops are mixed with water, cooked, and fermented with yeast to make beer.

Differentiation
Group activity 1
To support children, give them 'Top tips for saving water' (green), which includes fewer examples of water use than the core sheet. To extend children, give them 'Top tips for saving water' (blue), which asks them to explain how water is wasted as well as how it can be saved.

Explain to the children that we are using more water than ever before. *Where are we going to get the extra water from?* Elicit the answer that more water will have to be taken from rivers, and more reservoirs will have to be built. Stress the environmental consequences of this (see Background). Say that everyone needs to reduce their water consumption. Explain that car and paper manufacturers now have to recycle their water and use it again and again.

Show the children an enlarged version of page 135. Look at each activity in turn and discuss ways in which water is wasted. Ask the children to suggest ways of saving water. Write a couple of answers in the appropriate cells of the table as an example for those children who attempt Group activity 1. When you have discussed each water-saving idea with the children, ask them to suggest three ideas that they could implement at home. Ask them how they could persuade other members of their family to save water.

GROUP ACTIVITIES
1 Give the children a copy each of photocopiable page 135 and ask them to complete it individually.
2 The children can design a poster (to display in school) that presents two or three good ideas for saving water.

ASSESSMENT
During the Plenary, ask the children to identify things at home that use a lot of water. Ask them why we need to save water.

PLENARY
Ask the children to tell you which they think is the most wasteful activity listed on the photocopiable sheet. Ask for their reasons. Look at the posters from Group activity 2. Ask the children how effective these posters are at suggesting water-saving ideas and at explaining why we should conserve water.

OUTCOMES
● Recognise some activities that require a great amount of water.
● Can explain the need for water conservation.
● Can describe simple ways in which we can conserve water.

LINKS
PSHE: care of the local and wider environment.

Lesson 6 ▪ A frog's guide to ponds

Objective
● To know that water can be polluted by waste from human activities.

Vocabulary
pollution, polluted, algae, conditions, discarded, sewage, sludge worm, rat-tailed maggot, water louse, caddis fly larva, dragonfly nymph

RESOURCES
Main activity: An A3 copy of photocopiable page 136 (also 'A frog's guide to ponds' (red) available on the CD-ROM); the table from page 127 copied onto a flipchart; large piece of paper or displayed on an interactive whiteboard using the diagram 'Pond life' from the CD-ROM.
Group activities: 1 Copies of the table on page 127; writing materials. **2** Copies of photocopiable page 136 (also 'A frog's guide to ponds' (red) available on the CD-ROM); paper; glue; scissors; writing materials.
ICT link: 'A frog's guide to ponds' interactive and 'Pond life' diagram on the CD-ROM.

PREPARATION
Prepare the visual aids and sheets needed.

Differentiation

BACKGROUND

Even though fresh water resources are limited, human development has damaged much of this precious and vital resource. Many areas of waterway in Britain have been polluted by industrial and agricultural activity. The problem has often been compounded by ignorance and neglect. Organisations such as the National Rivers Authority have begun to make some improvement. They have successfully prosecuted industries and farmers who have failed to take proper action to prevent pollution, and have enforced compliance with 'anti-pollution' regulations.

Simple biological indicators, such as those described on photocopiable page 136, can be used to determine the existence of pollution. Water containing a wide range of species is likely to be less polluted than water that carries a concentration of a narrow range of species.

STARTER

Remind the children of the main points of the previous lessons: water is essential for our survival; fresh water resources are limited; we need to conserve water as the demand for it increases.

MAIN ACTIVITY

Tell the children that even though water is precious, human activity has been spoiling the resource. Ask them whether they know a word that describes dirty water (Pollution). Ask them whether they have seen or know of any polluted areas of water. Discuss their observations and knowledge. Show the children the enlarged version of photocopiable page 136 and read through the 'Frog's guide to ponds' with them.

Show the children a large copy of the table below. Using the information in the 'Frog's guide', show the children how the empty cells can be filled. For example, ask: *What did the frog say the water looked like in very polluted conditions?* (Lots of human litter and waste; liquids and junk from factories.) *What is living in very polluted water?* (Nothing.)

GROUP ACTIVITIES

1 Give the children a copy each of the 'Is there pollution?' table and photocopiable page 136. Ask them to use the information on the sheet to complete the table.
2 Ask the children to complete the questions on the photocopiable sheet using scissors, paper and glue.

ICT LINK

Use 'A frog's guides to ponds interactive, on the CD-ROM, as part of the Plenary.

ASSESSMENT

During the Plenary session, ask the children how they would find out whether a pond or stream was polluted. Ask them to tell you some of the main causes of pollution. (Industry, farming, sewage and thoughtless humans.)

PLENARY

This session is a particularly important part of this lesson. Write the main causes of pollution on a board or flipchart: 'industry', 'farming', 'sewage' and 'thoughtless humans'. Ask the children what they would do to prevent pollution by each of these causes. Listen to the children's suggestions; then inform them that there are laws to prevent water pollution, and that these are gradually being enforced.

Ask the children what equipment they would need to check on water pollution in a local stream or pond. Ask them why they think the rat-tailed maggot has a strange tube extending from its nose.

Is there pollution?		
Clean or polluted?	What the water looks like	What is living in the water
Very polluted		
Polluted with algae		
Polluted with sewage		
A little pollution		
No pollution		

(This is a natural snorkel to breathe in air from the surface, as the creature lives in stagnant, oxygen-starved water.)

OUTCOMES
- Can identify sources of water pollution.
- Know how water pollution can be assessed using biological indicators.
- Know some of the effects of water pollution.
- Know some ways to reduce water pollution.

LINKS
PSHE: care of the local and wider environment.

Lesson 7 ▪ A pond survey

Objective
- To use pollution indicators to monitor a local pond or stream.

RESOURCES
An enlarged, filled-in 'Is there pollution?' table from Lesson 6; pond-dipping nets; hand lenses; white plastic trays; copies of photocopiable page 137 (also 'A pond survey' (red) available on the CD-ROM); clipboards; pencils. You will need a safe, accessible area of local waterway, with no deep water, for a 'pond-dipping' lesson. Check with your school or LEA policy on out-of-school visits; organise appropriate supervision, first aid and so on. Inform parents and carers of the arrangements and purpose of the visit. Ensure that the children are appropriately dressed for the activity.

MAIN ACTIVITY
Tell the children they are going to investigate an area of local water for pollution. Use an enlarged, filled-in table from Lesson 6 to discuss the indicators they should look for.

Demonstrate how to use the pond-dipping nets safely and effectively. The children should work in pairs for safety and practical effectiveness. There are usually three ways of catching a representative selection of water life: a slow horizontal sweep near the surface; a vertical sweep up the stems of water plants; a very slow sweep along the bottom of the waterway.

Encourage the children to use all three methods. After each sweep, the net should be carefully emptied into a tray part-filled with stream or pond water. After observation and monitoring, the water creatures should be carefully returned to their environment. Show the children how to complete photocopiable page 137, and carry out the visit to a pond or stream.

ASSESSMENT
On return to school, ask the children to explain the purpose of the two sections of the photocopiable sheet.

Differentiation 💿
Support children by giving the, 'A pond survey' (green) from the CD-ROM, a simplified version of the core sheet, with illustrations. To extend children, give them 'A pond survey' (blue), which omits the prompts for activity 2.

PLENARY
Ask the children for their assessment of the water quality, and the reasons for their decision. If the water is polluted, plan the action that you and the children will take to inform the appropriate local authority.

OUTCOME
- Can assess water quality in the local environment.

Lesson 8 ▸ Air pollution

RESOURCES

Main activity: Three visual aids (see Preparation); marker pens; a bucket and spade; a globe; a pair of swimming armbands.
Group activities: 1 and **2** Paper; writing and drawing materials.
ICT link: 'Buildings', 'Forest' and 'Island diagrams from the CD-ROM.

PREPARATION

Draw the three diagrams shown below and on the following page on large pieces of paper or flipchart pages. Alternatively, display 'Buildings', 'Forest' and 'Island diagrams from the CD-ROM on an interactive whiteboard.

BACKGROUND

There is now agreement among world scientists that climate changes are taking place due to global warming. 'Greenhouse' gases are trapping larger amounts of infra-red radiation from the Sun, warming the surface and atmosphere of the Earth. The three main 'greenhouse gases' are carbon dioxide, methane, and nitrous oxide. Carbon dioxide is the least potent of these, but by far the most abundant. The increased levels of carbon dioxide in the atmosphere are due to the burning of fossil fuels (coal, gas and oil). In Britain, fossil fuels are consumed by homes, vehicles, factories and power stations.

It is certain that one of the effects of climate change is a rise in sea level. This is due to the expansion of sea water as its temperature increases, and to the melting of some polar ice. Some islands and low-lying countries are already threatened by the rise in sea level. Parts of eastern Britain are likely to be affected too.

The burning of fossil fuels and emissions of sulphur dioxide pollution have caused acid rain locally and in nearby Scandinavian countries. Lakes and forest soils have undergone an increase in acidic conditions, with the result that many fish and trees have died.

This lesson establishes a clear chain of events between the creation of air pollution and damage to both the regional and the global environment.

STARTER

Ask the children to tell you some of the causes of water pollution mentioned in Lesson 6. (Sewage, fertiliser from farms, industrial pollution and human carelessness.) Explain that you are going to show them how we are all accidentally polluting the air and damaging the habitats of other people and animals.

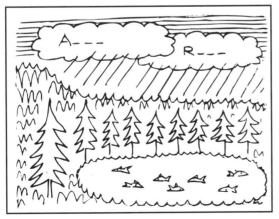

MAIN ACTIVITY

Show the children your first visual aid: a simple drawing of a house, power station, vehicles and factory (see left, or 'Buildings' diagram on the CD-ROM). Ask the children to tell you where air pollution might come from in this picture. Draw black clouds rising from the house chimney, power station, factory flues and vehicle exhaust as the children indicate these sources of air pollution.

Ask the children whether they have ever caused unnecessary air pollution. *Do you ever leave the TV on when you are not watching it? Do you ever leave a light on in an empty room? Do you ever leave the door open when the heating is on? Do you ever ask a parent to drive you*

somewhere when it would be easy to walk there?

Most children will admit to these 'errors'. Choose a child with a good sense of humour. Ask this 'unfortunate child' to come to the front of the class, and say that you are going to act the part of a very angry teacher. Now overact! Explain that wasting electricity or heat, or making unnecessary car journeys, adds to air pollution. Tell the child that you are very angry because he or she has caused extra air pollution (point to the black clouds on the visual aid.)

Show the children a second visual aid: a simple drawing of a lake and wood beneath a black rain cloud, with the initials 'AR' on the cloud. Ask: *Has anyone heard the name for rain that has been spoiled by pollution?* Elicit the answer: 'Acid rain'. The children may not have heard of it before because we don't get acid rain in this country. Explain that the pollution from our country causes acid rain, which kills trees and poisons fish, in other countries. Tell the 'unfortunate child': *Leaving a TV on without watching it helps to cause more acid rain.* Explain why this is.

Still in role, tell the child that you are so angry with him or her for causing air pollution that you are going to send him or her to a desert island.

Reveal the third visual aid: a child with bucket and spade, standing on a desert island. The sun is shining, but a single black cloud of pollution (with the initials GW) is in the sky. Give the child a bucket and spade to hold. Say that air pollution causes another problem. Point to the cloud and the initials. Tell all the children that air pollution is making the whole world warmer. *Has anyone ever heard of the name of this problem?* (Global warming.)

Pick up a globe and point to the North and South Poles. *What is it like at the North and South Pole?* Establish that there is ice there. *What will happen to the ice as the world gets warmer?* Establish that the ice will melt and the water will go into the sea. Now point to the visual aid and ask: *What will happen to the water around the island if the ice at the North and South Poles is melting?* On the visual aid, draw a deepening sea that gradually covers the island and the child. Turn to the 'unfortunate child' and take away the bucket and spade. Explain that because he caused unnecessary air pollution, he won't need a bucket and spade any more. Give the child a pair of swimming goggles and ask him to 'swim' back to his seat.

Go through the chain of events again to remind the children that wasting heat and electricity and burning fuels can cause air pollution, which in turn causes acid rain and global warming. Remind the children that global warming is not a joke. Some children who live in flat countries close to the sea, such as Bangladesh, already know that the sea level is rising: their land is often flooded by the sea.

On the board or flipchart, list the children's ideas for ways to reduce air pollution. The list should include ways of reducing electricity consumption, conserving heat in buildings, reducing car use and producing power by sustainable means (such as solar energy).

GROUP ACTIVITIES

1 Ask the children to make their own copies of the visual aids, then add stick characters and speech bubbles to create a comic strip explaining the effects of air pollution.
2 The children can make a poster to encourage people to reduce air pollution.

ASSESSMENT

At the start of the Plenary session, ask the children to list some of the activities that produce air pollution and explain the damage that is caused.

Differentiation
Both Group activities are differentiated by outcome.

PLENARY

Warn the children that there is evidence that polar ice is melting, and that our weather is gradually changing. Discuss their ideas for reducing air pollution. Ask them whether they have any ideas that could be implemented in the classroom.

OUTCOMES

- Recognise some activities that cause air pollution.
- Can describe some effects of air pollution on the environment.
- Can describe some ways in which air pollution can be reduced.

LINKS

Chapter 2, Unit 5b, Lesson 20, Song thrush survival.
PSHE: responsibility for the environment.

Lesson 9 ▪ A fisherman's tale

Objectives
- To know that human activities are affecting fish stocks.
- To understand why an indigenous fish species is in danger of extinction.
- To know that fish stocks need to be conserved if species are to survive.

Vocabulary
salmon, fish farm, fish stocks, sand eel

Salmon life cycle	Problems
Eggs are laid in patches of gravel	
Small fish live in a river	
Young fish migrate to the sea	
Fish growing in the sea	

RESOURCES

Main activity: One copy per pair of photocopiable page 138 (also 'A fisherman's tale' (red) available on the CD-ROM); an A3 copy of photocopiable page 138; a copy of the chart shown below (see Preparation); a highlighter.
Group activities: 1 and **2** Writing materials; paper.

PREPARATION

Practise reading the play 'A Fisherman's Tale' on photocopiable page 138 with a confident child or adult. Copy the chart shown below onto a large sheet of paper or a flipchart.

BACKGROUND

The North Atlantic Wild Salmon is in danger of extinction. A huge decline in its population occurred at the end of the 20th century. At least four factors are thought to have contributed to this decline:

1. Pollution of streams and rivers by agricultural, industrial and social waste.
2. Diseases contracted by the wild fish from their proximity to populations of fish-farmed salmon. Large numbers of the latter are reared intensively. They are prone to infectious and parasitic diseases.
3. Global warming is believed to be affecting the food chain of the wild salmon. While at sea, salmon feed on species that thrive in cold Arctic water.
4. Intensive 'forage farming' of fish species that are part of the salmon's food chain. Huge quantities of sand eels and other species are dredged from the floor of the ocean. They are dried, then used as 'fishmeal' in poultry and pig feeds, as pellets to feed farmed fish, as fertiliser, and as a fuel for power stations in some countries (such as Denmark).

The North Atlantic Salmon Conservation Plan is a project of detailed research into the plight of the fish, particularly their life at sea. Currently, a 'catch and release' policy is advocated for fishermen who catch the species. Releasing caught fish will prevent further depletion by fishing, and might allow the remaining salmon to spawn.

There are good reasons for the conservation of salmon stocks. The large tourist industry in Scotland and Ireland is partly dependent on salmon fishing. Also, the salmon possesses behavioural skills that are only partially understood, such as the ability to return to the river where it spent its infancy.

Differentiation

Group activity 1
Children who have difficulty writing a playscript could record their play on a cassette recorder.

Group activity 2
The problems facing the salmon are highlighted in bold text in the play. Children could cut out the bold sections of text from an enlarged version of page 138 and paste them into a copy of the table.

STARTER

Remind the children of the lessons in this unit that involved water pollution and global warming. Help them to remember the causes of both problems. Water pollution is caused by agricultural, industrial, and social waste. Global warming is caused by the burning of fossil fuels in homes, industries, vehicles and power stations.

MAIN ACTIVITY

Tell the children that they are going to learn about the danger of extinction facing a famous fish, the wild salmon. Explain that this fish used to be common in most rivers in Britain.

Give each pair of children a copy of photocopiable page 138. Read the play aloud, with you and a confident child or another adult reading the two parts. Ask questions to make sure the children understand the text. Now display an enlarged version of the play. Ask the children to help you highlight words that give information about the life cycle of the salmon. Use a highlighter for this. Highlight phrases such as 'eight thousand eggs', 'patches of gravel' and 'the place where I hatched'. When all the appropriate phrases are highlighted, use them to discuss the life cycle of the wild salmon.

Show the children the flipchart or large sheet of paper marked with the table on the previous page. Ask them to tell you what problems human beings have caused for each stage of the wild salmon's life cycle. Discuss each stage of the development of the fish, but only fill in a couple of cells in the table as examples.

Finally, inform the children that in order to help the wild salmon increase in numbers, fishermen who catch them are being asked to release them again.

GROUP ACTIVITIES

1 Ask the children to write a second short play, presenting a conversation between the fisherman and a friend when they meet at their holiday hotel later that day.
2 Ask the children to copy and fill in the table, using information from the play.

ASSESSMENT

In the Plenary session, ask the class to explain the problems facing salmon at different stages of their life cycle.

PLENARY

The class could listen to some of the plays written by the children. Finally, discuss how the children think wild salmon could be conserved. This is an important part of this lesson.

OUTCOMES

● Understand how human activities reduce fish stocks.
● Know the life cycle of an important indigenous fish species and understand some of the problems facing it.
● Can suggest some ways in which fish stocks can be conserved.

LINKS

PSHE: care of other living things.
Geography: rivers, seas and migration routes.

Lesson 10 ▪ Assessment

Objectives
● To assess the children's knowledge of the water cycle and where water appears in the environment.
● To assess the children's knowledge of the effects of human activity on the quality and distribution of water in the environment.

RESOURCES
Photocopiable pages 139 and 140 (also 'Assessment – 1' (red) and 'Assessment – 2' (red) available on the CD-ROM); writing materials.

STARTER
Start with a 'warm-up' of oral questions on the content of Lesson 9 (the demise of the wild salmon).

ASSESSMENT ACTIVITY 1
Give the children a copy each of page 139 and let them complete the sheet individually.

ANSWERS
A: 1. evaporates; 2. water vapour; 3. condense; 4. rain/snow; 5. rivers and streams; 6. sea.
D: Sentences that imply: clean water fit for drinking is a precious commodity; excessive extraction from rivers and streams is causing environmental damage; increased demand leads to increased sewage and pollution; building extra reservoirs damages the appearance of a landscape.

LOOKING FOR LEVELS
All the children should be able to complete parts A and B. Most children should be able to complete the rest of the sheet. The most able children will provide cogent answers to part D.

ASSESSMENT ACTIVITY 2
Give the children a copy each of page 140 and let them complete the sheet individually.

ANSWERS
A: 1. with water; 2. covered with ice or desert; 3. a small fraction of the Earth's surface.
B: Accept sentences that imply two of the following: humans pollute water through waste that emerges from factories; through excessive use of fertilisers by farmers; through sewage that enters the water.
C. A sensible order is as follows: I switch on the light in my bedroom; The electricity that makes my light work comes from a power station; Most power stations make electricity by burning coal, oil or gas; The pollution from the power station helps to cause global warming; Ice at the North and South Poles melts; The seas and oceans are deeper; Low countries such as Bangladesh are flooded.

LOOKING FOR LEVELS
This assessment sheet is more demanding than the first. All children should be able to attempt part A. Most children should be able to complete the rest of the sheet. The most able children will probably provide the most cogent answers to parts A and B.

PLENARY
The answers to both sheets should be discussed. Page 139 could be marked with the children at the end of the session. A discussion about the range of acceptable answers to both sheets will be an informative process for the teacher and the children. Children may argue cogently that there is more than one sensible order for the sentences in part C of page 140.

Changing water levels

Dear Editor,

Can you help me please? Last year I built a wildlife pond in my garden. I fill the pond with rainwater collected from the roof of my house. I want to encourage birds, frogs and other creatures into my garden to eat the slugs and snails that damage my plants. Sadly am I having some problems with my pond. Sometimes in winter, we get too much rain and my pond gets flooded with water. In summer, the sun evaporates lots of water from my pond and it occasionally dries up. I don't want to fill my pond with water from the tap, because I know I would be damaging the environment. Here is a diagram of my pond. - A Gardener

Dear Reader,

We think the solution to your problem is to make a reservoir where you can store water when you have enough in your pond. Then, when your pond is in danger of drying up, you can fill it with water from your reservoir. We suggest you get a large barrel and direct the water from the roof of the house into it. When the barrel is full, you can divert extra water into the drains. – Editor

Cut out the pond diagram and stick it on a separate sheet. Cut out the barrel and glue it onto the pond picture where it can become a reservoir. Then, beneath your diagram, write sentences to answer these questions:

◼ Why did the reader want a wildlife pond in the garden?

◼ Where did the water come from to fill the pond?

◼ What was the problem with the pond in winter?

◼ Why did the pond sometimes dry up in summer?

◼ Why didn't the reader want to fill the pond with water from the tap?

◼ What is a 'reservoir'?

◼ What happens when the reservoir is full?

◼ The editor has not told the reader how to move the water from the barrel into the pond. How could this happen?

◼ SCHOLASTIC

Top tips for saving water

■ Fill in the missing spaces in this table.

Water that is used by everyone	How to waste water	How to save or conserve water
Cleaning your teeth	Leave the tap running while you brush your teeth.	
Washing your hands	Leave the tap running while you wash your hands.	
Making a really cold drink	Run the cold tap until the water feels really cold.	
Making a hot drink	Fill the kettle right to the top.	

Here are some more ways that water can be wasted:

Water used mainly by adults	How to waste water	How to save or conserve water
Washing vegetables	Leave the tap running as you wash the vegetables.	
Washing a car	Use a hosepipe to rinse the car.	
Washing clothes in a washing machine	Wash clothes every day, even if the machine is not full.	
Watering the garden	Use a hosepipe or a sprinkler.	

Which of these activities do you think would waste the most water?

Illustration © Robin Lawrie

PHOTOCOPIABLE

A frog's guide to ponds

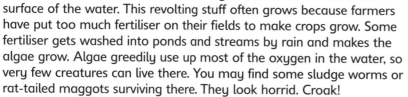

I spend a lot of time hopping around the neighbourhood. I know a lot about the local ponds, lakes, streams and canals. Croak!

The worst places for frogs to visit are waters that are full of human litter and waste. They often stink from liquids and junk that has been discarded by factories. Nothing can live in polluted places like that. It's a dead area that needs cleaning up! Croak!

Some ponds and rivers I visit look green and inviting from a distance. However, when you get close to them, they are polluted too. The colour is caused by green or blue algae that float like scum on the surface of the water. This revolting stuff often grows because farmers have put too much fertiliser on their fields to make crops grow. Some fertiliser gets washed into ponds and streams by rain and makes the algae grow. Algae greedily use up most of the oxygen in the water, so very few creatures can live there. You may find some sludge worms or rat-tailed maggots surviving there. They look horrid. Croak!

Sometimes I come across streams that are polluted with sewage. One creature that seems to enjoy crawling around in this stuff is the water louse. It seems to love feeding on rotting waste. If I see lots of these creatures but very few others, I keep well away. It probably means there's sewage in the water, and that can make you ill. Croak!

I do visit some ponds and streams that are a little polluted. They have lots of wildlife. As well as water lice munching up the waste, there will be the hunchbacked freshwater shrimps eating decaying water plants. Hiding on the bottom, you'll also find caddis fly larvae. These small creatures hide in a tube that they've made out of sticks or sand. They eat tiny water creatures that crawl or get washed into their tube. Croak!

The best and cleanest ponds contain all of these creatures: worms, lice, maggots, shrimps and caddis fly larvae. They also contain the enemies I had as a tadpole. At that time, I had to keep clear of the jaws of the dragonfly nymph. It's a ferocious hunter. Unfortunately, it likes the same clean unpolluted habitats as frogs do. Croak!

Caddis fly larva

Fresh water shrimp

Water louse

Rat-tailed maggot

Sludge worm

Dragonfly nymph

🖥 On a separate sheet, write the answers to these questions in sentences. Cut out or copy the pictures of the water creatures and put each one alongside a suitable answer.

1. What lives in the dirtiest, most polluted water?
2. What makes the blue and green algae grow?
3. When algae grow, how do they spoil and pollute the water?
4. If there are lots of water lice but few other creatures in the water, what might you suspect is happening?
5. Which two creatures would you expect to find in fairly clean water?
6. What would be the condition of the water if you found dragonfly nymphs and lots of other creatures living there?

Illustration © Robin Lawrie

A pond survey

Activity 1: Pond-dipping

◼ Carefully collect in your tray a sample of the wildlife living in the pond.

◼ Look at the sample carefully, then tick the correct boxes.

Creature	0–5 (write the number)	5–20 (tick the box)	More than 20 (tick the box)
Worm			
Rat-tailed maggot			
Water louse			
Freshwater shrimp			
Caddis fly larva			
Dragonfly nymph			
Other creature			
Other creature			

Activity 2: Evidence of pollution

◼ Look and listen around the area. Write in the table any evidence that will help you to decide whether the water is polluted.

Evidence of:	What did you see or hear?
1. Litter	
2. Insects Flies Butterflies and moths Dragonflies Others	
3. Birds and mammals Signs (tracks, droppings, feathers)	

When you have completed both activities, discuss this question with your partner: 'Is this water polluted?'

Very polluted	Polluted	A little polluted	Not polluted

If the water is polluted, write what you can do to improve it. If the water is not polluted, write how you can make sure it stays that way.

Illustration © Robin Lawrie

PHOTOCOPIABLE

A fisherman's tale (a play for two people)

A fisherman is alone on holiday, fishing from the bank of a clean river. Suddenly the fishing line goes tight. After a long struggle, a huge salmon is pulled to the side of the river. The hook is taken from the mouth of the exhausted fish, which is dropped into a large net.

Fisherman What a brilliant fish. The largest I've ever caught! I've been trying to catch wild salmon for weeks! (Pause as he admires the fish.)

Salmon (Puffing and panting.) I've got eight thousand eggs inside me. If you kill me, you'll be killing all my babies too (Pause). Let me go!

Fisherman A talking fish – I don't believe it!

Salmon (Gradually puffing less). I was going back to the place where I hatched, to lay my eggs. Stupidly, I ate your fly and you caught me. Wild salmon like us are becoming extinct. Let me go!

Fisherman Why are you becoming extinct?

Salmon Many of the rivers where we lay our eggs have been **polluted**. Young salmon can only live in clean water where there are lots of insects, such as dragonfly nymphs, to feed on. You humans have allowed **sewage**, **fertilisers** and **rubbish** to pollute so many rivers. Please let me go!

Fisherman This river isn't polluted. You can lay lots of eggs. Why aren't there lots of salmon living here?

Salmon After the eggs hatch out we live in clean rivers like this for about six years. Then, we swim down the river to the sea. Let me go!

Fisherman You live in fresh water and in sea water? That's clever. I didn't know that.

Salmon We swim down to the sea, past the places where you keep large numbers of our cousins, the farmed salmon, inside prisons. We wild salmon try to keep well away from those poor creatures. The water around them is full of water lice and diseases that can kill us. Let me go!

Fisherman So lots of wild salmon die from the **diseases** and **pests** which they catch as they pass the fish farms? Is that why you're becoming extinct?

Salmon Partly yes, but there are other problems for us out at sea (Pause). While living in the sea, we have to eat sand eels and other tiny sea fish. These fish live in the colder parts of the sea. The sea has been getting a little warmer lately. These little fish don't like the new conditions. Let me go!

Fisherman Global warming is heating the seas. I knew that but I didn't know it affected fish too.

Salmon Well, it does (Pause) and there's another problem with our food supply. Lots of **fishing boats** catch sand eels and tiny fish. Sometimes these fishing boats scoop up wild salmon too! What do you humans want those tiny fish for? They're our food!

Fisherman Fisherman catch tiny fish, dry them and feed some of the bits to chickens and pigs. Other bits are fed to the salmon in the fish farms and some is burned in things we call 'power stations' to make electricity.

Salmon What a stupid waste! Can't they feed the pigs and chickens other stuff? Can't they make electricity in other ways? It's our food they're catching. We will become extinct! Let me go!

Fisherman You really do have a lot of problems! **Water pollution**, **fish farming**, **global warming**, **fishermen scooping up tons of sand eels and tiny fish**... (Pause while the fisherman thinks). I'd better put you back in the river or there will be no more wild salmon to catch.

Salmon (As it is gently tipped from the net into the river). Thanks! I wish more people would listen like you.

Fisherman Good luck! I'm going back to the hotel to tell other fishermen about your problems.

Illustration © Robin Lawrie

■SCHOLASTIC

Assessment – 1

A. Use these words to complete the sentences below:

> sea   rivers and streams   rain and snow   water vapour
> condense   evaporates

1. The heat of the sun _____ water from the sea.

2. Air over the sea moves _____ over the land.

3. Some of the water vapour in the air begins to _____ into clouds.

4. _____ falls to the ground.

5. Water runs into _____.

6. Eventually the water finds its way back to the _____.

B. Label this diagram of the water cycle with the numbers of the sentences in part A.

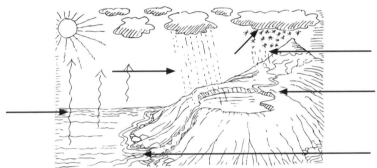

C. Fill in this table by writing ways that we can waste or conserve water.

	How to waste water	How to save or conserve water
Cleaning teeth		
Washing hands		
Washing a car		

D. Write down two good reasons why we should try to conserve water.

_____

_____

PHOTOCOPIABLE

Assessment – 2

A. Look at these facts about the Earth's surface:

Fraction of the Earth's surface that is covered by water	71%
Fraction of the Earth's surface that is covered by ice	3%
Fraction of the Earth's surface that is desert (very little water)	10%
Fraction of the Earth's surface that nearly all humans live on	16%

Use the table to complete these sentences:

1. Most of the surface of the Earth is covered _____

2. A lot of the land is difficult for humans to live on because it is _____

_____

3. Humans have to live on _____

B. Explain, using sentences, two ways in which humans pollute water apart from litter and rubbish.

_____

_____

C. Here are seven sentences that describe how switching on an electric light can help to cause flooding in Bangladesh. Write these sentences in a sensible order.

Ice at the North and South Poles melts.
I switch on a light in my bedroom.
Low countries such as Bangladesh are flooded.
The electricity that makes my light work comes from a power station.
The pollution from the power station helps to cause global warming.
The seas and oceans become deeper.
Most power stations make electricity by burning coal, oil or gas.

_____

_____

_____

_____

_____

_____

_____

Illustration © Robin Lawrie

📖 **SCHOLASTIC**

CHAPTER 6   Earth, Sun and Moon

Lesson	Objectives	Main activity	Group activities	Plenary	Outcomes
Lesson 1 Round Earth or flat Earth?	• To know that the Sun, Earth and Moon are approximately spherical. • To know that sometimes the evidence for an idea is indirect.	Model the indirect evidence for a flat Earth and a round Earth. Discuss the difference between direct and indirect evidence.	Decide what an observer would see in 'flat Earth' and 'round Earth' situations. Write a news report about the discovery that the Earth is round.	Review the shape of the Earth. Look at photographs of the Earth, Moon and Sun from space. Discuss the shape of the Moon and Sun.	• Know that the Sun, Earth and Moon are approximately spherical. • Can use indirect evidence to draw scientific conclusions.
Lesson 2 Raising questions	• To elicit children's existing ideas about Earth and space. To stimulate question-raising.	Brainstorming 'things we know' and 'things we want to know' about Earth and space.	Modelling the Earth, Sun and Moon in Plasticine.	Considering how the questions raised could be answered.	• Have elicited existing ideas. • Can raise questions.
Lesson 3 Sizes and distances	• To know the relative sizes of the Sun, Earth and Moon. • To know the relative distances of the Moon and Sun from the Earth.	Compare relative sizes and distances, using near and far objects. The children model the positions of the Earth, Sun and Moon.		Decide where to place cardboard models of the Earth, Moon and Sun to represent the relative distances.	• Can describe the differences in size between the three bodies. • Can compare the distances between the three bodies.
Lesson 4 Directions	• To know that directions can be found using a compass. • To be able to use a compass to find north, south, east, west, and midpoints between them, for example north east.	Explaining the four points of the compass and how to use a compass.	Using compasses to identify directions in the playground and recording features observed there.	Feedback of observations.	• Can use a compass to find the different directions on the ground.
Lesson 5 The Sun in the sky	• To track the apparent movement of the Sun across the sky during the day. • To relate this movement to the points of the compass. • To carry out systematic observations over a period of time.	Recording the apparent movement of the Sun using a shadow stick.		Interpreting results, including discussing how it seems like the Sun is moving, but actually it is the Earth.	• Can recognise that the Sun appears to move across the sky during the day. • Can explain that the Sun rises in the east, travels across the sky and sets in the west.
Lesson 6 Day and night	• To use scientific knowledge to explain observations. To know that the Sun's apparent movement across the sky is caused by the Earth spinning on its own axis. • To know that the Sun appears to rise in an easterly direction and set in a westerly direction. • To identify patterns of change in sunrise and sunset through the year.	Model how day and night are caused. Repeat with a torch and globe. Discuss how the amount of daylight varies throughout the year.	Plot graphs of the sunrise and sunset times throughout the year. Complete a 'day and night' crossword.	Summarise how day-length changes through the year. Use a torch and globe to show that this is due to the Earth tilting.	• Can describe how the Sun's path in the sky changes through the year. • Can explain that the spin of the Earth makes the Sun appear to move across the sky. • Can explain how day and night occur. • Can draw line graphs and use them to identify patterns.
Enrichment Lesson 7 Planet days	• To know that other planets have different day-lengths from Earth. • To think logically about causes and effects.	Discuss the scientific meaning of 'day'. Look at the length of a day on different planets. Imagine living on a planet with a different day-length pattern.		Discuss the children's stories. Talk about artificial 'day' and 'night' on space stations.	• Understand that other planets may have a different day-length from Earth. • Can deduce the effect that time of rotation has on day-length.
Enrichment Lesson 8 Shadows	• To know that the Sun's rays may be slanting at different angles. • To investigate how shadows change when the angle of the Sun changes. • To identify relevant variables.	Identifying variables for an investigation into the effect of changing the angle of the light source on the shadows produced.	Carrying out investigations as planned.	Discuss how the angle of the torch affects the length of the shadow and relate back to shadows in the playground.	• Can explain that the Sun's rays slant at different angles. • Can recognise how shadows change when the angle of the light source changes. • Can identify and control relevant variables.

Lesson	Objectives	Main activity	Group activities	Plenary	Outcomes
Enrichment Lesson 9 The angle of the Sun	• To know that the way the Sun heats the Earth depends on the slant of the Sun's rays. • To measure temperature.	Demonstration of how changing the angle of the light source affects how 'spread out' the spot of light is.	Measuring the temperature under the light source at different angles. Pictures to represent the seasons.	Discussion relating the angle of the Sun to the seasons of the year.	• Can recognise that the Sun's rays may slant at an angle and that this affects the temperature of the Earth. • Can measure temperature.
Enrichment Lesson 10 Star light	• To know that stars are sources of light.	Representing constellations by holes punched in black paper.		Discussion about what stars are like	• Can recognise that stars are sources of light. • Can explain that some stars are easier to see because they are bigger.
Enrichment Lesson 11 Star patterns	• To know that groups of stars are constellations. • To be able to identify some constellations.	Looking at pictures of constellations and naming them.		Discussing the real names and sharing 'better' names.	• Can explain what a constellation is. • Can recognise some constellations.
Enrichment Lesson 12 The Earth and time	• To know that the time on a clock varies around the world. • To know that some units of time are linked to the motion of the Earth, and some are artificial.	*Discuss the meanings of 'time' words. Look at how time zones are related to the rotation of the Earth. Divide 'time' words into 'natural' and 'artificial'.		*Discuss how time zones affect travellers. *Check the children understand that changing 'artificial' time units would have no effect on what we observe.	• Can distinguish between 'natural' times and 'artificial' times. • Can use a globe to model the movement of the Earth.
Lesson 13 The seasons	• To know that the Earth travels in an orbit around the Sun once a year, and this causes the seasons we experience.	Model the Earth's orbit around the Sun. Work out which regions are hot and which are cold. Discuss the orbits of other bodies.	Answer questions about the causes of summer and winter. Make information cards on heavenly bodies.	Children present their information cards. Discuss the effects of the Earth's axis if it horizontal or vertical.	• Can describe the orbit of the Earth. • Know that the cycle of seasons is evidence that the Earth orbits the Sun.
Enrichment Lesson 14 The Earth's tilt	• To know that the pattern of seasons is related to the Earth's tilt and its orbit around the Sun.	Discuss the effect on seasons if the Earth's axis were horizontal and research what animals live in these conditions.		Children share what they have found out about animals. Recap on how our seasons are caused.	• Understand that if the tilt of the Earth were different, the pattern of seasons would also be different.
Enrichment Lesson 15 Solar eclipse	• To know that an object moving in front of a light produces a shadow. • To know that a solar eclipse is a shadow caused by the Moon. • To know that the Earth turning makes the shadow seem to move.	Model a solar eclipse allowing the children to observe the shadow created when the 'moon' passes across the 'sun'.	Imagine they have seen a real eclipse. Write a postcard to a friend, describing what watching the eclipse was like.	Draw a shadow on a globe/world map and ask the children to identify where people who could see the eclipse would be living.	• Know that the relative positions of Sun, Earth and Moon during a solar eclipse. • Can describe what you would see during a solar eclipse. • Can explain how a solar eclipse is caused.
Lesson 16 The Moon	• To know that the Moon moves around the Earth. • To know that the Moon's changing appearance is evidence of a 28-day orbit. • To use scientific knowledge to explain observations.	Model the phases of the Moon using the children, a lamp and a football.	Draw phases of the Moon in the correct places on a diagram of the Moon's orbit.	Review the model of the Earth, Sun and Moon, looking at how day and night, seasons, and phases of the Moon arise.	• Know that the Moon goes around the Earth. • Can explain why the shape of the Moon appears to change.
Lesson 17 The Moon changes shape	• To know that the Moon moves around the Earth. • To model the movement of the Moon around the Earth, relating this to the Moon's phases.	Discuss why the Moon's shape appears to change. Demonstrate using a ball and OHP.	Use a diary to work out the phases of the Moon. Use secondary sources to identify how our ideas about the Moon have changed.	Review what causes the phases of the Moon and recap the movements of the Earth and the Moon.	• Know that the Moon goes around the Earth • Can describe how this causes the phases of the Moon.

Assessment	Objectives	Activity 1	Activity 2
Lesson 18 Sun, Moon and Earth	• To assess the children's understanding of the movements of the Earth and Moon. • To assess the children's ability to extract information from a graph.	Extract information from a line graph of sunrise times. Draw conclusions about the effects of daylight saving time. Add information to the graph.	Mark phases of the Moon in the correct places on a diagram of the Moon's orbit around the earth. Draw conclusions about the time of rising of the Moon.

SC1 SCIENTIFIC ENQUIRY

How does the appearance of the Moon change?

LEARNING OBJECTIVES AND OUTCOMES
- Interpret pictorial information about the phases of the Moon.
- Use this information to predict other phases.
- Check their predictions against secondary sources.
- Identify ways in which our ideas about the Moon have changed.

ACTIVITY
Children use their knowledge about phases of the Moon to complete information in calendars or diaries where only some of the phases have been filled in. They also predict phases of the Moon on given dates 7, 14, 21 or 28 days from the dates they have information for. They look at ancient and modern ideas about the Moon and identify how ideas have changed, possibly suggesting some reasons for the changes.

LESSON LINKS
This Sc1 activity forms an integral part of Lesson 18, Sun, Moon and Earth.

Lesson 1 ▶ Round Earth or flat Earth?

Objectives
- To know that the Sun, Earth and Moon are approximately spherical.
- To know that sometimes the evidence for an idea is indirect.

Vocabulary
spherical, eclipse

RESOURCES 💿
Main activity: Cardboard models of the Earth (see below); two small model people; Blu-Tack®.
Group activities: 1 Photocopiable page 167 (also 'Round Earth or flat Earth' (red) available on the CD-ROM); colouring pencils. **2** Paper; pencils; colouring pencils; secondary sources of information about the Earth (for extension activity).
Plenary: Photographs of the Earth and Moon taken from space, star constellation charts; photographs of lunar and solar eclipses; a globe. NASA has a website (www.nasa.gov) with copyright-free images. www.teachingideas.co.uk gives pointers to websites that are useful for all aspects of primary science and ICT.
ICT link: 'Earth models' diagram on the CD-ROM.

PREPARATION
Make 'flat Earth' and 'round Earth' models as shown in the diagrams below. Load appropriate secondary sources of information onto available computers.

BACKGROUND
Since the 1950s and 1960s, we have been able to see photographs of the Earth taken from space by rockets and satellites, showing that it is almost spherical. However, ancient Greek philosophers first deduced this in about

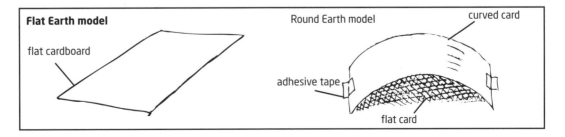

Flat Earth model — flat cardboard

Round Earth model — curved card, adhesive tape, flat card

Differentiation
Group activity 1
To support children, give them 'Round Earth or flat Earth?' (green) which omits the extension question included on the core sheet.
Group activity 2
Extend children by asking them to use secondary sources to find out about more discoveries that led to the knowledge that the Earth is round. They might refer to lunar eclipses, *Philolaus* or Ferdinand Magellan.

450BC from the indirect evidence of stars, ships, eclipses and shadows:
● They suggested that the Earth curved in a north-south direction because a traveller moving north sees some star constellations 'disappear' behind the southern horizon, while new ones appear over the northern horizon. (The rotation of the Earth hides this effect from a traveller travelling in an east-west direction.)
● Ships sailing away from all known ports 'disappear' hull-first, just as if they are sailing over a hill. This is indirect evidence that the Earth curves in all directions.
● During lunar eclipses, the Earth's shadow on the Moon always appears circular. The only shape that always casts a circular shadow is a sphere.

Understanding that the Earth is spherical is crucial to understanding how night and day occur, how seasons happen and how some places on Earth are always hot while others are always cold.

STARTER
Ask the children: *What shape does the land around us appear to have? Early people thought the Earth was flat, apart from the hills and valleys.* Discuss Ancient Greek ideas about the Earth and sky (see Background). Some children may be familiar with Terry Pratchett's *Discworld*, based on an Ancient Indian model. (If you wish to read this description to the children, it can be found in *The Colour of Magic*, published by Corgi.)

MAIN ACTIVITY
Show the children the 'flat Earth' model. Place two model people near one edge of the 'land', then move one away. *What will the person left behind see?* Repeat with the 'round Earth' model. *What will the person left behind see now?* Establish that when a person disappears over a hill, the figure disappears feet-first instead of just looking smaller and smaller. Compare this with ships sailing away from land. *What does this tell us about the shape of the Earth?* Explain the difference between direct evidence (things we can actually see or measure) and indirect evidence (where we draw conclusions about something by looking at the effect it has on something else). Discuss other early evidence for a round Earth. *Is our evidence for a round Earth direct or indirect?* (All the evidence for a round Earth was indirect until we had photographs taken from space.)

GROUP ACTIVITIES
1 Give the children a copy each of photocopiable page 167 and let them work through it.
2 Ask the children to write a newspaper report about the discovery that the Earth is round. If they know enough about Greek history, they could try writing a Greek newspaper report.

ICT LINK
Children can use secondary sources, such as CD-ROMs, or internet to find out more about the discoveries that the Earth is spherical.

ASSESSMENT
Show the children star charts of the constellations visible in the northern and southern hemispheres, and ask them to suggest why these are different.

PLENARY
Review what the children have learned about the shape of the Earth. Look at photographs of the Earth taken from space. Use a globe to identify different places on the Earth. *Can you tell where the photographs were taken from?* Look at pictures of the Moon, taken from Earth and from space. *Do they show the same view of the Moon? What shape is the Moon? Can*

you guess what shape the Sun might be? Show them photographs of solar eclipses to help them decide whether they were right. Remind them of the importance of never looking directly at the Sun, because its rays can damage the light-sensitive cells in the eye.

OUTCOMES
● Know that the Sun, Earth and Moon are approximately spherical.
● Can use indirect evidence to draw scientific conclusions.

LINKS
Geography: using globes and photographs of the Earth.
History: Ancient Greek astronomy and cosmology.

Lesson 2 ▪ Raising questions

Objectives
● To elicit children's existing ideas about Earth and space.
● To stimulate question-raising.

Vocabulary
Earth, Moon, sky, Sun

Differentiation
Some children may use flat discs rather than spheres to represent the Earth, the Moon or the Sun. Ask them about this and begin to challenge their ideas by showing them a globe, or showing them how you would represent the Moon as a sphere. If children seem confident about their models, probe their understanding further by asking them to arrange the models to show how they relate to each other. Ask questions, such as: *Do you think the Sun and the Moon are the same distance from Earth?*

RESOURCES
Group activity: Plasticine® in various colours.
Main activity: Flipchart and marker pens.

PREPARATION
Put the Plasticine® out on tables for the Group activity. Have the resources for the Main activity to hand.

BACKGROUND
Earth and space can be a difficult topic to teach because you are reliant on models and secondary sources. It also involves working in three dimensions, and these lessons try to give as many opportunities as possible for children to develop their spatial awareness. In this lesson, Plasticine modelling is useful to help children to communicate their ideas without struggling to make them into two-dimensional representations. The Group activities come before the Main activity to facilitate this.

STARTER
Ask the children to discuss in pairs their ideas about what the Moon and Sun are like. Invite the pairs to feedback their ideas to the class. Ask: *What do you think the surface of the Moon is like? What shape do you think the Sun is? What do you think the temperature on the Moon is?*

GROUP ACTIVITY
Ask the children to work in pairs or threes to make models in Plasticine of the Earth, the Sun and the Moon. Circulate and ask the children questions such as: *Why have you shown the Moon like that? What makes you think the Earth is that shape? Can you show me how they would be placed in space? Do you think the Earth is smaller or bigger than the Sun? Do you think the Moon or smaller or bigger than the Earth?*

MAIN ACTIVITY
On the flipchart, make two columns and give them the following titles: 'Things we already know' and 'Things we want to find out'. Record the children's existing ideas, such as 'The Sun is a sphere'; 'The Sun shines', ensuring that different children contribute their ideas. Then ask them to think about things that they may want to find out or learn about during the topic, for example, '*Is the Sun hotter in the summer?*', '*How far away are the stars?*' Don't worry that you will not be able to answer all their questions through the topic – they are worth raising to stimulate thought and interest.

ASSESSMENT

From observing and discussing the children's models, what are their existing ideas about the Earth and the Sun? Do any of them hold ideas that need to be addressed in future lessons? Are they able to raise appropriate questions about the topic?

PLENARY

Ask: *How do you think we might be able to answer our questions?* (By tests; observing the Sun and sky; reading books; using CD-ROMs; asking people.) Remind the children that it is not safe to look directly at the Sun and they must not do so in their investigating.

OUTCOMES

- Have elicited children's existing ideas.
- Can raise questions.

LINKS

Literacy: myths, legends, creation stories about the Sun.

Lesson 3 ▪ Sizes and distances

Objective
- To know the relative sizes of the Sun, Earth and Moon.
- To know the relative distances of the Moon and Sun from the Earth.

RESOURCES 💿

Photos showing a solar eclipse and solar flares; coloured clothing or hats to represent the Moon (grey), Sun (yellow) and Earth (green); various spherical objects (beach ball, football, tennis ball, golf ball, pea, mustard seed); coloured collage materials.
ICT link: 'Size/distances tables' diagram on the CD-ROM.

MAIN ACTIVITY

Copy Table 1 onto the board or flip chart, or display 'Size/distances tables' diagram on the CD-ROM on an interactive whiteboard, and talk through it. The children can look at their hands and distant trees or buildings to demonstrate that closer objects look larger. Let them select appropriate-sized spheres to represent the Sun, Earth and Moon and experiment to find out that the Sun has to be very distant to look the same size as the Moon.

Table 1

	Moon	Earth	Sun
Relative diameter	1	4	400
Distance from Earth	30 Earth diameters	-	12 000 Earth diameters

Table 2

	Sun	Earth	Moon	Moon to Earth	Earth to Sun
Model A	Football				
Model B			Marble		
Model C		Marble			

Differentiation
Let children who need support make collages of the Sun, Earth and Moon, using a simple scale. Extend children by asking them to select a scale model from Table 2, suggest appropriate objects for it and work out the approximate distances between them, then make the model.

ASSESSMENT

Assess the groups' models or collages. Invite other children to assess the accuracy of these, giving reasons for their judgement.

PLENARY

Show cardboard models of the Earth (1cm diameter), Moon (0.25cm) and Sun (1m). Decide where these must be hung from the classroom ceiling to make an accurate model. You may have to take the Sun outside the classroom! Hang them as accurately as possible.

OUTCOMES
- Can describe the differences in size between the three bodies.
- Can compare the distances between the three bodies.

Lesson 4 ▪ Directions

Objectives
- To know that directions can be found using a compass.
- To be able to use a compass to find north, south, east, west, and midpoints between them, for example north east.

Vocabulary
compass, east, north, point, south, west

RESOURCES 💿
Main activity: A globe compass; compass points drawn up on a sheet of sugar paper.
Group activities: 1 A compass for each group, a copy of photocopiable page 168 (also 'Directions – 1' (red) available on the CD-ROM) for each child. **2** Photocopiable page 169 (also 'Directions – 2' (red) available on the CD-ROM).

PREPARATION
Draw the compass points as on photocopiable page 168 onto a sheet of sugar paper, but with only 'north' written on. Copy photocopiable page 168 for each child. Have the class sitting in a circle.

BACKGROUND
This activity is a preparation for the subsequent lesson on the path of the Sun, and is also useful background for the work on star constellations. Remember that the intermediate points of the compass are referred to using the North Pole or South Pole first, for example, it is south-east, not east-south.

STARTER
Show the class a globe. Point to the North Pole and South Pole, asking: *Can you tell me the names of these points?* Find the UK. Say: *We could travel north or south, but we could also travel this way* (point east), *or this way* (point west). Ask: *Does anyone know the names of these directions?* Ask: *Why do we have names for directions? How does it help us?* Establish that it provides a way of communicating information about position. Explain that this will help them in their topic about Earth and that they will be learning how to find different directions.

MAIN ACTIVITY
Reveal the sugar paper drawing of compass directions. Ask the children to identify the four points of the compass, writing them on the paper as you go. They may know mnemonics such as 'Never Eat Shredded Wheat' that help them to remember the points. Explain that they will be using a real compass to find out the different directions in the playground. Pass around compasses and ask the children to try turning them around so that the needle lines up with the N for north. Explain that the needle will always point to north because the North Pole is a bit like a magnet and pulls the needle towards it. Together, point to the direction of north. Put the sugar paper in the middle of the circle and turn it, asking the children to tell you when to stop so that the paper 'north' is pointing to the real north. Ask children who are sitting at the south of the circle to put their hands up. Repeat this with the east and west. Explain that when they go outside they will need to use the compass to find out which direction is north, and work out the other directions from that.

Differentiation

Some children can record using drawing rather than writing. It may be necessary to limit the task by asking children only to record north and south. Other children can have the task extended by learning about the midpoints, for example south east.

GROUP ACTIVITIES

1 In the playground, give each group a 'base' by marking a place with a hoop. Ask each group to use the compass to identify north. On photocopiable page 168 they can write down some features that they see in that direction. They then work out the other points and record what they can see looking in those directions.

2 Give pairs of children a copy of photocopiable page 169. Ask them to work with a partner and take turns to decide on a starting place and a destination. They give their partner directions using 'north', 'south, 'east' or 'west' for them to follow to reach the destination. For example, a child could choose a journey from the fish and chip shop to the bank and could say 'Start at the fish and chip shop. Walk south until you reach the newsagent, then go east. You will find the bank on the south side of the road'.

ASSESSMENT

Can the children use the compass to identify the direction of north? Can they use the compass to work out the direction of the other compass points?

PLENARY

Bring the children together. Ask them to point to north, south, east, and west as they have identified them and to share what they have recorded as features in that direction.

OUTCOME

● Can use a compass to find the different directions on the ground.

LINKS

Geography: map work.
PE: orienteering.

Lesson 5 ▪ The Sun in the sky

Objective

● To track the apparent movement of the Sun across the sky during the day.
● To relate this movement to the points of the compass.
● To carry out systematic observations over a period of time.

RESOURCES

A sunny area (check that it does not become shaded later in the day) for each group; a stick mounted in a container of sand; compass; large sheet of paper (possibly several sheets of sugar paper taped together); felt-tipped pens.

MAIN ACTIVITY

This activity develops observations made in Year 3/Primary 4 by asking children to consider the direction of the apparent movement of the Sun, building in progression. Ask the children if the Sun stays the same all day. (It appears to move across the sky.)

In the morning, each group should record the shadow cast by the stick. Discuss with the class what would be appropriate time intervals to come back and check the shadow. Ask the children to draw around the shadow at intervals throughout the day and use the compass to mark the direction the shadow is pointing in. Point out to them that the Sun will be coming from the opposite direction to the way the shadow is pointing.

ASSESSMENT

Can the children describe the apparent movement of the Sun across the sky? Can the children recognise the different parts of the sky the Sun passes through during the day?

Differentiation

Have mixed groups so that the children can support each other.

PLENARY

Bring the children together with their records. Ask them: *Which way was the shadow pointing first thing this morning? So which way does that mean the Sun was shining from? What happened to the shadow during the day?* (It moved around.) *Which direction did it move? Where was the shadow pointing at the end of the day? What does that tell us about where the Sun is at the end of the day? If we could stay at school and record where the shadow was going next, where do you predict it would go? Can you tell me which compass direction the Sun rises from and in which direction it sets?*

Explain that actually, it is not the Sun that is moving; it is the Earth, but it seems like the Sun is moving.

Ask: *Was it just the direction of the shadow that changed or did anything else change?* (The length of the shadow.)

OUTCOMES

- Can recognise that the Sun appears to move across the sky during the day.
- Can explain that the Sun rises in the east, travels across the sky and sets in the west.

Lesson 6 ▫ Day and night

Objectives

- To use scientific knowledge to explain observations.
- To know that the Sun's apparent movement across the sky is caused by the Earth spinning on its own axis.
- To know hat the Sun appears to rise in an easterly direction and set in a westerly direction.
- To identify patterns of change in the sunrise and sunset times through the year.

Vocabulary

rotation, axis, spin, sunrise, sunset

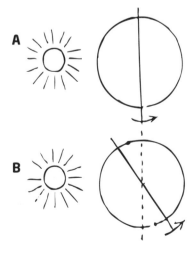

RESOURCES ⊙

Main activity: A compass; a yellow item of clothing; hat or ball; a large globe; a toy person; Blu-Tack®; a bright torch with a narrow beam; simplified sunrise and sunset times; graph paper; rulers; chalk; a large open space, such as the school playground.
Group activities: 1 Graph paper; rulers; colouring pencils. **2** Photocopiable page 170 (also 'Day and night' (red) available on the CD-ROM); pencils; squared paper (for extension activity).
ICT link: 'Day and night' interactive and 'Day/night' and 'Sunrise' diagrams on the CD-ROM.

PREPARATION

Obtain or record simplified sunrise and sunset times (these are found in most diaries). For each month, record the sunrise and sunset times closest to the 15th of the month. Record times to the nearest quarter- or half-hour. Draw a large chalk circle in the playground.

BACKGROUND

The Sun appears to rise in the east, travel across the sky and set in the west each day, giving shadows that change in shape and position. One conceivable explanation for this is that the Sun and the other stars move around the Earth. The second, and correct, explanation is that the Sun and stars stay still, but the Earth moves. The rotation of the Earth on its own axis makes the Sun appear to move across the sky.

If the Earth's axis of rotation were vertical (as in diagram A), day and night would always be the same length: 12 hours each. However, because the Earth's axis of rotation is tilted, day and night are different lengths in different places (see diagram B). Throughout the year, the Earth moves in its orbit around the Sun (see Lesson 13, The seasons), so the northern hemisphere is sometimes tilted towards and sometimes tilted away from the Sun. This change of tilt causes there to be different day-lengths at different times of the year.

STARTER

Review earlier years' work on shadows. Check that the children know how shadows change throughout the day, and that this change is because the

Sun appears to move across the sky. Shadows are shortest at midday, when the Sun is highest in the sky. Ask: *Why do you think the Sun appears to move?* Record the children's ideas. Discuss where the Sun rises and sets. If appropriate, encourage the children to use a compass to find out the direction of the Sun at the start and end of the school day, and at midday. Discuss the position of the Sun in the sky at different times of the year (see opposite).

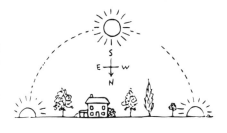

MAIN ACTIVITY

On the playground, help the children model how the Sun seems to move. Give one child something yellow. This child represents the Sun. Stand other children around a large chalk circle, facing straight outwards, toes touching the chalk line. They represent people standing in different places around the Earth. The 'Sun' stands outside the circle. *Put your hand up if you can see the 'Sun' without turning your head. What time of day is it when you can see the real Sun?* Encourage the children to suggest reasons why we can sometimes see the Sun and sometimes cannot. Lead them to the idea that they may stay in the same place on the Earth, but the Earth moves round. Ask the 'Earth' to move round in a ring, carefully.

Back in the classroom, demonstrate day and night using a large globe and a torch. Use Blu-Tack® to attach a toy person to the globe in different places. Rotate the globe, encouraging the children to say when it is day for the person and when it is night. Discuss how the amount of daylight varies throughout the year. *What is it like when you get up in winter? What activities can you do on summer evenings?*

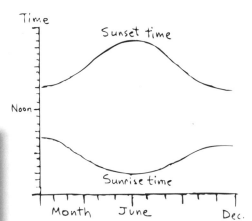

GROUP ACTIVITIES

1 Ask the children to plot a graph of the sunrise times each month. They should then plot the sunset times on the same axes, but using a different colour (left):
2 Give each child a copy of page 170 to complete. The answers are: 1. night-time; 2. shadow; 3. longer; 4. morning; 5. rotate; 6. daytime; 7. facing; 8. noon; 9. dusk; 10. spherical. The shaded word is 'twenty-four', which is the answer to a question such as 'How many hours are there in a day?'

Differentiation

Group activity 1
Support children by giving them prepared axes on which to plot separate bar charts of the sunrise and sunset times to the nearest half-hour.
Group activity 2
Support children by giving them 'Day and night' (green), which provides initial letters for each clue to help them complete the crossword. To extend children, ask them to work together to plan their own small crossword on squared paper, and then challenge another friend to solve it.

ICT LINK

Show 'Day/night' and 'Sunrise' diagrams from the CD-ROM on an interactive whiteboard as a starting point for discussion and revision.
Children can use the 'Day and night' interactive from the CD-ROM.

ASSESSMENT

Ask the children to compare their graphs within their groups. *Do they look similar?* Ask them questions such as: *Is it dark at 7 o'clock in the morning in April?* Let them decide and then explain to you how they used their graphs to find the answer. Look for ability to use the axes to find particular points, and for an understanding that the area between the sunrise and sunset lines is 'day' and the rest is 'night'.

PLENARY

Discuss how the day-length (the number of hours of daylight) changes through the year. Use the globe and torch to demonstrate how, if the Earth were 'upright', day-length would always stay the same (12 hours light, 12 hours dark). Show them the Earth tilting; use the torch to show how, when we are tilted towards the Sun, we spend more time in sunlight and so the day-length is increased. Practise this until the children are confident. *In winter, do you think we are tilted towards the Sun or away from the Sun? Why do you think that?*

OUTCOMES

- Can describe how the Sun's path in the sky changes through the year.
- Can explain that the spin of the Earth makes the Sun appear to move across the sky.
- Can explain how day and night occur.
- Can draw line graphs and use them to identify patterns.

LINKS

Literacy: poetry and descriptive writing about summer and winter.
Art: sunrise or sunset paintings.

ENRICHMENT
Lesson 7 ▪ Planet days

Objective
- To know that other planets have different day-lengths from Earth.
- To think logically about causes and effects.

RESOURCES 💿
Main activity: An A3 copy of the table shown below.
ICT link: 'Planet days' diagram on the CD-ROM.

Name of planet	Mercury	Venus	Earth	Mars	Jupiter
Time of rotation	59 days	243 days	1 day	25 hours	10 hours

Name of planet	Saturn	Uranus	Neptune	Pluto
Time of rotation	10 hours	18 hours	19 hours	6 days

MAIN ACTIVITY 💿

Ask the children to define a day. Make sure they all understand that a day is the time taken for the Earth to turn once on its own axis, and this rotation gives rise to our 'night' and 'day'. Explain the distinction between the everyday and scientific meanings of the word 'day'. Show the children the table on a flip chart, or display 'Planet days' diagram from the CD-ROM on an interactive whiteboard. Explain that it tells us how long different planets take to turn round once on their own axis. Ask them to describe the effect that the time of rotation would have on the length of 'daytime' and 'night-time' observed. Ask them to write short stories describing 'a day on Venus' or another planet of their choice, imagining what effects the length of 'day' or 'night' would have. Ask questions to help the children, such as: *What would people do if the nights were much longer? What kind of job would you like to do if it were light for much longer?*

Differentiation
All the children should be able to participate fully in this activity.

ASSESSMENT

Ask some children to state roughly how long 'night' and 'day' would be on their chosen planet, explaining how they worked this out.

PLENARY

Read out, or let children read out, some of the short stories. Discuss what it might be like to live on a planet with a very long or very short day-length. Talk about astronauts living on space stations: their experience of light and dark, and how space stations use lights and blackouts to simulate an 'Earth' environment.

OUTCOMES

● Understand that other planets may have a different day-length from Earth.
● Can deduce the effect that time of rotation has on day-length.

ENRICHMENT
Lesson 8 ◗ Shadows

Objectives
● To know that the Sun's rays may be slanting at different angles.
● To investigate how shadows change when the angle of the Sun changes.
● To identify relevant variables.

Vocabulary
angle, light, shadow, torch

RESOURCES 💿

Main activity: A large matchbox; a small matchbox; two different torches; a ruler; a felt-tipped pen; a large sheet of white/pale coloured paper.
Group activities: 1 A domino or matchbox; torch; paper; and a ruler for each group; a copy of photocopiable page 171 (also 'Shadows - 1' (red) available on the CD-ROM) and writing materials for each child. **2** Photocopiable page 172 (also 'Shadows - 2' (red) available on the CD-ROM).

PREPARATION

Put the resources for the Group activities out on the tables. Have the resources for the Main activity to hand.

BACKGROUND

This work links with the children's understanding of light. They need to have previous experience of shadows and understand that a shadow is formed when light is blocked. In this lesson, the focus is on how the length of the shadow changes as the angle of the light source changes. This can then be related back to the shadows that the children have seen cast by the Sun, and used to provide evidence that the angle of the Sun with respect to the Earth must be changing. This will begin to give children some insight into seasonal change.

   The lesson also aims to help children identify the variables that will need to be controlled to carry out a fair test.

STARTER

Stand the matchboxes on a large sheet of paper and shine the torch at the large one so that a shadow of the box is formed on the paper. Ask the children to describe what is happening.

MAIN ACTIVITY

Ask the children to brainstorm all the different things that could be changed about the situation. Demonstrate some examples to start them off, such as using a different torch or a smaller matchbox. Record their ideas on a flip chart. Make sure that the list includes changing the position of the torch and clarify different aspects of the torch position that could be changed, for example distance away, position around the box, angle.

   Now ask the children what things could be measured or recorded about the shadow, for example its direction, width, length, shape. Record these in a separate list. Explain that in this investigation you want them to explore

Differentiation
Group activity 1
Some children may need support with the measurement. If they are not ready to use standard units, children could cut strips of coloured paper to the length of the shadow and make a visual representation of the results. To extend children, give them 'Shadow – 1' (blue), from the CD-ROM, which asks them to measure and record the area of the shadow.
Group activity 2
For children who need support, give them 'Shadows – 2' (green), from the CD-ROM, which includes fewer questions than the core sheet.

the changes of the length of the shadow. Ask: *How could we measure the length of the shadow?* (Use a ruler; use squared paper; draw around it, then measure it.)

Return to the list of things that could be changed. Explain that you want the children to focus on the angle of the torch, because this will help them to understand more about the Sun. Without saying anything, shine the torch on the large matchbox and mark the length of the shadow on the paper with the felt-tipped pen. Then say: *Now I'm going to try putting the torch at a different angle*, and do so, but shine it onto the small matchbox. Ask: *Which angle made the shadow longer, the first or the second?* One of the children may well suggest that it is not a fair comparison because of the change in size of the matchbox. If not, you will need to 'realise' it yourself. Explain that it must be the same matchbox, or we won't know if the shadow is different because the angle of the torch is different, or if it's to do with the matchbox.

Repeat this process using the same matchbox, but changing to a different torch, and then holding the torch exaggeratedly close and far away. Discuss the need to keep everything the same except the one thing you are investigating. Refer back to the list and go through it item by item, identifying that each needs to be kept the same, except the angle of the torch. Remind the children that this is what we mean by a 'fair test'.

GROUP ACTIVITIES

1 Give each child a copy of photocopiable page 171, explaining how you want them to record their investigation on the sheet. The children carry out the investigation.
2 Give the children a copy of photocopiable page 172. Ask them to look carefully at the graph and then answer the questions.

ASSESSMENT

Are the children aware of the need to control the different variables and do they try to do so in their investigation? Do they recognise that the shadow changes in length with the angle of the torch? Can they relate this knowledge to what happens to shadows cast by the Sun?

PLENARY

Ask the groups to report back on what they have found. Ask: *Does changing the angle of the torch affect the length of the shadow?* (Yes.) *In what way?* (When the torch is low/flat, the shadow is long and when the torch gets higher/more angled the shadow is shorter.) Ask the groups to demonstrate their findings to the class.

Ask: *Do shadows stay the same length when we are out in the Sun?* (No.) The children may have observed this in previous years in science. Look back at some of the recordings made in Lesson 5, The Sun in the sky and note that the shadows changed length as well as direction. Ask: *What does this tell us about the angle of the Sun?* (It must be changing.) Say: *So we know two things about the Sun.* Write these on the board: 'The Sun seems to move across the sky, and it changes its angle.'

OUTCOMES

● Can explain that the Sun's rays slant at different angles.
● Can recognise how shadows change when the angle of the light source changes.
● Can identify and control relevant variables.

ENRICHMENT
Lesson 9 ▷ The angle of the Sun

Objectives
● To know that the way the Sun heats the Earth depends on the slant of the Sun's rays.
● To measure temperature.

Vocabulary
angle, autumn, degrees Celcius, season, spring, summer, temperature, winter

RESOURCES
Main activity: An 'angle-poise' lamp; a sheet of white card; a model person (such as LEGO® products or Plasticine®); a thermometer; an electronic temperature sensor or data-logging equipment with temperature sensor.
Group activities: 1 and **2** Writing materials; colouring pencils; photographs and books showing different seasons.

PREPARATION
If the room has blinds or curtains, close them for the Main activity.

BACKGROUND
The Sun shines on the Earth at different angles. This is the case at different times of the day, but the angle of the Sun also varies through the year, being higher in the sky in the summer and lower in the winter. When the Sun is high in the sky, the light hits the ground straight-on, and so the heat is 'concentrated' in one place. If the Sun is lower and the light hits the ground at an angle, it is spread over a larger surface area and so each part of the ground is heated less. (See diagram on page 155.)

STARTER
Ask the children what they have learned about light and the Sun so far. (The Sun seems to move across the sky, it changes angles – which we know because of the way the shadows change position and length.) Explain that the children are going to find out more about the effect of the angle of the Sun.

MAIN ACTIVITY
Shine the lamp on the white card from directly overhead. Explain that this is like the Sun in the summer. Ask: *What does the spot of light look like?* (Round and bright.) Now move the lamp so it is shining at an angle. Explain that this is more like the Sun in the autumn. Ask: *What does the spot of light look like now?* (Stretched out and not as bright.)

Repeat this with the model figure standing in the spot of light. Ask: *I wonder what it would feel like to this person?* (Bright and hot/Not as bright, not as warm.)

Ask: *We can see that it is not as bright when it is at an angle; how can we tell if it is not as hot?* (Measure the temperature.) Explain that each group will have the opportunity to come and measure the temperature.

GROUP ACTIVITIES
1 One group at a time will, with support, measure and record the temperature with the light directly above and at a low angle. The difference is not huge, so the two angles need to be exaggerated as much as possible. Work with the groups, ensuring that they are waiting for the thermometer/ sensor to adjust and are able to read the scale and record the units (degrees Celsius).
2 Ask other groups to work independently on drawings to represent the different seasons of the year. They could either work as a group to produce one large picture of their season, or each child could produce a drawing to show their own representation of the seasons. The books and photographs will stimulate ideas for a discussion in the Plenary session.

Differentiation
Group activity 1
Extend children by asking them to try a third lamp position and record the temperature.
Group activity 2
Some children may need more guidance with the drawing and they can be given a paper circle folded into quarters on which to show their ideas about the seasons.

ASSESSMENT
Can the children state that the light coming at a low angle produces less heat than that coming from directly above? Can they relate this to their ideas about the seasons?

PLENARY

Ask: *What did we find out about the effect of the angle of the light?* (It is hotter when the torch is directly above.) *Is it generally hotter in summer or winter?* Use the pictures from Group activity 2 to stimulate discussion about the sunshine in different seasons. *Can someone come and show me with the lamp how they think the Sun is shining in the summer/winter?* Invite a child to use the lamp to demonstrate. *Can you explain why you think that?*

The pictures could be displayed alongside the following poem:

The spring Sun is young,
The summer Sun is bold,
The autumn Sun is quiet,
The winter Sun is old.

A discussion about global warming and its possible impact on our seaside resorts would provide a contemporary angle.

OUTCOMES
- Can recognise that the Sun's rays may slant at an angle and that this affects the temperature of the Earth.
- Can measure temperature.

LINKS
Geography: seasons.

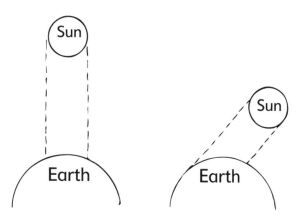

ENRICHMENT
Lesson 10 ▪ Star light

Objective
- To know that stars are sources of light.

RESOURCES
A room, blacked-out with blinds or curtains; black card; torches; Plasticine®; tools for making holes (bradawls); sharp pencils; knitting needles.

MAIN ACTIVITY
Discuss the children's experiences of seeing stars in the night sky: *Do they always seem the same? Can you always see the same number of stars?*

Recite the rhyme 'Twinkle, Twinkle, Little Star'. Ask: *What do you think a star is?* Listen to the children's ideas. Explain that stars are like the Sun: they are balls of fire and give out light, but as they are further away from the Sun they look smaller.

Ask the children to make some different-sized holes in their pieces of black card, showing them how to make a hole safely by pushing the bradawl through the card into the Plasticine.

Working in small groups, ask the children to shine their torches through the cards and experiment with moving nearer and further from each other to explore how that changes what they can see. Ask: *Are all the 'stars' as easy to see? What makes some easier to see than others?* (The brightness of the torch, the size of the hole.)

ASSESSMENT
Do the children realise that stars are sources of light? Are they aware that stars vary in size and brightness?

PLENARY
Ask a group at a time to stand together, shining torches through their cards to give the effect of a patch of night sky. Ask: *What can you tell me about stars?* (They are like the Sun, they give out light, they are balls of fire, some are brighter than others, they are different sizes.)

OUTCOMES
- Can recognise that stars are sources of light.
- Can explain that some stars are easier to see because they are bigger and brighter than others.

ENRICHMENT
Lesson 11 ◗ Star patterns

Objective
- To know that groups of stars in the sky are known as constellations.
- To be able to identify some constellations.

RESOURCES 💿
Copies of photocopiable page 173 (also 'Star patterns' (red) available on the CD-ROM) cut up into individual cards; books and CD-ROMs with information about constellations including *The Plough, Great Dog, Orion, Leo, Cassiopeia, and Gemini.*

MAIN ACTIVITY 💿
Ask the children what they can say about stars. Explain that when we look at the night sky we can see groups of stars. These are arranged in patterns. In the ancient past, people have imagined that these look a bit like a person or an animal and have given them special names. Give out books with the named constellations in and a set of cards to each group.

You may want to display 'Star patterns (red) on an interactive whiteboard and use the drawing tools to add the lines between the stars. This will help make it easier to recognise the 'pictures' like a dot-to-dot pattern.

Challenge the children to name each constellation. Ask: *What do the constellations look like to you? Can you draw new, twenty-first century shapes around the constellations and rename them?*

ASSESSMENT
Can the children explain what is meant by a constellation? Have they successfully identified the constellations?

PLENARY
Check that the constellations have been correctly named and share the names the children have devised. Suggest the children take a copy of page 173 home with them and look at the night sky with their parents for homework. (Note they will not be able to see all the constellations at all times of the year.)

OUTCOMES
- Can explain what a constellation is.
- Can recognise some constellations.

ENRICHMENT
Lesson 12 ▪ The Earth and time

Objective
● To know that the time on a clock varies around the world.
● To know that some units of time are linked to the motion of the Earth and some are artificial.

RESOURCES
Globes; torches.

MAIN ACTIVITY
Discuss the meanings of some 'time' words. *How do we know when it is morning? When it is night?* Establish that some time words are connected to the movement of the Earth. It is morning when the Sun rises. Use a globe and torch to show that morning happens at different times around the world. Make sure the children know that the Earth rotates anticlockwise (if looking down on the North Pole). Show the 'time zones' on the globe and count them. Explain that moving east by one time zone moves the clock forward 1 hour and moving west moves the clock back. Explain what the International Date Line is and why it is there: so we can't go around the world and come back a day earlier than we left! Talk about 'time' words that are artificial, such as an hour. *Would it matter if we split the day into 4 parts instead of 24?* Ask the children to work in small groups to list 'time' words and divide them into those that are 'connected to the motion of the Earth' and those that are 'artificial'.

ASSESSMENT
Start the Plenary with questions such as: *Can you find a place where it is morning later than in Britain?* to test the children's understanding of what they have been practising.

Differentiation
Children who need support could make up some questions such as: 'When the Sun is just rising in Britain, where will it still be dark?', then use a globe and a torch to practise finding the answers. Extend children by asking them to find out the time at different places in the world when it is 6am in Britain, then make up related questions and find answers.

PLENARY
Discuss how time zones affect people travelling around the world. We have to put our watches forward if we go east on holiday. Make sure the children understand thoroughly which time units are artificial. For example, if we said a day was longer, it would eventually mean that the Sun came up in the middle of the night; but if we said an hour was longer, it would not matter – there would just be fewer hours in a day.

OUTCOMES
● Can distinguish between 'natural' times and 'artificial' times.
● Can use a globe to model the movement of the Earth.

Lesson 13 ▪ The seasons

Objective
● To know that the Earth travels in an orbit around the Sun once a year, and this causes the seasons we experience.

Vocabulary
orbit, comet, meteor, rotation, angle, axis

RESOURCES ●
Main activity: A yellow item of clothing; hat or ball; a large globe; a torch; a dry-wipe marker pen.
Group activities: 1 Photocopiable page 174 (also 'The seasons' (red) available on the CD-ROM), pencils. **2** Secondary sources of information about comets and meteors, A6-sized cards, pencils.
ICT link: 'Sun's rays' diagram on the CD-ROM.

PREPARATION
Make sure that there is space to model the orbit of the Earth around the Sun where all the children can see it. Have the chosen secondary sources of information to hand.

BACKGROUND
The seasons happen because the Earth orbits the Sun and is tilted relative to the plane of its orbit. The tilt of the Earth means that the northern

hemisphere is sometimes tilted towards the Sun and sometimes tilted away from the Sun, depending on where the Earth is in its orbit. Summer in the northern hemisphere occurs when it is tilted towards the Sun, winter when it is tilted away from the Sun (180° further around the orbit). In the southern hemisphere, winter and summer occur in the opposite halves of the calendar year – in Australia, Christmas is commonly celebrated with a barbecue! This is a very difficult concept for most children, and it is worth spending plenty of time on modelling the situations to make sure they understand thoroughly.

Sun's rays spread over small area   Sun's rays spread over large area

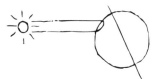   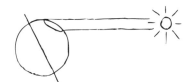

Summer in northern hemisphere   Winter in northern hemisphere

STARTER
Ask the children to describe what the weather is like in different seasons, concentrating on it being warmer in summer than in winter. Remind them of the work covered in Lesson 6 Day and night. Can they explain *why* we have summer and winter?

MAIN ACTIVITY
Explain that the seasons happen because as the Earth moves around the Sun sometimes we are tilted towards the Sun and sometimes away from the Sun. Stand a child in the centre of the room with a yellow hat, ball or item of clothing, to be the Sun. Stand a second child, holding a large globe with the axis of rotation vertical, some way from the Sun. Use the term 'axis of rotation' or 'axis the Earth is turning on'. Ask the class to describe where on the Earth it will be hot and where it will be cold, and to explain why. If necessary, show them the area covered by a torch beam shone at different places on the globe.

Mark where you live on the globe. *How could we make our country hotter?* (Moving the Earth nearer to the Sun is not allowed.) *What happens if we tilt the globe?* Now say that the globe must be kept at the same angle, and encourage the children to think of another way of moving the globe so that it becomes cold in our country. Lead them to suggest moving the globe to a different place in its orbit, so that your country is on the far side of the Earth from the Sun. Repeat the orbital movement until the children understand clearly how your country is moving from warm to cold and back again. *Describe the movement of the Earth around the Sun. How long does it take for the Earth to orbit the Sun once?* (365.25 days.) *How do you know this?*

Discuss the fact that the Earth is not the only body orbiting the Sun: it is also orbited by planets, comets, meteors ('shooting stars') and meteorites. The planets all have names, and many comets have been named after the people who first described them.

GROUP ACTIVITIES
1 Give each child a copy of page 174 to work through. The answers are as follows: 1. A diagram showing the Earth's northern hemisphere pointing towards the Sun; 2. The correct sentences are: 'The South Pole is in constant darkness.'; 'The North Pole is in constant daylight.'; 'Sunlight reaching Britain is spread over a small area'; 3. As the Earth orbits the Sun, the Northern hemisphere gradually moves until it is tilting away from the Sun. When this

happens, the Sun's radiation is spread over a larger area, making it cold. This is winter. The Earth has to move 180° around its orbit for the change from summer to winter to take place. This takes six months, as the entire orbit takes a year.

2 The children should work in pairs, using secondary sources to prepare brief information cards about comets, meteors or meteorites. Let them choose a specific comet to research if they wish. They should try to describe how it moves through space.

ICT LINK

Display 'Sun's rays' diagram from the CD-ROM on an interactive whiteboard. Use this as another visual aid to explain how the tilt of the Earth results in different seasons.

Children could use CD-ROMs or the Internet to find out about other bodies in the solar system, such as comets, meteors or meteorites. Children could possibly, with relevant help, download pictures, and use the computer to produce writing to contribute to a class display.

ASSESSMENT

At the start of the Plenary session, ask groups to use the yellow ball and large globe to model different seasons, explaining why they have put the objects in the positions they have chosen. Collect in the children's information cards, or ask some children to read their card out loud. Look for evidence of how much they have understood about the motion of their chosen body around the Sun.

PLENARY

Talk briefly through the answers to page 174. Ask some children to share the information on their cards with the class. Discuss what would happen to the seasons and the day-length if the Earth's axis were vertical or horizontal. (In the first case, day and night would be constantly equal in length. In the second case, half the world would be in constant daylight with the Sun circling in the sky; the other half would be in constant darkness. There would be no seasons in either case.)

OUTCOMES

● Can describe the motion of the Earth around the Sun (as a 'circular' or 'almost circular' orbit).
● Know that the cycle of seasons is evidence of the Earth's orbit.

LINKS

Literacy: imaginative writing about living in constant daylight or darkness.

ENRICHMENT
Lesson 14 ▪ The Earth's tilt

Objective
● To know that the pattern of seasons is related to the Earth's tilt and its orbit around the Sun.

RESOURCES
A large globe; a lamp; a small model person; secondary sources of information about animals in different environments.

MAIN ACTIVITY
Remind the children how the tilt and movement of the Earth causes the seasons. *What effect would it have if the tilt of the Earth were different?* Show the children a large globe, with a lamp to represent the Sun. Tilt the globe so that its axis of rotation is in the plane of the Earth's orbit around the Sun, with the North Pole pointing directly at the Sun. Place a model person at points on the globe and discuss how, for that person, the Sun would appear to move. (Permanent darkness in one half, the sun

permanently circling in the sky in the other.) Discuss the effects this would have on temperature in different parts of the world. Let the children use secondary sources to find out about animals that could live in permanent light and heat and in permanent dark and cold.

ASSESSMENT

In the plenary, ask the children to describe the daylight and temperature patterns at particular positions on the globe and at particular points in the Earth's orbit.

PLENARY

Review the effect that making the Earth's axis of rotation horizontal would have on daylight in different places. Discuss what the children have found out about the effects this could have on animals. Finish the lesson by asking the children to model the movement of the globe with its true tilt. Recap on how our actual seasons are caused.

OUTCOME

- Understand that if the tilt of the Earth were different, the pattern of seasons would also be different.

ENRICHMENT
Lesson 15 ▪ Solar eclipse

Objectives
- To know that an object moving in front of a light produces a shadow.
- To know that a solar eclipse is a shadow caused by the Moon.
- To know that the Earth turning makes the shadow seem to move.

Vocabulary
light, shadow, Moon, Earth, solar eclipse.

RESOURCES

Starter: Video of a solar eclipse, particularly concentrating on the experience of seeing an eclipse, showing scenes of it getting dark, as at night time.
Main activity: A bright lamp; a plain wall; a cardboard circle fastened to a thin stick to represent the Moon.
Group activities: 1 Video of solar eclipse playing in background if possible. **2** Prepared sentences or sentence pieces explaining what happens in a solar eclipse.

PREPARATION

If possible, dim the lighting in the room and set up a bright light so that it shines onto a plain wall. Attach a cardboard circle, large enough to completely cover the light, to a thin stick. This will represent the Moon. Find out where to position the lamp and the 'Moon' so that a shadow is cast on the wall, at about child head height and at least about football size. As the 'Moon' is moved from left to right in front of the lamp, the shadow should be large enough to pass in turn across the faces of children of all heights if they stand in a row against the wall.

BACKGROUND

During a solar eclipse, the Moon passes between the Earth and the Sun. Although the Moon is only about 1/400th the size of the Sun, it is able to cover the Sun completely because it is also only about 1/400th the distance from the Earth to the Sun. The Moon blocks the light from the Sun, casting a shadow onto the surface of the Earth. Because the Earth is rotating on its own axis, this shadow appears to move across the surface of the Earth. Solar eclipses are rare in any particular place because the orbits of the Earth and the Moon are such that the Earth, Sun and Moon very rarely line up exactly. A solar eclipse is visible from somewhere on the Earth's surface about twice a year. The next solar eclipse to be visible from Britain will happen in 2090.

Differentiation

Group activity 1
All children should be able to do this activity.
Group activity 2
Provide differentiation in the complexity of the sentences.

STARTER

Ask the children: *What light sources can you name? What's the biggest light source that you know?* Establish that the Sun is a light source and discuss what happens if something moves in front of a light source.

Show the children a video of a solar eclipse, and discuss what they see, concentrating on what it is that moves in front of the Sun (the Moon), and the fact that it goes dark during an eclipse because they are in the shadow that the Moon is creating. Tell the children that they are going to model a solar eclipse to see if they can explain exactly what is happening.

MAIN ACTIVITY

Show the children the lamp and the cardboard circle and tell them that they represent the Sun and the Moon. Show them how moving the 'Moon' in front of the 'Sun' casts a shadow on the wall. Once children have seen how the 'Moon' casts a shadow, line up half the class along the wall, with the other half behind the 'Sun' to watch. Move the 'Moon' gradually across in front of the 'Sun'. Ask the children against the wall to describe what they see as they 'Moon' passes in front of the 'Sun'. Swap over the two groups of children and repeat. Help the children to 'pool' their observations from both positions to realise that as the shadow passes over them, against the wall, they become unable to see the 'Sun', just as in a real solar eclipse.

Encourage the children to remember what happens to ordinary shadows formed by the Sun throughout the day, and help them to deduce from this that the reason the Moon's shadow moves across the Earth is because the Earth is turning on its own axis, not because the Sun is moving, and that this explains why a solar eclipse never lasts long in one place.

GROUP ACTIVITIES

1 Ask the children to imagine that they were present during a real solar eclipse. They should use what they have learned from the video to write a postcard to a friend, describing what the eclipse was like.
2 Working in groups, give children a series of prepared sentences (or sentence pieces) explaining how a solar eclipse happens. Ask the children to work together to put the sentences in the correct order.

ASSESSMENT

Ask children to explain in their own words how a solar eclipse happens, linking this to what they saw during the main activity from against the wall and from behind the 'Sun'.

PLENARY

Recap on the positions of Earth, Sun and Moon during a solar eclipse. Are children able to draw a diagram showing the relative positions? Draw a diagram of the Moon's shadow being cast onto a small section of the Earth's surface. Are children able to decide who, from a selection of people in different positions on the Earth's surface, would be able to see the eclipse, and who wouldn't?

OUTCOMES

- Know the relative positions of Sun, Earth and Moon during a solar eclipse.
- Can describe what you would see during a solar eclipse.
- Can explain how a solar eclipse is caused by the Moon's shadow on Earth.

Lesson 16 ◾ The Moon

Objectives
● To know that the Moon moves around the Earth.
● To know that the Moon's changing appearance over 28 days is evidence of a 28-day orbit.
● To use scientific knowledge to explain observations.

Vocabulary
phases, full Moon, new Moon, half Moon, crescent Moon, gibbous Moon

RESOURCES

Main activity: A football, another football painted half black and half white, a lamp; a torch. (NB It is very important to use a ball for this activity, not a balloon as the light shines through a balloon and makes the phases hard to see.)

Group activities: 1 Large pictures of the complete cycle of the Moon's phases (see Preparation) with days 1 and 2 labelled and the rest unlabelled. For support: small photocopied pictures of the Moon's phases; scissors; adhesive. **2** Large sheets of paper; colouring pencils. For support: pictures of the Moon's main phases; scissors; adhesive.

ICT link: 'Moon phases' diagram on the CD-ROM.

PREPARATION

One month or more in advance of the lesson, collect pictures of the daily appearance of the Moon. This information often appears in daily newspapers. Paint a football so that one hemisphere is black, the other white or yellow. (NB You will not need to dim the lights in the classroom for this lesson; the activities can take place in normal light.)

BACKGROUND

The Moon is spherical. As with the Earth, half of the Moon's surface is brightly lit by the Sun's light falling on it while the other half is in darkness. As the Moon orbits around the Earth, we see different proportions of the light and dark sides. It is this (and not the shadow of the Earth, which we see only during a lunar eclipse) that causes the appearance of the Moon to change during its 28-day orbit, giving us the phases of the Moon.

STARTER

Ask the children: *What do you know about the Moon?* Once you have basic information such as 'It's in the sky' and 'It's spherical', discuss the appearance of the Moon. The children will have noticed that they see the Moon at night; a few may have noticed that occasionally the Moon is visible in the daytime, and that sometimes it is not visible at night. Draw their attention to the fact that the Moon is there all the time – but in the daytime, it is so dim compared to the Sun that it is usually invisible. *Does the Moon always look the same shape?*

MAIN ACTIVITY

Tell the children that they are going to model how the Moon can look different at different times. Place a reading lamp on one side of the classroom (the Sun). Hold up a football (the Moon). *What would this look like in bright sunlight?* Make sure the children understand that it will always be half light and half dark. Take the half white, half black ball and hold it so that the white side points to the 'Sun'. Sit the children as shown in the diagram below and stand in the position marked 'M'. Ask: *What does the 'Moon' look like?* (It will be a full Moon.) *Where can the 'Moon go so it looks all black?* Help the children to discover that it must be between them and the Sun (this is a new Moon). *How do you think the 'Moon' might be moving?* (It moves in an orbit around the Earth.) Orbit around the children so that they can see the phases of the 'Moon'. Repeat the orbit a few times until all the children are confident about which phase of the Moon they see in each position of the 'Moon's' orbit.

Differentiation

Group activity 1

Support children by giving them pictures of the Moon phases and asking them to put them in the correct order.

Group activity 2

Children who need support can stick their pictures of Moon phases from Group activity 1 in the correct places.

Extend children by asking them to work out, in groups, what part of the Moon we will see if the Moon also takes 28 days to turn once on its own axis - as is actually the case. (The same part of the Moon will always be facing us.)

GROUP ACTIVITIES

1 Display a set of large pictures of all the phases of the Moon. The pictures should be in a random order and unlabelled, except for the first two (labelled 'day 1' and 'day 2'). Ask the children to draw the pictures in the correct order, labelling the full Moon, new Moon, half Moon and crescent Moon. They should use this set of pictures to work out the length of time of the Moon's orbit around the Earth.

2 Give each child (or small group) a large sheet of paper. Show the children where to draw the Sun and the Earth. Ask them to draw a circle representing the Moon's orbit and draw onto the circle the phases of the Moon that they would see when the Moon is at various positions in its orbit. They should colour the Moon yellow where it is visible and black where it is in shadow.

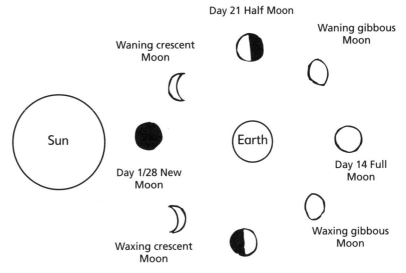

ICT LINK

There are many websites that allow you to view the phases of the Moon on specific dates, such as on forthcoming birthdays, or allow you to view how the phases of the Moon change.

ASSESSMENT

Ask one or two groups to show their pictures of the phases of Moon, and ask others to assess them for accuracy. Check that the children have worked out the time for the Moon's orbit is 28 days, and that they understand how we can work this out from the visual evidence.

PLENARY

Recap on the complete model of the movements of the Earth and Moon. Key points for the children to know are:

1 The Earth orbits the Sun once in a year, giving rise to our seasons.

2 The Earth spins on its own axis once in a day, giving us night and day.

3 The Moon orbits the Earth once every 28 days (28.25 days precisely), giving rise to the phases of the Moon.

OUTCOMES

- Know that the Moon goes round the Earth.
- Can explain why the shape of the Moon appears to change.

Lesson 17 ▪ The Moon changes shape

Objectives
● To know that the Moon moves around the Earth.
● To model the movement of the Moon around Earth, relating this to the Moon's phases.
● To use the phase of the Moon's on given dates to predict, then check the phase of the Moon at other times.

Vocabulary
phases, full Moon, new Moon, half Moon, crescent Moon, gibbous Moon

RESOURCES 💿

Main activity: A football; another football painted half black and half white; a lamp; a torch. (NB It is very important to use a ball for this activity, not a balloon as the light shines through a balloon and makes the phases hard to see.)
Group activities: 1 Calendar or diary for one month, showing the 'full moon', 'new moon' and 'half moon' phases. **2** Access to legends and stories, CD-ROMs or Internet sites about the Moon. **3** Photocopiable page 175 (optional) (see also 'The Moon changes shape' (red) available on the CD-ROM).

PREPARATION
Select suitable legends or early stories about the Moon. Select suitable CD-ROMs or internet sites with information about Moon exploration.

BACKGROUND
As the Moon travels around the Earth in its orbit, half the Moon is always brightly lit by the Sun, and half is in darkness. From Earth, we can only see the brightly lit side. The proportion of the brightly lit side that we are able to see depends on where the Moon, Earth and Sun are in relation to each other. As the Moon orbits the Earth its position relative to the Earth and the Sun changes in a regular and predictable way, leading to the phases of the Moon (the proportion of the bright side we see) also changing in a regular and predicable way. The Moon completes one orbit of the Earth in 28 days, but a calendar does not show the phases repeating in an exact 28 day cycle because the Earth is also moving around the Sun, leading to a slight change each month in the relative positions. This slight distortion of the 28 day cycle each month is ignored here, as it is too complicated for children.

STARTER
Ask the children: *Why do we see the Moon?* Ensure that children remember that the Moon is not a light source, we only see it because it reflects light from the Sun. *Can you explain why we usually only see the Moon at night time?* The light straight from the Sun is so much brighter than the reflected light from the Moon, that during the day we can't see the reflected light at all (compare with a candle and a floodlight) but the Moon is always there.

MAIN ACTIVITY
Assist the children to remodel what they learned in Lesson 16 about the movement of the Moon around Earth. Can they, with appropriate help, work out what phase of the Moon they will see when the Moon, Earth and Sun are in given positions relative to each other? Check their understanding using a globe and a model 'Moon' to ask questions such as, *'Who will not be able to see the Moon at all, when we are seeing a full moon? Why not? (*The people on the opposite side of the Earth, because the Earth gets in the way and because for them it is daytime, so the Moon wouldn't show up, even if it was in the sky above them.)

GROUP ACTIVITIES
In these Sc1 activities the children look up secondary sources of information and relate these to the information they have been given as well as investigating how scientific ideas have changed over time, possibly giving reasons for some of these changes.
1 Give children a calendar or a diary covering a time span of a month, or just over, with the 'full moon', 'new moon' and 'half moon' phases drawn in. In pairs or small groups, ask the children to use what they have learned about

Differentiation

Group activity 1
Let children who need support cut out a complete set of phases of the Moon for one calendar month and put them into the correct order.

Group activity 2
All children should be able to complete this activity. Provide differentiation in the complexity of secondary sources provided.

the phases of the Moon to work out, then draw in, the missing phases of the Moon. Can they also work out when the dates of the previous, and the next 'full moon' and 'new moon' phases. Provide completed calendars or diaries, or websites showing moon phases on different dates, for children to check their ideas, helping them to do this if necessary.

2 Provide children with some early stories or legends about the Moon, and access to modern, secondary sources of information about the Moon. Ask the children to work together to identify some ways in which our ideas about the Moon have changed and, with help if necessary, suggest ideas about why these ideas changed.

3 Give the children photocopiable page 175 to work through (optional).

ASSESSMENT

Ask one or two groups to describe what they have found out and ask others to discuss whether or not they agree. Check that the children know that the time for the Moon's orbit is 28 days and explain, if necessary, that it doesn't always look like that in calendars because the Earth moves too.

PLENARY

Recap on the complete model of the movements of the Earth and Moon, ensuring that the children know that the phases of the Moon are caused by the reflection of sunlight from the Moon and the orbit of the Moon around the Earth. Ensure that they can predict the times of new moons, full moons and half moons given some appropriate information.

OUTCOMES

● Know that the Moon goes round the Earth.
● Can describe how this causes the phases of the Moon.

Lesson 18 ◗ Assessment

Objectives

● To assess the children's knowledge and understanding of the movements of the Earth and Moon.
● To assess the children's ability to extract information from a graph.

Vocabulary

phases, full Moon, new Moon, half Moon, crescent Moon, gibbous Moon

RESOURCES 💿

Photocopiable pages 176 and 177 (also 'Assessment – 1' (red) and 'Assessment – 2' (red) available on the CD-ROM); pencils.
ICT link: 'The Moon ' interactive and 'Moon orbit' diagram on the CD-ROM.

STARTER

You may wish to start the lesson with the Assessment activities, or to start with a brief 'question and answer' session covering important facts. You may wish to check orally that the children have understood all the new vocabulary introduced in this unit by giving words and asking for definitions, or giving definitions and asking for the correct words.

ASSESSMENT ACTIVITY 1

Give out copies of page 176 for the children to complete individually. The answers can be collected in to be marked; alternatively, the children can exchange and mark them in class, which will encourage them to discuss the answers.

ANSWERS

1. 6.45; 2. 3.50; 3. 1 July; 4. Earliest time 3.50, latest time 8.00, difference is 4 hours 10 minutes; 5. 5.45; 6. 4.45; 7. It makes the early morning darker. 8. Each point on the graph should be 1 hour (2 blocks) higher up the y-axis.

LOOKING FOR LEVELS

This activity has questions that require children to read from the graph, questions that require them to use information read from the graph, and questions that require them to draw conclusions from that information. All the children should answer questions 1, 2 and 3. Most of them should answer questions 4, 5 and 6. More able children will answer questions 7 and 8.

ASSESSMENT ACTIVITY 2

Give out copies of page 177 for the children to complete individually. As with Assessment activity 1, the answers can either be collected in for marking or marked in class.

ANSWERS

(See diagram opposite, and on CD-ROM.)
1. New Moon;
2. Half Moon;
3. See diagram;
4. The Earth has to turn a bit further before the Moon comes into view, so the Moon will rise later.

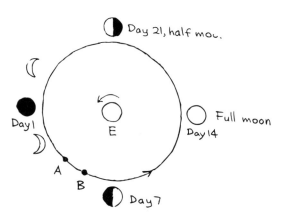

LOOKING FOR LEVELS

All the children should answer question 1 and place the full Moon correctly. Most of the children should answer questions 1, 2 and 3. Some children will answer question 4. It is expected that:

● Most children will know that the Earth, Sun and Moon are spherical and know some evidence supporting this; be able to explain how the motion of the Earth makes the Sun appear to move across the sky; understand how day and night occur; know that the Moon orbits the Earth; and identify patterns in sunrise and sunset times.

● Some children will know that the Earth, Sun and Moon are spherical, and be able to describe how shadows change as the Sun appears to move across the sky.

● Some children will be able to explain how the phases of the Moon arise and how they are evidence for a 28-day orbit of the Moon around the Earth; and be able to work independently to represent sunrise and sunset times in graphs.

ICT LINK

Complete 'The Moon' interactive as a class, or in small groups, as part of the Plenary.

PLENARY

If you allow the children to mark each other's answers, the Plenary session can be used to go through the questions and discuss the correct answers. Encourage the children to ask questions about topics in the Assessment activities that they were unsure of, and any related topics that they would like to know more about. If you are going to mark the answers later, encourage the children to say which parts of the Assessment activities they found easy or difficult and why. Take time to clear up any obvious misconceptions, and encourage the children to ask any other questions they may have about the Earth, Sun or Moon, even if the answers are not covered by any of the lessons. If there are any questions that you cannot answer, help the children to decide how they can find out the answers.

OUTCOMES

● Know that the Moon goes around the Earth.
● Can describe how this causes the phases of the Moon.

Round Earth or flat Earth?

■ Draw three pictures to show what the observer on land would see as the ship sails further and further away.

1. If the world is flat.

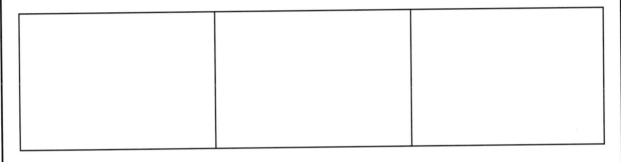

2. If the world is round.

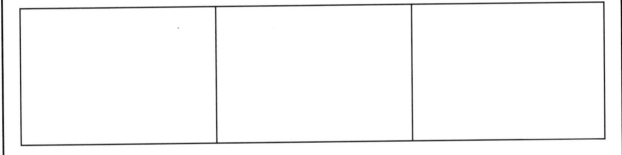

■ As a ship approaches land anywhere in the world, the sails come into view first. What does this tell you about the shape of the Earth?

_____

■ Colour in blue the stars that observer A would be unable to see. Colour in red the stars that observer B would be unable to see. Explain to a friend what observer C notices about the stars she can see as she walks from A to B.

Illustration © Robin Lawrie

Directions – 1

■ Draw what you can see in each compass direction.

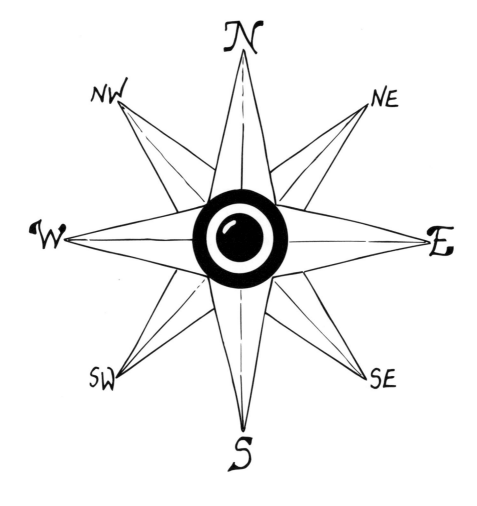

■ SCHOLASTIC

Directions – 2

◼ Work with a partner. Take it in turns to choose a starting place and a destination. Tell your partner where you want them to start and tell them where to go using 'north', 'south', 'east' and 'west'. For example, you could choose a journey from the fish and chip shop to the bank and you could say 'Start at the fish and chip shop. Walk south until you reach the newsagent, then go east. You will find the bank on the south side of the road.'

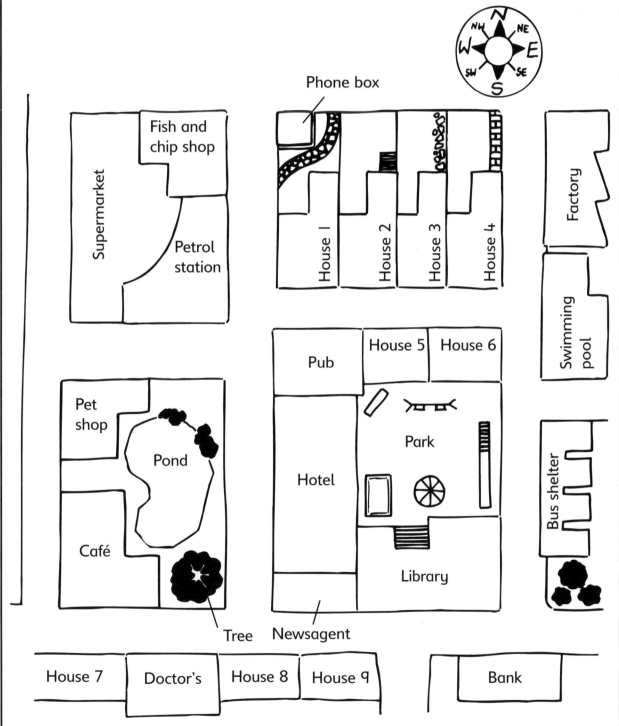

PHOTOCOPIABLE

Day and night

◼ Fill in the answers to the clues. Make up a question about the Earth with the answer that you find in the shaded squares.

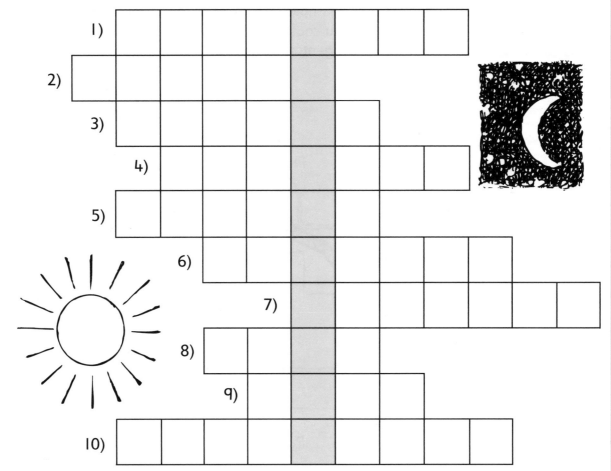

1. It is this time when you cannot see the Sun.

2. A stick in sunshine will have one of these.

3. As the afternoon passes, shadows will get _____ .

4. The time when shadows are gradually getting shorter.

5. The Earth does this once every day.

6. It is this time when you can see the Sun in the sky.

7. Cold places are _____ away from the Sun.

8. This is the time when shadows are shortest.

9. This is the time when the Sun disappears below the horizon at the end of the day.

10. The Earth is approximately this shape.

SCHOLASTIC

Shadows – 1

■ Our question: What happens to the length of the shadow when we change the angle of the torch?

What we changed: _____

_____

What we kept the same: _____

_____

_____

Our table of results

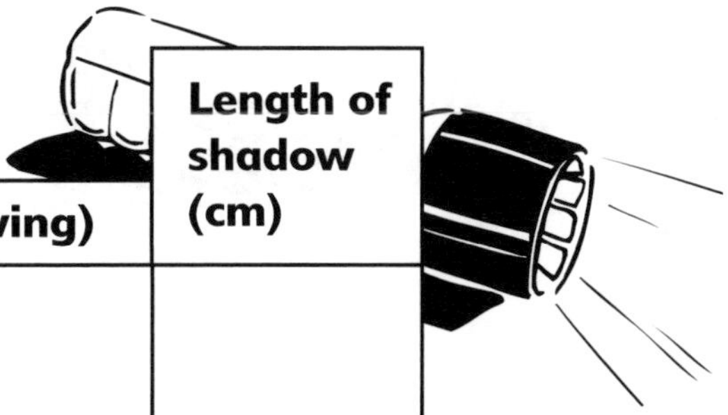

Angle of torch (drawing)	Length of shadow (cm)

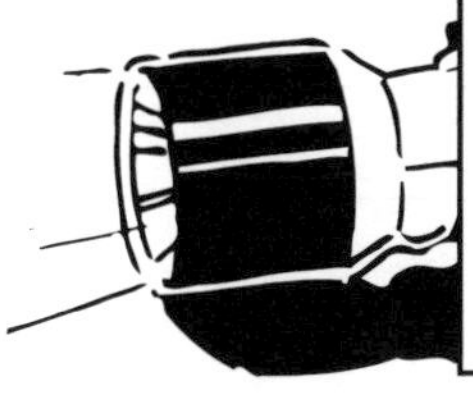

We found out that when the torch _____

_____

then the shadow gets _____

_____ .

Illustration © Robin Lawrie

Shadows – 2

■ These children measured a shadow at different times of day.

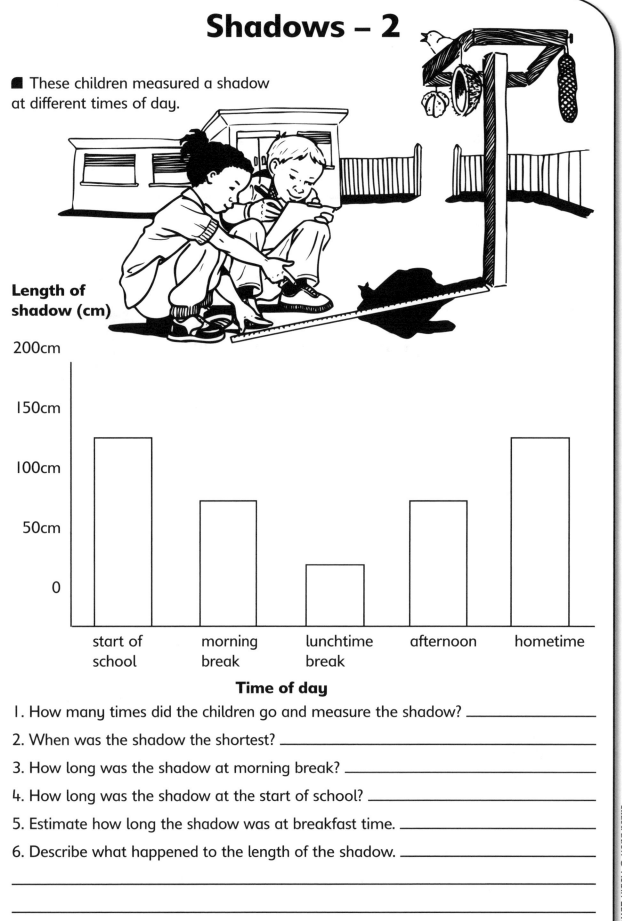

Length of shadow (cm)

200cm

150cm

100cm

50cm

0

| start of school | morning break | lunchtime break | afternoon | hometime |

Time of day

1. How many times did the children go and measure the shadow? _____

2. When was the shadow the shortest? _____

3. How long was the shadow at morning break? _____

4. How long was the shadow at the start of school? _____

5. Estimate how long the shadow was at breakfast time. _____

6. Describe what happened to the length of the shadow. _____

_____

_____

Illustration © Robin Lawrie

■ SCHOLASTIC

Star patterns

Illustration © Robin Lawrie

PHOTOCOPIABLE

The seasons

1. Draw a diagram of the Earth and Sun to show the position that the Earth will be in when it is summer in Britain.

2. Some of the sentences below are correct when it is summer in Britain. Tick the ones that are correct. Remember: the Earth is rotating on its own axis.

The South Pole is in constant darkness.	
The sunlight reaching Britain is spread over a large area.	
The North Pole is in constant daylight.	
The sunlight reaching Britain is spread over a small area.	
The South Pole is in constant daylight.	
The North Pole is in constant darkness.	

3. Describe what happens to the seasons as the Earth orbits the Sun. Explain why the changes happen, and say how long the changes take.

_____

_____

_____

_____

_____

SCHOLASTIC

The Moon changes shape

- Choose the Moon shapes.
- Cut them out and stick them in the grey circles to make Moon shapes.

Assessment – 1

The graph below shows the time that the Sun rises on the first day of each month throughout the year.

The jumps on April 1st and October 1st show when daylight saving time begins and ends. The dotted line shows the time when the Sun would have risen without daylight saving time.

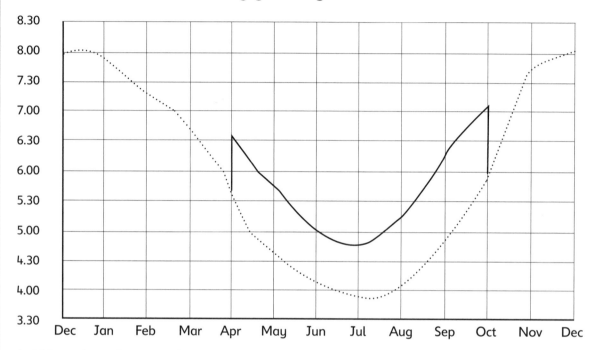

1. What time does the Sun rise on March 1st? _____

2. What is the earliest time the Sun rises? _____

3. When does this happen? _____

4. What is the difference between the earliest sunrise time and the latest sunrise time? _____

5. What time does the Sun rise on May 1st? _____

6. What time would it have risen on May 1st without daylight saving time? _____

7. What effect does daylight saving time have on how light it is early in the morning? _____

8. Draw a line to show how the graph would look if the sunrise times were all 1 hour later. Ignore daylight saving time. _____

Illustration © Robin Lawrie

Assessment – 2

The first diagram shows the Moon's orbit around the Earth. The arrows show the direction the Moon moves and the direction the Earth is spinning in.

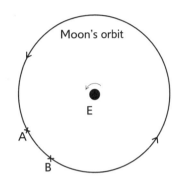

The second diagram shows the phases of the Moon that we see.

Day 1   Day 7

1. Put a 1 on the Moon's orbit where you would see Day 1 of the phases of the Moon. What is this phase called?

_____

2. Put a 7 where you would see Day 7. What is this phase called?

_____

3. Draw the other four phases of the Moon in the correct places on the Moon's orbit.

4. When the Moon is at A on its orbit, it 'rises' (is first visible) at 7pm. When it has moved to B, will it 'rise' earlier, later or at the same time? Why?

_____

_____

_____

Illustration © Robin Lawrie

CHAPTER 7 Changing sounds

Lesson	Objectives	Main activity	Group activities	Plenary	Outcomes
Lesson 1 Sound survey	• To know that there is a wide variety of sound sources. • To be able to plan a fair test, make observations and judgements. • To be able to draw conclusions.	Looking at natural and non-natural sound sources.	Carrying out a school sound survey. Describing sounds.	Identifying quiet and noisy areas around school.	• Can recognise sound sources. • Can understand that humans are responsible for making, and so controlling, much noise. • Can plan a fair test, make observations and judgements. • Can draw conclusions.
Lesson 2 Producing sounds	• To know that a range of vibrating objects produce different sounds. • To make observations and draw conclusions. • To make and test predictions.	Describe the sounds produced by a range of objects.	Use hearing, sight and touch to observe things that make sounds. Record observations and deduce what all sound-making objects have in common.	Discuss the fact that all sound is made by vibration. Predict the effect of making something unfamiliar vibrate, and ways to make sound louder or quieter.	• Can make a generalisation that sound is made by something vibrating.
Lesson 3 Vibrations	• To understand what is meant by 'vibration'. • To recognise that sound is the result of vibration. • To recognise that different things vibrate differently and this makes different sounds. • To observe carefully using different senses. • To make connections between different experiences and ideas.	Using the word 'vibration' to describe observations.	Circus of activities exploring vibration.		• Can recognise that sound is the result of a movement called a vibration. • Can recognise that different things vibrate differently and so make different sounds. • Can observe carefully using hearing, sight and touch, and link ideas to observations.
Lesson 4 Recording sound levels	• To know that sound travels in straight lines and can reflect off things, making echoes. • To record data on a line graph.	Use the task of locating a sound source to demonstrate that sound travels in straight lines.	Plot graphs to show volume of sound recorded from different directions by a sound meter. Use secondary sources to study animals' ears.	Check all the children know that sounds travel in straight lines from source to hearer. Discuss advantages of large ears and ears that swivel.	• Can describe the path of a sound from its source to the ear. • Can draw a line graph using data from a table.
Lesson 5 Sound paths	• To know that sound can travel through solids, water and air.	Demonstrate that sound travels through solids, water and air. Describe different sound paths.		Recap on how sound travels. Discuss creatures that use underwater sounds.	• Recognise that sound can travel through solids, water and air (a gas).
Enrichment Lesson 6 The speed of sound	• To know that sound travels at a certain speed through air and that this is slower than the speed of light.	Taking advantage of a thunderstorm to compare when we observe the thunder and lightning.			• Know that sound travels slower than light. • Can recognise that sound travels at a certain speed.
Lesson 7 String telephones	• To know that it is possible to change some solids so that sound travels better though them. • To make a prediction and test it, choosing appropriate equipment for the test.	Discuss how sound travels from one end of a string telephone to the other. Consider what type of design would be best.	Build a string telephone. Test predictions about when it will work well. Write about how it was made and tested, including predictions and conclusions.	Children explain how the string telephone works, and when it works best. Discuss whether using wire instead of string would work better.	• Can predict what factors make a solid able to transmit sound. • Can test a prediction.
Lesson 8 Materials for reducing sound	• To know that some materials reduce sound. • To plan and carry out a fair test.	Discuss what types of material would be suitable as sound reducers.	Assess the sound reduction properties of different materials. Design a poster.	Discuss what materials reduce sound the most and why. Where might these materials be used?	• Know that some materials can reduce sound. • Can plan a fair test.
Lesson 9 Elastic band sonometers	• To know that the pitch of some musical instruments can be altered by changing the size or tension of the vibrating part. • To know how to make a test fair.	Listen to an elastic band sonometer. Discuss possible ways of producing higher or lower notes. Discuss and try ways of changing the note produced by a model drum.	Investigate the effect on an elastic band sonometer of changing one factor.	Identify similarities between the sonometer and a real instrument.	• Can describe how the pitch of a drum or a stringed instrument is altered. • Understand how to make a test fair.

Lesson	Objectives	Main activity	Group activities	Plenary	Outcomes
Lesson 10 Pitch	• To recognise high and low pitch. • To recognise that the pitch of a sound is related to the size of the vibrating part of an object. • To notice patterns in their observations and to make generalisations.	Introducing '-er' statements (generalisations) to relate pitch to length of chime bar.	Looking for patterns in the sounds made by collections of objects and musical instruments.		• Can recognise high and low pitch. • Can recognise that the pitch of a sound is related to the size of the vibrating part of an object. • Can notice patterns in their observations and make generalisations in the form of '-er' sentences.
Lesson 11 Higher or lower?	• To consolidate recognition of high and low pitch. • To know that the pitch of a sound is related to the size of the vibrating part.	Exploring how changing the length of a ruler 'twanged' on a table changes the pitch and express this as an '-er' statement.		Groups describe what they have found out. .	• Can recognise high and low pitch in a variety of contexts. • Understand that pitch is related to the size of the vibrating part of a musical instrument.
Lesson 12 Changing pitch and volume	• To explore and understand how the pitch and loudness of a sound can be changed.	Examine how a musical instrument has been built, and how it is used to make different sounds. The children build their own simple instruments.		Conduct the children as they play their instruments together; focus on how the notes are made and discuss the pitch of notes produced.	• Can describe musical sounds in terms of loudness and pitch. • Can suggest ways to change the sound an instrument makes.
Enrichment Lesson 13 DIY instruments	• To know that the loudness of musical instruments can be altered by changing how much they vibrate.	Build musical instruments using knowledge gained earlier in unit. Create tunes. Vary the loudness of the notes.		Groups play the tunes they have made.	• Can make simple musical instruments and describe how to change the loudness of the note they produce.
Lesson 14 Different instruments	• To know what parts of a musical instrument vibrate to produce sounds. • To know that sounds can be described in terms of loudness and pitch.	Demonstrate how to play low and high notes on an instrument, then loud and soft notes. Demonstrate that the latter correspond to greater and lesser degrees of vibration.	Use secondary sources to look at musical instruments from around the world. Find out how different notes are played on them.	Discuss 'families' of musical instruments and how they are used to make different notes.	• Can explain how sound is produced from string, wind and percussion instruments. • Can describe musical sounds in terms of loudness and pitch.
Lesson 15 Making wind instruments	• To know that the pitch of a wind instrument can be altered by changing the length of the vibrating air column.	Look at different wind instruments. What are the similarities and differences?	Make milk bottle instruments and drinking straw buzzers. Find out how to change the note produced.	Discuss how different notes are obtained on a real instrument.	• Can relate the pitch of a sound made by a wind instrument to the length of the air column.
Enrichment Lesson 16 Recycled instruments	• To apply knowledge of sound in a design and technology context. • To apply scientific understanding.	Designing and making a musical instrument from junk materials.		Designing and making a musical instrument from junk materials.	• Can apply knowledge and understanding of sound in a design and technology context.
Lesson 17 Echoes	• To know that sound can be reflected. • To introduce 'echoes'.	Discussing experiences of echoes.	Modelling echoes using ropes.		• Can recognise that sound can be reflected and create an echo.
Enrichment Lesson 18 Loud and quiet	• To know that loud sounds can be an environmental problem.	Ask the children to concentrate on a task in a noisy environment. Discuss the use of soundproofing. The children investigate what materials reduce noise.		Ask the children to try concentrating in silence, then with 'background' music.	• Recognise the need for quietness at times. • Can identify causes of loud noises. • Can test a material for its sound reduction properties.

Assessment	Objectives	Activity 1	Activity 2
Lesson 19	• To assess the children's knowledge of how sound travels from a source to a listener, and how well it travels through different materials.	Draw sound paths from a source to different listeners. State which listener will hear the sound first. Describe and explain the effects of echoes and of sound-reducing materials.	Answer questions about musical instruments and how to change pitch and volume.

SC1 SCIENTIFIC ENQUIRY

Which material is best at stopping sound?

LEARNING OBJECTIVES AND OUTCOMES
- Use a sound meter to measure the loudness of sound.
- Repeat measurements.
- Plan and carry out a fair test.
- Use results to draw a conclusion.

ACTIVITY
The children work together to plan an investigation to find out which type of material is best at reducing the sound heard from a given sound source. They consider what they have to do to make a fair comparison between the different materials they try. They should repeat readings and present their results in a table.

LESSON LINKS
This Sc1 activity forms an integral part of Lesson 8, Materials for reducing sound.

Lesson 1 ▪ Sound survey

Objective
- To know that there is a wide variety of sound sources.
- To be able to plan a fair test, make observations and judgements.
- To be able to draw conclusions.

Vocabulary
detect, hear, loud, noisy, quiet, sound, transmit, vibrate

RESOURCES
Main activity: A flipchart or board, pens.
Group activities: 1 Simple plan of the school; clipboards; pens; pencils.
2 Paper; pens; pencils.

PREPARATION
Copy a plan of the school for each child or group.

BACKGROUND
Sound originates from very many different sources - some natural, some made by human activity or intention. But whether it is pleasant or unpleasant, all sounds are produced, transmitted and detected in the same way. All sound sources produce their sounds by causing a vibration.

STARTER
Begin the lesson by playing some music, banging about, singing, opening and shutting doors and generally making a great deal of varied noise. Suggest it's a little noisy in the classroom and ask the children to suggest where all the sounds are coming from - own up to it being you! Tell the children that they are going to be thinking about and listening for sounds.

MAIN ACTIVITY
Ask the children to close their eyes for one minute and to listen very carefully for all the sounds they can hear. Compile a class list of those sounds. Ask the children to name where all these sounds were coming from and they will soon begin to realise that there is a wide variety of sources of sound. Highlight that these 'sources' can be divided into those that are natural and those that are made by human actions or inventions. Talk about the sounds the children like and those they do not. Introduce Group activity 1. Tell the children to imagine they are 'Sound consultants' who have been called in to school to carry out a 'Sound survey'. Their task is to walk around the school, in groups, inside and/or outside on a 'Sound survey walk'.

Differentiation
Group activities
Support children by giving
them a word bank of
descriptive words to describe
the sounds.

GROUP ACTIVITIES

1 The children should mark on a plan of the school the locations and types of sounds that they hear as they walk around. They should prepare a 'Sound consultants' report' to be presented at the end of the survey.

2 The children remaining in class while the sound consultants tour the school should make two lists identifying a variety of sound sources and describing the sound that is produced. These sounds can be divided into 'natural' (such as birds, animals, humans, the weather and so on) and 'not natural' (such as machinery, music, doors banging and so on).

ASSESSMENT

Have the children been able to identify a variety of sound sources? Expect a good range, with perhaps ten examples in each section for higher-attaining children. Can the children offer any judgements about the noises around school – should there be talking in the 'Quiet reading area'? Why? Why not?

PLENARY

Ask each group of 'Sound consultants' to present their findings from the sound survey walk. Encourage them to draw conclusions from their data . *Can you see where the quiet areas are? What goes on there? What is the source of most of the sound?* Ask: *If you were to carry out the survey at different times of day would your findings be the same or not?* (Consider the playground at break time and during assembly time.) Point out that one survey (or experiment) may not be enough for scientists to get the whole picture. Emphasise the importance of carrying out a fair test and being able to make judgements based on the evidence collected.

Explain that loud sounds are produced when more energy is expended: hitting a drum hard produces a louder sound than gently tapping it.

OUTCOMES

- Can recognise sound sources.
- Can understand that humans are responsible for making, and so controlling, much noise.
- Can plan a fair test, make observations and judgements.
- Can draw conclusions.

LINKS

Literacy: non-fiction writing.

Lesson 2 ◗ Producing sound

Objective
- To know that a range of vibrating objects produce different sounds.
- To make observations and draw conclusions.
- To make and test predictions.

Vocabulary
detect, hear, loud, noisy, quiet, sound, transmit, vibrate

RESOURCES

Main activity and Group activity: A flipchart and marker pen; a selection of sound-producing objects (for example: a drum, a stretched elastic band, a tuning fork, a ruler clamped to a table); a recording of familiar sounds; paper; writing materials.
Plenary: A glass; a handbell.

PREPARATION

Check that all the sound sources you will use can either be seen or felt to be vibrating.

BACKGROUND

This lesson should be aimed at finding out how much the class already knows about sound, and teaching that all sounds are made by objects vibrating. Asking children to describe sounds is a good way of checking both their understanding and their knowledge of the relevant vocabulary.

Differentiation
Support some children could use pictures to record which parts of some objects are vibrating to make sounds.

Extend children by asking them to think of things around the home that make sounds. Ask them: *What is vibrating to make the sound?*

STARTER

Tell the children that in the next few lessons, they are going to be finding out about sounds. *What do you know about sounds?* Brainstorm all the children's ideas about sounds; record their knowledge, including any misconceptions, on a flipchart. Keep this to be referred to at the end of the unit. Check that the children are aware that the words 'sound' and 'noise' mean the same thing, but that we usually use 'noise' to refer to sounds that we don't like.

MAIN ACTIVITY

Study a selection of things that produce sound, and listen to a recording of various familiar sounds. Ask the children to describe the sounds produced. Look for vocabulary such as 'high/low', 'loud/quiet' and 'getting louder/quieter'. Make sure the children understand words such as 'high', 'low' and 'soft' that have different meanings in other contexts. Discuss when particular sounds will seem louder or quieter. At this stage, you should be looking only for the knowledge that any sound seems louder when you are closer to what is making it.

GROUP ACTIVITY

Ask the children to examine various things that make sounds (see Resources). Using hearing, sight and touch, they should make very careful observations of the sound-producing objects. They should then record their observations using writing or drawing, and try to deduce what all the things making sounds have in common. (They are vibrating.)

ASSESSMENT

Ask the children to choose one object and tell their friends what they observed about it. Can they describe what was moving and how they detected the movement?

PLENARY

Make sure the children understand what vibration is. If they have used language such as 'All the things had bits that were moving', explain that when something keeps moving backwards and forwards (for example, a 'twanged' ruler) we use the word 'vibrating'.

Look at a less familiar situation, and ask the children to predict what will happen if you do something to cause vibration. Examples could be rubbing a damp finger around the top of a glass or tapping a handbell. For some familiar objects, ask the children to predict ways of making the sound produced louder or quieter. Test all their predictions.

OUTCOME

● Can make a generalisation that sound is made by something vibrating.

LINKS

PE and drama: fitting appropriate sounds to moods and actions.

Lesson 3 ▪ Vibrations

RESOURCES 💿
Main activity: A guitar, a tuning fork.
Group activity: A guitar; ping-pong balls threaded on to thick thread; a bowl of water; two tuning forks; a drum; rice; a tank of water; pebbles; a slinky (three would be ideal); a cymbal and soft beater; photocopiable page 201 (also 'Vibrations' (red) available on the CD-ROM); card.

Objective
● To understand what is meant by 'vibration'.
● To recognise that sound is the result of vibration.
● To recognise that different things vibrate differently and this makes different sounds.
● To observe carefully using different senses.
● To make connections between different experiences and ideas.

Vocabulary
hear, see, sound, touch, vibration

PREPARATION
Copy photocopiable page 201 on to card, enlarged to A3 if possible. Cut the page into individual cards. Set up the Group activities on tables around the room with their appropriate instructions.

BACKGROUND
When things are made to vibrate, perhaps by being struck, they vibrate in different ways according to what they are made of and their size and shape. The vibrations move the air next to the object, which moves the air a bit further away and so on. This is what is called a sound wave; every time the vibration pushes the nearby air it sets off a 'ripple'. This moves out in all directions, like when a pebble is dropped in a pond. The ripple may reach the air near our ears; the ears are really vibration detectors and our brains construct the idea of a 'sound'.

STARTER
Ask the children to put their hands gently on their throats (on their voice box) and make a humming noise. Ask: *What does it feel like?* (A 'buzzing'; a vibration.) Some children may find it easier to feel on a partner. Demonstrate playing a chime bar and ask some children to feel the bar. Ask: *What do we call that 'buzzing', that tiny up and down movement?* (A vibration.) Write the word 'vibration' on the board or hold up the card with the word written on it.

This lesson is structured with a short Main activity to help the children focus their attention on the Group activities, but has a longer Plenary in which important ideas are clarified.

MAIN ACTIVITY
Explain that the children are going to experience all sorts of vibrations using their senses of hearing, sight and touch. Explain that you will demonstrate some first, but that they will all be able to experience them for themselves in their groups.

Ask a child to gently touch the body of the guitar. Pluck a string of the guitar and ask the child to describe what they see, hear and feel. Now ask: *Can you use the word 'vibration' to explain what you have noticed?*

Demonstrate how to use a tuning fork, holding it by the unforked end and striking a prong on a hard surface. Show how it makes a note by holding the unforked end onto a surface. Ask: *What do you think will happen if I touch the end of the fork on some water?* Show interest in the children's suggestions and then try them! Don't get involved in explanations at this stage.

Briefly outline the Group activity, reminding the children to use their senses and to think about vibrations. Explain that they will have 5 minutes on each activity and you will discuss their ideas in the Plenary.

GROUP ACTIVITY
The children need to be in groups of about four, though these can be larger if equipment is scarce. The activities are set up as a circus. Tell the groups to try each activity for five minutes, then move on to the next activity.

Circulate, asking questions, for example: *What have you noticed? What did that feel like?* Help the children to use the equipment effectively if necessary.

ASSESSMENT
Do the children understand what is meant by the term 'vibration'? Can they describe different examples of vibration? Are they making links between vibration and sound?

PLENARY
Gather the children together. Invite different children to comment briefly on

Differentiation
Support
● Target questions differently, asking some children to focus on description and others to try to form explanations.

each activity, bringing the equipment to the circle. Ask: *Did all the things make the same sound?* (No.) *What differences did you notice in how the things vibrated?* (This one was difficult to feel; this one vibrated a lot and so on.) Ask: *What do we mean by a vibration?* (Something moving backwards and forwards very fast.) *What have vibrations got to do with sound?* Listen to the children's ideas and draw on them in your explanation. Explain that our ears are 'vibration detectors' so when something vibrates they notice and our brain calls it a sound. Ask: *How do our ears up here* [indicating up] *pick up a vibration down there* [point to an object]? Listen to the children's ideas. Explain that the sound travels through the air, a bit like a ripple travels through water or along a slinky and gets to our ears.

OUTCOMES
● Can recognise that sound is the result of a movement called a vibration.
● Can recognise that different things vibrate differently and so make different sounds.
● Can observe carefully using hearing, sight and touch, and link ideas to observations.

LINKS
Music: musical instruments have a vibrating part.

Lesson 4 ▪ Recording sound levels

Objective
● To know that sound travels in straight lines and can reflect off things, making echoes.
● To record data on a line graph.

Vocabulary
sound, source, echo, volume

RESOURCES 💿
Main activity: A device that ticks; such as a metronome or timer; a long scarf; a cardboard ear tube.
Group activities: 1 Photocopiable page 202 (also 'Recording sound levels' (red) available on the CD-ROM); graph paper; pencils; rulers. **2** Secondary sources of information about animal ears.

PREPARATION
Make an ear tube: a sheet of cardboard rolled and taped to make a tube about 7cm in diameter and about 30cm long.

BACKGROUND
Sound waves travel outwards in all directions from a source of sound. A listener hears sound that has travelled in a straight line from the source to the ear, but he or she will also hear sound waves that have bounced off hard objects: echoes. The echo is always heard after the original sound, because the sound wave that has been reflected has always travelled further than the sound wave that has travelled directly from source to listener. Whenever sound waves hit a material, some of the sound energy is absorbed, so the sound that has travelled directly from source to listener is always louder than the echoes from surrounding materials. This means that the source of a sound can be located by identifying the direction in which it is loudest.

STARTER
Remind the children that vibrating objects make sounds. Ask: *How does the sound get to us?* (It travels to us through the air.) *Do all sounds reach us?* (Obviously not, or we would be able to hear everything that was happening in the next classroom. Explain that we can work out how sound travels to us by finding out what sounds we hear best.

MAIN ACTIVITY
Show the children a source of sound. Something that ticks, such as a metronome or a timer, will be better for this than a variable source such as

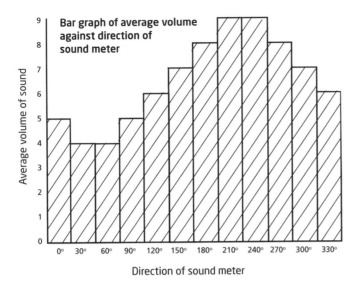

Bar graph of average volume against direction of sound meter

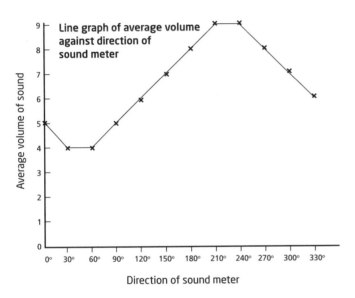

Line graph of average volume against direction of sound meter

music. Adjust the volume by moving it until the children can still hear it, but it is quiet. Turn the sound source off. Ask for a volunteer to help work out how the sound travels from the source to our ears. Give him or her a scarf, or something soft and padded, to cover one ear (absorbing sound), and a cardboard tube to hold to the other ear. Ask the child to shut his or her eyes, then start the sound source again this time in a different part of the room. Keeping his or her eyes shut, the child has to turn around very slowly until the sound appears to be at its loudest, then stop with the tube pointing at the source of the sound. Repeat with other children, then discuss what this tells us. (The sound is travelling directly to us from the source.

GROUP ACTIVITIES

1 Give the children a copy each of page 202 and some graph paper, and let them work through the task. Explain that the units of sound volume are relative.

2 The children can use secondary sources to study animals that have large ears or ears that can swivel around easily. Ask them to write a few sentences for each animal, describing the advantage of these ears.

ASSESSMENT

In the Plenary session, ask some children to show the graphs they have drawn. Discuss the direction of the sound source, asking the children to explain why they chose the direction they did.

PLENARY

Remind the children that sounds appear louder when the ear is pointing directly at them. Make sure all the children know what the line graph (or bar chart) of sound volume against direction should look like (see diagrams). Discuss what this tells us about the direction of the source of the sound, and why this is the case. Discuss the questions at the bottom of the sheet; make sure the children understand that the readings were repeated in order to make sure that the results were reliable. They should suggest checking the readings at 90°, since the large difference between the two readings indicates a probable error. The precise direction of the sound source cannot be given, but is close to 225°.

Invite some children to share their have findings, drawing attention to why many animals have ears that can swivel. Relate this to what was discovered in the Main activity: a source of sound can be located because the sound appears louder when the ear is pointing directly at the source.

OUTCOMES

- Can describe the path of a sound from its source to the ear.
- Can draw a line graph using data from a table.

LINKS

Maths: calculating averages, plotting line graphs or bar charts.

Lesson 5 ▪ Sound paths

Objective
● To know that sound can travel through solids, water and air.

RESOURCES
A wooden or tin box with a lid; a bead or marble; a bowl of water; a source of underwater sound (such as two spoons to knock together); pictures of different situations showing a sound source and a listener.

MAIN ACTIVITY
Talk about the evidence we have that sound travels through different types of material. *How do we know that sound can travel through air (a gas)?* (We wouldn't be able to hear each other talk if it didn't.) Rattle a bead or marble in a closed wooden or tin box. *What does that sound travel through to reach us?* If the sound could not travel through the solid box, we would not hear anything. Tap two spoons together in a bowl of water (or use any other method of making a sound underwater). *Can you hear anything?* This tells us that sound must be able to travel through water.

Ask the children to put an ear close to the desk and tap their fingers so lightly on the desk that they cannot hear it, then rest their ear on the desk and repeat the soft tap. The second time, they can hear the tapping clearly - so sound travels better through solids than through air. Discuss why echoes are fainter than the original sound: some of the sound bounces off to reach us, but the rest travels into the solid object.

Give the children pictures of various situations showing a source of sound and a listener. Ask them to describe the possible paths that the sound can take to reach the listener and state what type of material the sound has to travel through on each path.

ASSESSMENT
Ask the children to talk about the sound paths they have found. Look for knowledge that sound can travel through solids, liquids and gases, and that it can reflect from some objects. Some children may be aware that sound travels better through solids than through air.

PLENARY
Recap on how well sound can travel through different materials. Discuss creatures that use underwater sounds. All the creatures that communicate over any but very short distances use low-pitched sounds, which are distorted less.

OUTCOME
● Recognise that sound can travel through solids, water and air (a gas).

Differentiation
Ask children who need support to draw the possible paths for the sound, using red where the sound travels through a solid, blue for a liquid and green for a gas. Extend children by asking them to make up and describe different situations in which sound has to travel through solids, liquids and gases.

ENRICHMENT
Lesson 6 ▪ The speed of sound

Objective
● To know that sound travels at a certain speed through air and that this is slower than the speed of light.

RESOURCES
A thunderstorm! Take advantage of this whenever it occurs.

MAIN ACTIVITY
Observe the flash of lightning and count aloud together until you hear the thunder. Ask: *Why don't the thunder and the lightning come at the same time?* Explain that although they are started at the same time, the light travels much faster than the thunder and so gets to us almost straight away. The sound of thunder travels more slowly and so we can use it to work out how far away the storm is.

Repeat, counting the time difference between the lightning and the thunder. If the time is getting shorter, then the storm is closer and vice versa. Ask: *What do you think is happening to the storm - is it coming closer or moving away?* Explain that for every second counted the thunder has travelled a distance of about a mile (1.6km) so that we can work out how far the thunder and lightning have travelled.

ASSESSMENT
Can the children state that in a thunderstorm we see the lightning before the thunder? Can they explain that this is because the sound takes a certain time to travel the distance to us.

PLENARY
Ask: *In a thunderstorm, which comes first, the thunder or the lightning?* (The lightning comes first.) Ask: *What does this tell us about the speed of sound?* (It is slower than light.)

OUTCOMES
- Can recognise that sound travels slower than light.
- Can recognise that sound travels at a certain speed.

Lesson 7 ▪ String telephones

Objective
- To know that it is possible to change some solids so that sound travels better through them.
- To make a prediction and test it, choosing appropriate equipment for the test.

Vocabulary
stiff, floppy, solid, vibrate, transmit

Differentiation
Some children will be familiar with this idea, so target questions at those for whom this is a new experience.

RESOURCES
Main activity: A ready-assembled string telephone.
Group activity: A selection of different plastic and cardboard cups or small containers (two of each type per pair); different types of string; scissors; paper; writing materials.

PREPARATION
Make a string telephone (using cardboard cups). Prepare a suitable set of questions (perhaps for a classroom assistant) in order to support children in describing how they built and used their string telephone.

BACKGROUND
Sound travels well through solids because the particles in a solid are tightly bound together, giving a stiff structure which transmits vibrations well. If there are good connections between the cups and the string, and the string is tight, a string telephone will transmit sounds well: the vibrations of one cup will be transmitted along the string to the other end. A poor connection stops the message being transmitted because the string does not vibrate. A floppy string will absorb the vibrations instead of transmitting them, so the message will not get through.

STARTER
Ask the children to suggest ways in which they could get a sound message to someone else. Emphasise that it has to be a sound message: a telephone or a radio does not count, because these devices send electrical signals or radio signals. The children could shout, and they could use something like a megaphone to make the shout louder - but what if they wanted to send a whisper? Remind them of their discoveries about what sound travels through well (see Lesson 5).

MAIN ACTIVITY
Show the children a string telephone, already assembled. Ask who has seen or made one before. *How does it work?* Make sure the children know that the sound travels along the string from one mouthpiece/earpiece to the

other. Tell them that they are going to work in pairs to make string telephones – but they have to think carefully about the design and how they will build it, so that it will work as well as possible. They need to consider, for example: *What is the best sort of cup to use? Does it matter how the string attaches to the cups? What sort of string is best?*

GROUP ACTIVITY

Ask pairs of children to write down predictions about when the string telephone will work and when it won't, then choose their own materials to build a string telephone and test their predictions. They should find that the telephone will work when the string is tight and will not work if the string is loose. This is because sound travels easily through a stiff solid, but poorly through a soft or floppy solid.

Ask the children to write a few paragraphs about how they made their telephone, describing how it was built (probably using a diagram), their prediction about when it would work, what they found out and their conclusions (including whether their prediction was correct).

ICT LINK

Children could use the computer to produce writing and pictures to show how they designed and used their string telephones. Use this work to contribute to a class display.

ASSESSMENT

Look at the children's predictions and conclusions about their telephones. They should show awareness that the string has to be taut for the telephone to work, and that this is the case because sound travels better through hard or stiff solids than through soft or floppy solids.

PLENARY

Ask children to explain how the string telephone works. (It works because vibrations caused by someone talking are transmitted along the string.) Ask them to report what they have found about when the telephone works. (It works when the string is tight, but not when the string is floppy.) *Do you think using wire in the telephone instead of string would make any difference?* (The telephone would work better with wire, because even when wire is bent it is still stiff enough to transmit sound vibrations.)

OUTCOMES
● Can predict what factors make a solid able to transmit sound.
● Can test a prediction.

Lesson 8 ▪ Materials for reducing sound

RESOURCES 💿
Main activity: A sound source (such as a ticking clock or a buzzer); a selection of sound-reducing materials (see Preparation).
Group activities: 1 Photocopiable page 203 (also 'Materials for producing sound' (red) available on the CD-ROM); writing materials; sound sources; sound-reducing materials; measuring tapes; metre rulers. **2** Art paper; colouring pencils; felt-tipped pens.

PREPARATION
Collect many samples of different materials that might be used around the home, such as foam, plastic, carpet and vinyl. Make sure that there is enough for each group, and that the children can use equal thicknesses of each material. Do not use fibreglass loft insulation as this can cause splinters.

Differentiation

Group activity 1

● To support children, give them 'Materials for reducing sound' (green) from the CD-ROM, which includes fewer and less complex questions than the core sheet. To extend children, give them 'Materials for reducing sound' (blue), which includes more open-ended questioning.

Group activity 2

All the children should be able to participate in this activity.

BACKGROUND

There are many circumstances in which materials are used to reduce sound, from the ear defenders used by operators of noisy machinery to the soundproofing used in buildings to shut out the sounds of nearby roads or railway lines. Occasionally, scientists may use specially-shaped foam rubber padding to line a laboratory in order to make it 'anechoic' – that is, completely free from all echoes. The one feature that all materials used in these situations share is that they are soft and squashy, and so do not transmit vibrations. Most household furnishings, such as soft furniture, curtains and carpets, reduce sound transmission; this is why empty houses always sound more 'echoey' than furnished houses.

STARTER

Ask the children to think of situations where they might not want to hear certain sounds, or where other people might be hearing sounds they do not want to listen to. Introduce the idea of 'noise pollution': disturbance of people's lives by sounds that are unpleasant or even dangerous. Discuss ear protection, soundproofing and situations where these would be used.

MAIN ACTIVITY

Set up a source of constant or regular sound. *What can we do to this buzzer to stop us hearing it?* Explain that there is no volume control so it can't be turned down. Mention that there are some very loud sources of sound (such as factory machines) where the volume cannot be turned down either. When they suggest covering up the sound source, discuss appropriate material. At this stage, they should be aware (see Lesson 7) that a soft material will be better than a hard one. Show them a selection of different soft materials. Say: *You have to plan and carry out a fair test to find out which of these materials is best at blocking the sound of the buzzer.*

GROUP ACTIVITIES

1 Ask the children to assess the sound reduction properties of different materials. They can use copies of page 203 to plan and record their results.
2 Let the children design a poster to advertise a soundproofing material. They should include information on what the material is like, what it is made from and where it might be useful.

ASSESSMENT

Ask one or two groups to present their investigations and findings to the class. The other children can review the work presented and decide on good features and limitations. Look for the ability to tell whether a test is fair, and whether there are questions that the test could not answer.

PLENARY

Look at the children's results and decide which material is best for reducing sound. Discuss the features of this material prevent sounds getting through. For example, it may contain pockets of air. Discuss situations where this material might be useful – and situations where (for other reasons) it would not be so good. For example, a flammable material would not be suitable near a blast furnace. Display the children's posters, picking out good points.

OUTCOMES

● Know that some materials can reduce sound.
● Can plan and carry out a fair test.

LINKS

PSHE: noise pollution and consideration for others.

Lesson 9 ▪ Elastic band sonometers

Objective
● To know that the pitch of some musical instruments can be altered by changing the size or tension of the vibrating part.
● To know how to make a test fair.

Vocabulary
elastic band sonometer, stringed instrument, tension, pitch, volume

RESOURCES 💿

Main activity: 1 An elastic band sonometer (see Preparation). **2** A model drum (see Preparation); balloon rubber; various jars or basins; strong elastic bands.
Group activity: Strong cardboard or plastic boxes; a large selection of elastic bands of different sizes and thicknesses; photocopiable page 204 (also 'Elastic band sonometers' (red) available on the CD-ROM).

PREPARATION

If possible, invite a musician (or ask a talented child) to attend the Plenary session, to play a stringed instrument and demonstrate how the it works.

Make an elastic band sonometer from a strong cardboard box with a variety of elastic bands stretched across it (see page 204). Make a model drum by stretching a circle of rubber from a balloon across the top of a jar or basin (with a lip) and holding it in place with a strong elastic band.

BACKGROUND

There are many different types of stringed instruments around the world, but they all produce a range of notes in very similar ways. There are only three ways to change the pitch of the note produced by a vibrating string: changing the length, thickness or tension of the string. The pitch can be increased by reducing the length, reducing the thickness or increasing the tension. Drums and other stretched-skin instruments work in a similar way to stringed instruments: they just have a 'two-dimensional string'. The pitch of the note produced can be increased by reducing the area of the vibrating skin, reducing the thickness or increasing the tension. The volume of the notes produced can be increased by making the vibrations bigger – that is, by plucking the string harder or hitting the drum harder.

STARTER

Tell the children that they are going to spend the next couple of lessons looking at musical instruments and finding out some of the ways that these instruments are used to make different notes. Ask the children to name some musical instruments. List them on the board and help the children to group them according to the way they produce sound. All instruments can be grouped broadly into those you blow, those you hit or shake, and those that have strings. This lesson looks at instruments with strings and instruments that you hit.

MAIN ACTIVITY 1

Show the children an elastic band sonometer (sound maker). *How many of you have ever made one of these? What will happen when I pluck one of the elastic bands? Will all these bands make the same sound when I pluck them?* Test the bands and listen to the notes produced. Ask the children to suggest things that could be changed to make higher or lower notes. Write their suggestions on the board. The things that will affect the note produced by the elastic band are: the length of band plucked, the thickness of the band used and the tension in the band (how stretched it is).

GROUP ACTIVITY

Each group should look at the effect on an elastic band's sound of changing one factor only. They should use copies of page 204 to help them carry out and record their investigation. Each group should then explain to a different group what they have found out. Talk to all the groups to produce a summary of their findings on the board.

Differentiation 💿
To support children, give them 'Elastic band sonometers' (green) from the CD-ROM, a simplified version of the core sheet. To extend children, give them 'Elastic band sonometers' (blue), which includes more open-ended questioning.

MAIN ACTIVITY 2

Show the children a model drum (see Preparation). Have jars or basins with different-sized mouths and more balloon rubber visible. Tap the drum lightly, listening to the sound it produces. Ask the children to suggest possible ways of making drums that produce different notes. Try out their ideas and record the results on the board or flipchart. Discuss which factors can be changed, and which factors you need to keep the same. You will find that using a container with a larger mouth produces a note with a lower pitch, provided that you stretch the balloon rubber by the same amount. Using a container with the same-size mouth, but stretching the balloon rubber more, produces a note with a higher pitch.

ICT LINK

Children could use CD-ROMs or the internet to find pictures or descriptions of different types of instruments, and identify what is vibrating to produce the sound in each instrument they find.

ASSESSMENT

At the start of the Plenary session, ask the groups to explain the results of their investigations. Ask the children to write down two ways of making the note higher for each instrument, and two ways of making it lower.

PLENARY

Show the children a guitar or other stringed instrument. Ask them to pick out things that the real stringed instrument has in common with the elastic band sonometer. If necessary, help them to identify that both have several strings and a hollow box that the strings stretch across. Discuss how different notes are obtained on a real instrument, again stressing the similarities. Show them how different notes can be obtained by changing the thickness of the string, changing the length of the string (putting your finger on the frets) and changing the tension of the string (adjusting the tuning screws). Make sure that all the children know the factors that change the note.

OUTCOMES
● Can describe how the pitch of a drum or a stringed instrument is altered.
● Understand how to make a test fair.

LINKS
Music: how musical instruments make sounds.

Lesson 10 ▪ Pitch

Objectives
● To recognise high and low pitch.
● To recognise that the pitch of a sound is related to the size of the vibrating part of an object.
● To notice patterns in their observations and to make generalisations.

RESOURCES
Main activity: A xylophone or a glockenspiel and beater; a flipchart; marker pens.
Group activity: Sugar paper and felt-tipped pens. Six different sets of equipment: 1. A collection of bottles with different amounts of water in them (not in order) and a beater. 2. A collection of different chime bars. 3. A collection of elastic bands and different boxes to stretch them around. 4. A collection of recorders or whistles of different sizes, for example descant, treble, tenor. 5. A collection of different-sized tins and a beater. 6. A collection of different-sized drums (or saucepans!) and beaters.

PREPARATION
Set up the equipment for the Group activities on tables around the room.

Vocabulary
elastic band sonometer, stringed instrument, tension, pitch, volume

BACKGROUND

Pitch is to do with the frequency of vibration. Short or small things vibrate quickly, and so have a high pitch. Large or long objects vibrate more slowly and so have a lower pitch.

Children often find it difficult to distinguish between a sound getting louder and a sound getting higher in pitch. Discuss the words used to describe different sounds to clarify this. This lesson also helps children learn how to express a relationship between two variables as a generalisation, such as 'the larger the object, the lower the pitch of the note.'

STARTER

Ask the children to hum the same note as you. Now hum a lower note, then a higher note and indicate that they should join in. Develop this by asking the children to raise and lower their hands as the humming gets higher and lower. They could stand up and move their whole bodies up and down in line with the pitch of the hum. Ask: *How are we making that humming noise?* (Something in our throats - our vocal chords in our voice box - is vibrating.) Ask: *What were we changing about the sound we made?* (It went up and down; higher and lower.) If some children are confusing pitch and volume, then explain that people often get muddled between them and demonstrate the difference by hitting one note on the xylophone loudly then softly, then hitting different notes to change the pitch.

MAIN ACTIVITY

Hold a xylophone or glockenspiel on its end in front of you so that the long bars are nearest the floor and the short bars are at the top. Play some different notes and ask: *What do you notice?* (The bars at the top are short; the bars at the bottom are long; they get shorter and shorter; some notes are higher; some notes are lower.)

Write on the board: 'The ____er the ____, the ____er the ____. Give the children an example of how to use this scaffold, for example: *The longer I walk, the hungrier I get.* Or, showing with your hand and humming: *The higher my hand, the higher the note.* Ask them if they can think of an '-er' sentence about the xylophone. (The longer the bar, the lower the note; the shorter the bar, the higher the note.) Write these sentences on the board, underlining the '-er' words.

Explain that the 'highness' and 'lowness' of notes is called the pitch. Demonstrate on the xylophone a high- and a low-pitched note. Write the word 'pitch' on the board.

Explain that in the Group activities, you want the children to think about the pitch of the sound and try to write some '-er' sentences. Explain that they need to be ready to tell the class what they have found out.

GROUP ACTIVITY

Give each group time to explore their collection of equipment and look for patterns. Ask them to write down some '-er' sentences on sugar paper. The group will feed back what they have found to the rest of the class. Circulate, supporting the groups.

ASSESSMENT

Can the children put the collection in order relating to the pitch of the sound? Can they make an '-er' sentence to generalise their findings. Are they correctly relating the pitch to the size of the object?

PLENARY

Ask each group to show the rest of the class their findings, demonstrating the change in pitch of their collection and reading out their '-er' sentences. Ask: *Do you notice anything about what we all found?* (There is a common relationship between the pitch and the size of the objects.)

Differentiation
Support children by writing the first or second half of the '-er' sentence for them, for example: 'The more water, the ___er'. Extend others by challenging them to add 'I think this is because ____', so they are providing explanations too.

The water and elastic band collections are the most challenging, and the chime bars are easiest because they are most similar to the example provided.

OUTCOMES
● Can recognise high and low pitch.
● Can recognise that the pitch of a sound is related to the size of the vibrating part of an object.
● Can notice patterns in their observations and make generalisations in the form of '-er' sentences.

LINKS
Music: the size of musical instruments is related to the pitch of the notes produced.

Lesson 11 ▪ Higher or lower?

Objective
● To consolidate recognition of high and low pitch.
● To know that the pitch of a sound is related to the size of the vibrating part.

RESOURCES
Rulers; writing and drawing materials.

MAIN ACTIVITY
Show the children how a ruler 'twanged' on a table can make different sounds depending on how much of the ruler is sticking out. Ask: *Which part of the ruler is vibrating?* (The part sticking out.) Ask: *Can someone give me an '-er' sentence about this?* (The shorter the part of the ruler sticking out, the higher the sound.) Ask the children to observe closely and look at how fast the ruler is vibrating. This produces other '-er' sentences: 'The longer, and the slower, the lower the sound', 'The shorter, and the faster, the higher the sound.'

Ask the children to try out the pitch of different ruler lengths for themselves. Ask them to record their findings as an annotated drawing and an '-er' statement. Some children could be encouraged to change the length of the ruler systematically, such as 2cm at a time.

ASSESSMENT
Can the children apply their knowledge and ideas from previous lessons to explain how the instruments make different sounds?

PLENARY
Ask: *What have you learned so far about sound?* (Sound is the result of a vibration; the pitch of a note can be changed; the pitch is related to the size of the vibrating part of the object.)

OUTCOMES
● Can recognise high and low pitch in a variety of contexts.
● Understand that pitch is related to the size of the vibrating part.

Lesson 12 ▪ Changing pitch and volume

Objective
● To explore and understand how the pitch and loudness of a sound can be changed.

RESOURCES
A selection of musical instruments in different musical 'families'; materials to make simple musical instruments (such as pop bottle flutes, rubber band guitars); paper; writing materials.

MAIN ACTIVITY
Show the children a real musical instrument. Together, examine how it was made and how the sound is changed when playing it. Ask the children to make their own simple instruments, and to write a description of how the sound their instrument makes can be varied.

Differentiation
● Differentiate by outcome, depending on the complexity of the instrument made and the method of recording. Some could make simple drums and shakers; others could make wind or stringed instruments (allowing them to alter the pitch and volume).

ASSESSMENT
Can the children make an instrument and record correctly how the pitch is changed and how the volume is changed?

PLENARY
Conduct your orchestra! Point out how the notes are being made. Keep the music fairly simple: Vivaldi may be a little too tricky.

OUTCOMES
● Can describe musical sounds in terms of loudness and pitch.
● Can suggest ways to change the sound an instrument makes.

ENRICHMENT
Lesson 13 ● DIY instruments

Objective
● To know that the loudness of musical instruments can be altered by changing how much they vibrate.

RESOURCES
Enough milk bottles; strong cardboard boxes; elastic bands; glass jars; balloon rubber and drinking straws for all groups to construct instruments.

MAIN ACTIVITY
Ask the children (working in groups) to use the knowledge they already have to build a simple musical instrument that will make enough different notes to play a simple tune that they know or make up. They should use strings/drums, wind, or a mixture of both. They should also experiment with ways of making the notes on their instrument louder or quieter.

Differentiation
Support children by asking them to focus on making a series of notes that gradually become higher or lower in pitch. Beware: this activity requires musical skill as well as scientific knowledge so children who usually need support in science may do well in this activity; a different set of children may require support.

ASSESSMENT
Ask some children to explain how they have obtained different notes, and to demonstrate how they made the notes louder or quieter.

PLENARY
Give all groups the opportunity to play the tune they have made. If you wish, you could allow the class to vote for a favourite tune or to run a concert performance.

OUTCOME
● Can make simple musical instruments and describe how to control the loudness of the note they produce.

Lesson 14 ● Different instruments

Objective
● To know what parts of a musical instrument vibrate to produce sounds.
● To know that sounds can be described in terms of loudness and pitch.

Vocabulary
pitch, vibration, loudness

RESOURCES
Main activity: A collection of musical instruments in various 'families'; a small drum; rice (optional).
Group activity: Research materials (books and CD-ROMs) on musical instruments; display materials (large sheets of paper, coloured pens).

BACKGROUND
This lesson will develop the children's understanding of how musical instruments work. The different 'families' of instruments – brass, woodwind, percussion and string – are played in different ways. In brass and woodwind instruments, it is the air inside the instrument that is vibrating. The vibrations in brass instruments are caused by the vibration of the musician's lips. Those in woodwind instruments are usually caused by the vibration of a reed; however, in the flute, piccolo and recorder, they are caused by the shape of the airhole in the mouthpiece. Percussion instruments are usually

Differentiation
The children can use methods appropriate to their ability for research and presentation of their information. More able children could use multimedia software, and include recorded sounds.

struck to make part or all of the instrument vibrate. String instruments are plucked, strummed or bowed to make the strings vibrate. Bowing (drawing a bow across a string), causes the bow to grip and then slip on the string.

The loudness of an instrument depends on the size (amplitude) of the vibration. The pitch depends on the frequency of the vibration (the number of vibrations per second). Middle C has a frequency of 256 Hertz (vibrations per second). Higher notes have more vibrations per second, lower notes have fewer. In order to change the pitch of a note, the length of the air or string that is vibrating must be made shorter (for a higher pitch) or longer (for a lower pitch). In stringed instruments, the thickness or tension of the string can also be changed to change the pitch of the note.

STARTER
With the children look at each instrument in turn, asking the children how it is played and what it does when you play it. When all of the instruments have been discussed, ask: *What do all these instruments have in common when they are played?* (They all vibrate.) Ask the children to feel their own instrument, their voice, vibrating by placing their fingers on the front of their throat (the windpipe) and saying 'Aaargh'. Encourage them to feel the difference as they change the sound they are making.

MAIN ACTIVITY
Select an instrument and make a high-pitched note and a low-pitched note. Can the children say which is which? Can they tell you how the instrument was played differently to make the different notes? Now make a loud and soft sound. Again, can the children tell the difference and say how each was made? This can be demonstrated effectively using a small drum sprinkled with dried rice. Hitting the drum softly to make a quiet sound causes the rice grains to move just a little; striking the drum harder to make a loud sound causes the grains to leap clear of the drum. This shows that loud sounds have greater vibrations than soft sounds.

GROUP ACTIVITY
The children can work in groups to look at musical instruments from around the world, using secondary sources such as CD-ROMs and books. They should find out how a range of instruments are played and how the note can be changed. They can build up a display of drawings, photographs and text to convey the information they have found out, then present this to the class. Combining the groups' findings would provide interesting material for an assembly, particularly if you can borrow some world instruments from your local multicultural support service for the children to demonstrate.

ASSESSMENT
Can the children explain how a particular musical instrument is played and how its sound can be changed? Can they use different research sources to build a coherent presentation?

PLENARY
Following up the group presentations, emphasise similarities between the instruments in a 'family' and the music produced with them. Look at how the note produced can be changed for instruments in that 'family'.

OUTCOMES
● Can explain how sound is produced from string, wind and percussion instruments.
● Can describe musical sounds in terms of loudness and pitch.

LINKS
Music: playing in a group.

Lesson 15 ▪ Making wind instruments

Vocabulary
wind instrument, air column

RESOURCES 💿
Main activity: A selection of real wind instruments; pictures (perhaps of an orchestra) showing a range of different wind instruments.
Group activities: 1 A large number of clean, washed, empty glass milk bottles (plastic bottles do not work as well, but it is important to warn the children of the dangers of using glass bottles); some tall glass jars with larger mouths than the bottles; jugs for pouring water. **2** Photocopiable page 205 (also 'Making wind instruments' (red) available on the CD-ROM); many plastic drinking straws; scissors.

PREPARATION
If possible, ask a musician (or a child) to attend the Plenary session, to play a wind instrument and demonstrate how the instrument works. Arrange for any children with wind instruments to bring them to school for this lesson.

BACKGROUND
Wind instruments all work because patterns of resonating air are set up inside the tubes of the instrument. These patterns develop because a sound wave travelling down the tube bounces off the other end and travels back up the tube, interfering with the wave travelling down. At a certain pitch for each pipe, the sound going down and the sound coming back reinforce each other to produce a loud, resonant note that we can hear. The note heard depends on the length of the air column that vibrates – that is why the note can be changed by changing the length of the tube, or by using valves or holes that alter the proportion of the air column that vibrates. In real musical instruments, several different patterns of vibration (called 'harmonics') are set up at once. These harmonics give real instruments a much fuller, more musical tone than simple buzzers or milk bottles.

STARTER
Remind the children of the three main types of musical instrument: those that you hit or shake, those that have vibrating strings, and those that you blow. Make a list of as many instruments as you can that work by blowing, including whistles and squeakers. *Could we call the human voice a musical instrument? How does it work?* The voice works by air vibrating in the larynx (let the children feel this); we use muscles to change the shape of the mouth and throat, and so make different sounds.

Differentiation 💿
Group activity 1
Children who need support could investigate whether the size of the bottle mouth affects the sound made. Extend children by asking them to work together to decide on a way of finding out whether it is the length of the air column or the amount of water that affects the sound.
Group activity 2
To support children, give them 'Making wind instruments' (green) from the CD-ROM, a simplified version of the core sheet. To extend children, give them "Making wind instruments' (blue), which includes more open-ended questioning

MAIN ACTIVITY
Look at a range of pictures showing different wind instruments, and at some real instruments if possible. *What do all these instruments have in common?* (They all have a column of air inside them that vibrates.) *What are the differences between them?* Some instruments are bigger, with longer air columns than others. Some instruments (such as organ pipes) have air blown across them mechanically, while others (such as recorders) have a person blowing them. Tell the children that they are going to find out how these instruments make different notes by making their own instruments.

GROUP ACTIVITIES
1 The children should try blowing across the tops of bottles that are part-filled with water, then investigate how they can adjust the note produced by the bottle. Tell them to be extremely careful when using glass bottles.
2 The children should make drinking straw buzzers, using copies of page 105, then find out the effect of (a) changing the length of the straw and (b) making holes in the drinking straw (as in a recorder). *Does it matter what size the holes are?*

ASSESSMENT
Ask some children to demonstrate how they can use their home-made instruments to make high or low notes. Can they relate what they have found out to the notes they would expect real instruments to make?

PLENARY
Ask some groups to describe what they have found out about the length of the air column and the note produced. Look at the real instruments from earlier, and discuss which ones will be best for producing high and low notes. Look at different types of recorder, and help the children to arrange them in order from the highest to the lowest.

OUTCOME
● Can relate the pitch of a sound made by a wind instrument to the length of the air column.

LINKS
Music: find out how a recorder works.

ENRICHMENT
Lesson 16 ◾ Recycled instruments

Objective
● To apply knowledge of sound gained in previous lessons.
● To apply scientific understanding in a design and technology context.

RESOURCES
A wide range of design and technology tools; junk materials; glue; sticky tape; paint .Or, set this activity as a homework project.

MAIN ACTIVITY
Design and make a musical instrument from junk/reclaimed materials. It must make more than one sound.

ASSESSMENT
Does the instrument make more than one sound? Can the children explain how the sounds are made in terms of vibration? Can they explain variation in volume or pitch?

PLENARY
Have a demonstration time in which children show and play their instruments. Ask them to explain how the sounds are made and the reason for their designs.

Differentiation
Support children who are finding it difficult to raise ideas by suggesting possibilities.

OUTCOME
● Can apply an understanding of sound in a design and technology context.

Lesson 17 ◾ Echoes

Objective
● To know that sound can be reflected.
● To introduce 'echoes'.

RESOURCES
Group activities: 1 Skipping ropes (one per pair); secondary sources on echoes and echo location. **2** *Echo and Narcissus* from *Let's Learn at Home: Reading 8–9* by Sue Palmer (Scholastic.)
Plenary: A Slinky.

Vocabulary
echo, reflect, wave

PREPARATION
The Group activities are best carried out in the playground or hall as they need some space. If there is a good place to hear an echo within the school grounds or reasonable walking distance then take the children there to experience echoes.

Differentiation
Support children who have poorer observational skills by spending more time with them and targeting questions at them, for example: *Can you describe to me what you see?*
Extend children by asking them to use secondary sources to explore echolocation.

BACKGROUND

Sound can be reflected - it can bounce back from hard surfaces. This is what is happening when we hear an echo. It also explains why, when we shut a door, the sound seems to be kept in a room, even though we know that sound can travel through solid materials. Although it is not possible to demonstrate this directly, it can be modelled.

STARTER

Invite children to tell the rest of the class about places where they have heard an echo. Ask: *What did it sound like? What do you think an echo is?* Do the children know how to be your echo?

MAIN ACTIVITY

Ask: *What do all those places that make good echoes have in common?* (A hard surface, usually large, often curved, like a cave or bridge.)
Explain that an echo is when sound bounces off a surface and comes back to us. Draw a parallel with what happens when light bounces off a mirror - it is reflected. Explain that because we can't actually see the sound travel we need to think of other similar things that we can see to help us understand it, and this is what they will be doing in the Group activities.

GROUP ACTIVITIES

1 Ask the children to work in pairs. Give each pair a skipping rope. Either tie one end of each rope to a fixed place, or ask one child to hold the end as still as they can. The other child needs to make a wave run along the rope by giving it a gentle flick. Explain that if they shake the rope too hard they won't notice what is going on! By observing carefully, they should be able to see the wave bounce back. Ask: *Is the wave that comes back exactly the same as the wave that went out?* (It may be smaller, or less definite.) Ask: *In what way is that like an echo?* (The sound is distorted.)
2 Ask the children to read the echo myth 'Echo and Narcissus', in which the talkative nymph Echo annoys Hera and is condemned only to repeat the words of others. Ask them to perform part of it as a play, working in collaborative groups.

ASSESSMENT

Can the children explain that an echo is the result of sound being reflected/bouncing back?

PLENARY

Gather the whole class around in a circle. Ask two children to sit opposite each other in the centre of the circle holding either end of a Slinky. Ask one child to hold their end still and the other child to make a wave. Together observe what happens. Ask: *What happened to the wave when it got to the end?* (It bounced and came back.) Ask: *How does this help us understand an echo?* (In an echo, the sound bounces back.)
Ask: *Does anyone know how bats use echoes to help them?* Explain that bats have poor eyesight and hunt in the dark so they need another way of knowing where their prey is. They make a high-pitched noise, and if something is in the way an echo is produced when the sound hits and it is the echo that the bat can detect.

OUTCOME

● Can recognise that sound can be reflected and create an echo.

LINKS

Literacy: myths, plays.
History: the Ancient Greeks.

Lesson 18 ▪ Loud and quiet

Objective
● To know that loud sounds can be an environmental problem.

RESOURCES
A selection of hard and soft materials; a small battery-operated radio; a shoebox.

MAIN ACTIVITY
Demonstrate the difficulty of working in a loud environment when concentration is needed: turn on the radio tuned to a foreign station, turn it up, then do a mental maths test. Discuss which parts of the school might be quiet or noisy. *Do any parts of the local environment have noise problems? Why?*

Discuss the use of soundproofing (for example, in a recording studio). Ask the children to investigate what materials reduce noise by packing a radio in a shoebox with material around it to see whether it reduces the volume.

ASSESSMENT
Are the children aware that the softer materials muffle the sound more effectively?

Differentiation
Ask children who need support to make a simple qualitative judgements of which materials make the radio less noisy. Extend children by asking them to record the distance at which they can no longer hear the radio when different 'soundproofing' materials are used.

PLENARY
Reinforce the idea that silence can aid concentration by repeating the mental maths test without the distraction of the radio. Now see whether the children perform better with suitable background music. You may also wish to try using a 'moods' tape as a concentration exercise.

OUTCOMES
● Recognise the need for quietness at times.
● Can identify causes of loud noises in the environment.
● Can test a material for its sound reduction properties.

Lesson 19 ▪ Assessment

Objective
● To assess the children's knowledge of how sound travels from a source to a listener, and how well it travels through different materials.

RESOURCES
Photocopiable pages 206 and 207 (also 'Assessment – 1' (red) and 'Assessment – 2' (red) available on the CD-ROM); pencils.

STARTER
You may wish to start the lesson with the Assessment activities, or to start with a brief 'question and answer' session to revise the most important facts in this unit. You could ask each child in turn to tell the class something about sound.

ASSESSMENT ACTIVITY 1
Give each child a copy of page 206 to complete individually.

ANSWERS
1. The red sound path goes straight through the log to Freda.
2. The blue sound path goes straight through the water to the fish.
3. The green sound path goes straight through the air to the heron.
4. Freda will hear Bertie's croak before the heron does, because sound travels better through wood than it does through air.
5. If Bertie sat in the middle of the clump of weeds, the heron and the fish would not hear him so well. This is because soft, squashy materials act as sound reducers.
6. Freda would not be able to hear Bertie croak so well either.

7. Freda might hear three croaks, one after the other: the first one travelling through the log, the second travelling straight through the air from Bertie to Freda and the third travelling through the air from Bertie to the boat, then reflecting off the boat back to Freda.

LOOKING FOR LEVELS

All the children should be able to draw the sound paths to the different listeners. Most children will be able to answer questions 5 and 6. More able children will answer questions 4 and 7.

Most children will be able to describe sound paths through various objects, including examples where sound bounces off objects. They will know that soft materials prevent sound travelling and can be used as sound reducers. Some children will not have progressed this far, but will know that vibrating things produce sound and that sound travels better through some materials than through others. Other children may be able to explain why some solids transmit sound better than others.

ASSESSMENT ACTIVITY 2

Give each child a copy of page 207 to complete individually.

ANSWERS

1. A and E.
2. D
3. The skin of the drum.
4. The string, or strings.
5. Blow harder.
6. Any two of: change the level of the water, change the material of the beater or container, blow across the top of the container.
7. Either of: make the buzzer shorter, cover fewer holes.

LOOKING FOR LEVELS

All the children should be able to answer correctly questions 1 and 2. Most children will be able to answer questions 3, 4 and 5. More able children will answer questions 6 and 7.

Most children will have learned that the pitch of a musical instrument can be changed by adjusting the part that vibrates. Some children will not have progressed this far, but will know that the pitch of a musical instrument can be changed. Other children may have made more progress: they may be able to explain how musical instruments produce sounds, and predict whether particular alterations will cause a rise or fall in pitch.

PLENARY

You may wish to go through the answers to these assessments with the children. Refer back to the chart you made in Lesson 2 to record the children's knowledge of sound. Discuss what they have learned, and how they have increased their knowledge.

Vibrations

fold

Guitar
Take it in turns to strum the guitar while the other children listen, look and feel. What do you notice?

Ping-pong balls and tuning fork
One person dangles the ping-pong ball on the thread. Someone else strikes the tuning fork and touches the ping-pong ball with it. Everyone looks, listens and thinks. Take turns. What is happening? Why?

Water and tuning fork
Take it in turns to strike the tuning fork and touch the water while everyone else watches carefully. What has this got to do with vibrations?

Drum and rice
Take it in turns to hit the drum while everyone else watches carefully. What happens to the drum skin? What happens to the rice?

Water and pebbles
Take it in turns to drop a small stone into the water while everyone watches carefully. Look and listen. What happens to the ripple? What has this got to do with sound?

Slinky spring
Two children sit cross-legged on the floor about two metres apart. Each of them holds one end of the slinky. Take it in turns to send ripples down the slinky. Everyone else watches carefully. What do you notice? Take turns watching and doing.

Cymbal and soft beater
One person hits the cymbal with the beater. Another person gently touches the edge of the cymbal. What does it feel like? Can you change the way the cymbal vibrates?

Illustration © Robin Lawrie

Recording sound levels

Some children set up a sound meter to measure how loud a sound was:

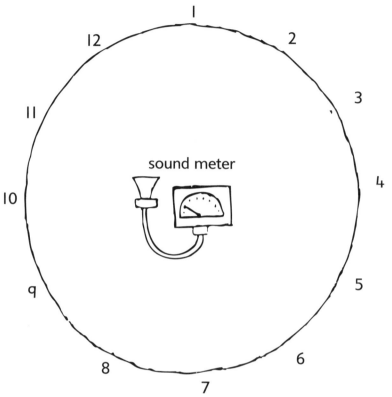

They pointed the sound meter at each position in turn and took two readings of the loudness. They recorded the following results:

Direction	Volume 1	Volume 2	Average volume	Direction	Volume 1	Volume 2	Average volume
1	4	6		7	9	7	
2	3	5		8	9	9	
3	5	3		9	8	10	
4	8	2		10	8	8	
5	7	5		11	6	8	
6	8	6		12	7	5	

◼ Work out the average volume (loudness) for each position. Write it in the 'average volume' column of the table.

◼ Plot a graph of 'average volume' on the y-axis (up the side) against 'position' on the x-axis (along the bottom). Your teacher will show you what scale to use or will give you prepared axes to plot your graph on.

◼ Use your graph to decide the direction the sound source is in. How could you tell?

◼ Why is it a good idea to take more than one reading for each position?

Illustration © Robin Lawrie

◼ SCHOLASTIC

Materials for reducing sound

◼ You need to test the materials you have been given to find out which is the best at reducing sound. You must decide where to put the material, what to measure and how to record your results.

1. Draw a diagram to show how you are going to do your test.
Write a few sentences to say what you will do and why you have chosen this way.

2. Use the space below to record your results.

3. Which material reduced the sound the most?

4. What do you think makes this material best at reducing sound?

5. Write down any things you did to make your test a fair test. For example, what did you keep the same?

6. Jessica said, 'I think it is a good idea to repeat our measurements.' Do you agree with her? Say why or why not.

Illustration © Robin Lawrie

Elastic band sonometers

This diagram shows you how to make an elastic band sonometer.

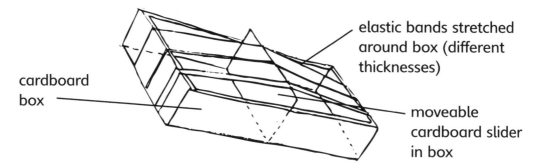

cardboard box

elastic bands stretched around box (different thicknesses)

moveable cardboard slider in box

The cardboard slider lets you change the length of elastic band that is being plucked.

1. What factor are you going to change?

2. What are you going to keep the same?

3. How many readings are you going to take? Why?

4. Draw a sketch diagram of the arrangement that gave you the highest note.

5. Draw a sketch diagram of the arrangement that gave you the lowest note.

6. Write down your conclusion.

7. What things did other groups find that changed the note produced?

Illustration © Robin Lawrie

■SCHOLASTIC

Making wind instruments

The instructions below show you how to make drinking straw buzzers:

    (a)   Cut straw to length.

                                 (b)   Cut one end to a point.

    (c)   Put cut end in mouth and blow hard.

I. Describe how you can make a buzzer that makes more than one note.

2. Describe how to make high and low notes.

3. Draw or describe another wind instrument. It can be a 'real' instrument or a 'home-made' one. Describe how to make the note higher or lower.

Illustration © Robin Lawrie

PHOTOCOPIABLE

Assessment – 1

Bertie Bullfrog croaks loudly to attract the attention of female Freda.
He has three listeners.

1. Draw in red the sound path that travels through a solid to a listener.
2. Draw in blue the sound path that travels through a liquid to a listener.
3. Draw in green the sound path that travels through a gas to a listener.
4. Who will hear Bertie's croak first, Freda or the heron? Explain why.

5. Where could Bertie sit to croak so that the heron and the fish would not hear him so well? Explain why this would work.

6. What would be the disadvantage of Bertie sitting there?

7. Describe what Freda might hear if a large boat was moored near the log. Explain why this might happen.

Illustration © Robin Lawrie

◢SCHOLASTIC

Assessment – 2

These children all have different musical instruments.

1. Which children have instruments that you blow? _____

2. Which child has an instrument that you pluck? _____

3. What vibrates to make the sound in the instrument Child B has? _____

_____

4. What vibrates to make the sound in the instrument Child D has? _____

_____

5. How could Child E make her instrument give a louder sound? _____

_____

6. Give two things that would change the sound from the instrument Child C has?

_____

_____

7. How could Child A get a higher note from his instrument.

_____